PLACES ALONG THE WAY:
FIRST FINDINGS ON THE M3

Places Along the Way:

first findings on the M3

Edited by Mary B Deevy and Donald Murphy

NRA SCHEME MONOGRAPHS 5

An tÚdarás um Bóithre Náisiúnta
National Roads Authority

First published in 2009 by
The National Roads Authority
St Martin's House, Waterloo Road, Dublin 4
Copyright © National Roads Authority and the authors

Library of Congress Cataloging-in-Publication Data are available for this book.
A CIP catalogue record for this book is available from the British Library.

Material from Ordnance Survey Ireland is reproduced with the permission of the Government of Ireland and Ordnance Survey Ireland under permit number EN0045206.

ISBN 978-0-9564180-0-5
ISSN 2009-0471
NRA Scheme Monographs 5.

Cover design: Nick Maxwell
Copy-editing: Aisling Flood
Typesetting and layout: Wordwell Ltd
Book design: Nick Maxwell
Index: Geraldine Begley
Printed by Castuera, Pamplona

Front cover photographs:
    Main photograph—souterrain capstone with megalithic art from Lismullin 1 (John Sunderland).
    Bottom left—blue glass bead found at Dowdstown 2 (John Sunderland).
    Bottom middle—bone motif piece from Phase 1A of the early medieval settlement at Roestown 2 (John Sunderland).
    Bottom right—copper-alloy object found in association with Burial No. 29 at Ardsallagh 1 (John Sunderland).
Back cover photograph: inner enclosure of the Lismullin Iron Age post enclosure, with four-post structure in foreground (John Sunderland).

CONTENTS

FOREWORD

In July 2005 the National Roads Authority (NRA) and Meath County Council published *The M3 Clonee to North of Kells Road Scheme Archaeology Research Framework.* This aimed to maximise the potential of archaeological discoveries on the M3 to contribute to archaeological research. The chief goal of the research framework is to transform the data generated by excavations and post-excavation analyses from 'information' into 'knowledge'. In this context I am delighted to present *Places Along the Way: first findings on the M3*, the first monograph dedicated to communicating the results of the M3 project.

The archaeological discoveries made on the M3 have been widely disseminated: reports on the excavations and on specialist analyses have been posted on the M3 website (www.m3motorway.ie); posters and brochures have been widely circulated; and articles have appeared in *Archaeology Ireland* magazine and in *Seanda*, the NRA's own archaeology magazine, as well as in the published proceedings of the NRA's annual Heritage Week seminar. *Roads, Rediscovery and Research*—the fifth volume in this series—includes five papers on the archaeology of the M3. Open days were held during the excavations, and many presentations have been given to local and national audiences, at conferences and seminars, by the excavation directors and NRA archaeologists. All of this activity honours commitments given in the research framework but also reflects standard practice for disseminating the results of archaeological investigations on national road schemes.

Places Along the Way presents a provisional description and interpretation of eight of the most significant archaeological sites excavated on the route. These were located between Navan and Dunboyne, Co. Meath—an area incorporating the broader landscape around the Hill of Tara. The book takes the form of eight papers authored by the excavation directors, two of which were co-authored by the project's archaeological researchers, and a ninth paper by the late medieval consultant historian to the project.

The authors have given us lucid, interesting and scholarly papers. Although the full results of the post-excavation analyses were pending, they have succeeded in producing informative readings of their excavated evidence and have explained the context of the discoveries in terms of both the landscape and the archaeological and historical background, on local and regional scales. This publication is a product of the NRA's general dissemination policy and adds to the growing number of scheme-specific monographs being produced to fulfil the NRA's responsibility to the archaeological heritage of Ireland. But it must also be remembered that this new book is just the first step in a comprehensive programme of publications that will aim to bring the results of the archaeological investigations on the M3 to the widest possible audience, among both the general public and professional archaeologists and historians. On the evidence of the present volume, we have much to look forward to.

Fred Barry
Chief Executive, National Roads Authority

PREFACE

The stated archaeological policy of the NRA is to make available as rapidly as possible access to the information about its important archaeological excavations that are conducted before development. The present volume represents an earnest of its intention to deliver on this promise, containing as it does substantial accounts of and reflections on a number of key excavations that took place on the line of the M3 motorway between Dunboyne and Navan in County Meath. The chapters describing the individual sites in this volume are all interim statements written while post-excavation research was continuing. A further, final publication of the sites is planned, but many of the conclusions tentatively proposed here are unlikely to be radically altered by further research.

While the evidence from the sites concentrates heavily on the early medieval period, there is substantial evidence of prehistoric burial at Ardsallagh, an Iron Age ceremonial enclosure at Lismullin and sporadic evidence for other prehistoric activity throughout the area examined. There is also the very welcome excavation of an important unenclosed later medieval settlement at Boyerstown.

The volume concludes with a chapter by Margaret Murphy on the evidence for later medieval settlement (essentially from the Anglo-Norman invasion onward), which draws together the documentary and archaeological evidence and points to ways in which the archaeological data, especially for continuity of occupation on a number of sites, enrich our understanding of the written record.

When reading the volume, it is important to bear in mind that the archaeological work was carried out on a narrow strip across the landscape defined by the land taken in for the construction of the motorway, and not by any archaeological research agenda, and that the footprint of many sites is greater than the width of the road corridor. The complex of earthworks at Roestown 2 is divided by the existing N3 roadway, and the excavator, Robert O'Hara, has performed prodigies of calculation to match the sequencing of the two severed areas of his excavation.

A number of the sites were not recognised before the archaeological prospection of the line chosen for the motorway and were indicated only by sporadic and faint magnetic anomalies that prompted further investigation. Trial-trenching initially by machine under archaeological supervision amplified the evidence of geophysical survey and provided further indications that the appropriate strategy of mitigation was to carry out full excavation of the areas affected by the road.

There are few parts of Ireland where major construction operations will fail to reveal substantial numbers of archaeological sites and by any international standards the approach to mitigation adopted on the line of the motorway stands in very favourable comparison with best practice elsewhere in Europe.

Among the interesting results of the excavations is the sequence of burials at Ardsallagh 1, which extends from the later Bronze Age into the early medieval period. This includes some interments that date to the Iron Age, and thus our knowledge of a period that is poorly known from the sites and monuments record is enhanced. One of the more striking achievements of the archaeological investigations conducted on the road is the discovery of the post enclosure at Lismullin. This ritual or ceremonial site consisted of an outer enclosure marked by a double ring of post-holes 80 m in diameter; inside and concentric with it was an enclosure of about 16 m in diameter, also indicated by post-holes. The complex was provided with an entrance feature that extended from a four-post structure at a gap on the eastern side of the perimeter toward the central enclosure. The monument was placed in a broad but shallow natural hollow that took the appearance of a natural amphitheatre. A souterrain and a ring-barrow and many cereal-drying kilns of much later date were found. The current dating evidence places the ritual site between the late sixth and the early fourth century BC and situates Lismullin firmly within the series of Early Iron Age ceremonial monuments.

The investigation of a number of human burials of the later Iron Age and early medieval period, not least at Collierstown, has shed new light on the gradual Christianisation of the landscape. It appears that traditional cemeteries continued in use but the burial practices gradually changed under the influence of ideas from overseas, not least from Anglo-Saxon England. The importation of exotic pottery from the Mediterranean lands gives a hint of the links that the new Christian world opened to the inhabitants of Meath at the beginning of the early medieval period.

The sites at Castlefarm 1, Roestown 2, Baronstown 1 and Dowdstown 2 were all early medieval enclosure sites, of basic ringfort type. All of them were heavily truncated—that is, the upper levels had been removed during agricultural and other activity, leaving only the basal layers and sometimes the negative impressions of posts, gullies, ditches etc. in the subsoil to be excavated.

In most cases these sites were not visible before the process of environmental assessment took place, and geophysical prospection and trial-trenching revealed their presence.

The frequent re-cutting of the original ditches of the circular or D-shaped enclosures that lie at the heart of these complexes and extensions in the form of what must have been paddocks, fields and pens for holding livestock all give the impression of thriving development in a settled landscape throughout the early medieval period. They certainly make it clear that research excavations of previous years were confined too closely to the visible ramparts of ringforts and related monuments and did not sufficiently explore the area outside the perimeters of these sites. Evidence of craftwork including fine metalworking and probably textile manufacture was recovered on some or all of the sites. Cereal-drying kilns were ubiquitous, and on several sites substantial wells were uncovered. It is difficult to know in all cases whether the sites were entirely secular or were in some sense dependencies of great religious houses.

It is, however, clear that they represent the habitations of people of substance in the area, and places like Roestown and Dowdstown may very well have been centres where wealth in the form of agricultural surpluses was accumulated and redistributed. We may see in their scale and elaboration an increasingly sophisticated reorganisation of the landscape during the second half of the first millennium AD. Such a reorganisation would be entirely in accordance with the increasing power of Irish regional kings who had political authority and coercive power that enabled them to redraw the map of early Ireland. It has long been argued, and it is reinforced by Margaret Murphy in this volume, that the Norman conquest of Meath was rendered comparatively easy by the settled and sophisticated nature of the landscape organisation that was taken over by the de

Lacy lords in the 12th century. They established a feudal system that managed to incorporate a considerable portion of the native population. The evidence for continuity of settlement on some sites—for example, Castlefarm—suggests as much.

In advance of full publication, the early dissemination of major statements on these important sites is a welcome achievement.

Michael Ryan
Director, Chester Beatty Library

ACKNOWLEDGEMENTS

The authors wish to thank the entire excavation crew (including Site Directors, Site Supervisors, Site Assistants and General Operatives) for their dedication and hard work throughout the entire excavation process, including Terry Connell, Stuart Elder, Stuart Reilly and Ken Wiggins (Site Directors), Allister Clark, Caroline Cosgrove, Olga Karmowska, Chris Kmiecik, Fiona Prenderville, Tony Kensell, James Lovely, Richard Morkan, Jim Kent, Michael Rozwadowski, Leigh Barker, Samantha Colclough, Ken Smith, Gearóid Kelleher, Aaron Henry, Wacław Cichocki, Jakub Dutkiewicz, Olga Karmovska, Dorota Kozłowska, Olga Sheehy, Tomas Westberg and Anja Bąkiewicz (Site Supervisors); special mention must go to Finds Supervisor Kasia Wieromiej for her excellent work in processing over 10,000 artefacts at Boyerstown 1, to all those involved in the post-excavation analysis (with special thanks to Maria Lear, Claire Grey, Hayley Foster and Rachel Sloane), surveying and draughting (Killian Murray, Martin Halpin, Aidan Kenny, Shane McArdle and Niall Gillespie), and logistics (Bill Hunter), and to Archaeological Consultancy Services Ltd, in particular Donald Murphy (Senior Archaeologist), who provided much-needed assistance and support and who was aided by John Harrison (Site Manager). The authors would also like to thank Meath County Council and the staff of the Roads Design Office, with special thanks to Mary Deevy and Maria FitzGerald of the NRA. Thanks are also due to Rónán Swan, James Eogan and Michael Stanley (NRA).

Thanks also to Professor Gabriel Cooney, Dr Aidan O'Sullivan and Dr Joanna Brück at the School of Archaeology, UCD, for their comments on these papers; Vicky Ginn for her comments and assistance on various sites and associated articles; Jonathan Kinsella and Eimear O'Connor who undertook background research; Tiernan McGarry for his comments on the ring-ditches at Ardsallagh; Claire Cotter for her information on the Dunboyne ringwork; Emily Gustafsson and Jenny Coughlan, who assisted with the analysis of the skeletal assemblage at Collierstown during and after excavation respectively; and Dr Amanda Kelly, who examined the imported pottery at Collierstown. Thanks are also due to the Lismullin Advisory Committee: Chief Archaeologist, Brian Duffy, Finian Matthews and Catriona Ryan (Department of the Environment, Heritage and Local Government), Director of the National Museum of Ireland, Dr Patrick Wallace, Professor Gabriel Cooney, Conor Newman (Department of Archaeology, NUI Galway) and Rónán Swan; Dr Elizabeth O'Brien for her opinions and advice with regard to Collierstown; Dr Michael Ryan, Dr Emily Murray and Eamonn P Kelly for their comments and assistance with regard to Dowdstown; and the [14]Chrono Centre, Queen's University Belfast, which provided a free radiocarbon date as part of 'Chrono: Project 3—The chronology of Irish early medieval settlement: the origin and demise of the ringfort'. Thanks also to David Sweetman, Professor Terry Barry and Dr Niall Brady for visiting Boyerstown 1 and for their helpful suggestions on comparative medieval sites. The comments of John Stafford-Langan on the medieval coinage from this site were also very helpful. We are also grateful to the previous landowner of Boyerstown 1, Jack Devine, who became a regular visitor during the excavations and shared his memories of the area with us.

Margaret Murphy would also like to extend her thanks to Dr Jim Galloway and Dr Mark Hennessy, who read an earlier draft of her paper and made many useful comments.

And finally the authors would like to extend their gratitude to Dr Eoin Grogan, who commented on many of the papers contained in this volume, and to all the individuals, of which there are far too many to name, who undertook the specialist reports associated with each of the aforementioned sites.

The editors would like to thank Vicky Ginn for editorial assistance on drafts of a number of the papers and, in particular, Michael Stanley for his major contribution to bringing the publication through the final stages.

INTRODUCTION

The archaeological discoveries made on the M3 Clonee–North of Kells motorway scheme in County Meath have attracted huge interest in recent years. The extent of the scheme—travelling 60 km north–south through Meath from the border with Dublin to the border with Cavan and covering approximately 700 ha—has resulted in an archaeological project of unprecedented size. An extensive programme of research, geophysical survey, trial-trenching and archaeological excavation has taken place over the eight years of planning for the road between 1999, when the first constraint reports were published, and 2007, when the excavations ended and road construction commenced. A total of 167 archaeological sites of varying size and date were excavated on the M3 by two archaeological consultancies—Archaeological Consultancy Services Ltd and Irish Archaeological Consultancy Ltd.

All investigations of the past landscape are a form of research, but traditionally development-led archaeological projects have not adopted formal research questions, methodologies and techniques. In order to ensure that the maximum knowledge would be extracted from the information generated by the M3 excavations, and to communicate how this was to be achieved, a formal research framework was developed in consultation with professional and academic archaeologists. The framework was published at the beginning of the excavations on the scheme in July 2005. A key element of the M3 research framework is to ensure that the newly uncovered archaeological data are placed in their archaeological, historical and palaeoenvironmental context.

Instead of waiting until the end of the programme of archaeological works to reflect on the excavation results, the M3 project employed full-time archaeological researchers to carry out research on the rapidly emerging results and to provide support to the excavation directors in the form of research papers to assist them in their interpretation and understanding of their sites as the excavations proceeded. Two of the papers in this volume are co-authored by the excavation directors and by archaeological researchers Neil Carlin and Jonathan Kinsella.

The professionalism, skill and dedication of what was at times a very large number of archaeologists working on the scheme, assisted by a wide variety of specialists, have led to very exciting and significant archaeological results. A selection of some of the key sites is presented in this volume. Undoubtedly the best-known discovery on the M3 was made at Lismullin 1 in the Gabhra Valley. The preliminary results of the excavation of the Iron Age post enclosure at Lismullin, which was declared a National Monument, are presented in the context of the initial site discovery and the subsequent use of a range of methodologies during the excavations. Although the majority of the sites on the scheme date from prehistory, it is arguably the results of research on the early medieval sites that will prove most exciting. Two early medieval burial sites are included in this volume—Collierstown 1 and Ardsallagh 1—which may span the prehistoric and early medieval periods. The excavations of early medieval settlement sites including Castlefarm 1, Roestown 2, Baronstown 1 and Dowdstown 2 are among the most important in the county since the work of the famous Harvard Archaeological Mission in the 1930s, and they will provide unique insights into how early medieval people lived and worked in this landscape.

A number of the early medieval sites displayed evidence for continuity and/or re-use into the late medieval period. In comparison to prehistoric and early medieval sites, opportunities to excavate rural late medieval sites such as Boyerstown 1 are relatively rare. The archaeology of historic periods requires an engagement with the documentary sources of the period, and hence consultant historians were commissioned to provide early medieval and late medieval historical overviews and, where possible, site-specific historical backgrounds to the excavation directors. In this volume historian Margaret Murphy presents a summary of current scholarship on late medieval rural settlement in Meath. Anne Connon's early medieval historical research will be presented in a future volume.

Since excavations ended in December 2007, specialist analyses have been continuing, and the majority of the final excavation reports are complete. The publication of *Places Along the Way* heralds the project entering its most meaningful phase. Plans for a suite of period-based publications dealing with the final results are well under way, including one dedicated to the excavations at Lismullin. The chapters describing the individual sites in this volume are interim statements written while post-excavation research was continuing but are quite definitive in their own right. These fascinating early reflections make the prospect of future M3 monographs all the more tantalising.

Mary Deevy
Senior Archaeologist, National Roads Authority
and
Donald Murphy
Senior Archaeologist, Archaeological Consultancy Services Ltd
September 2009

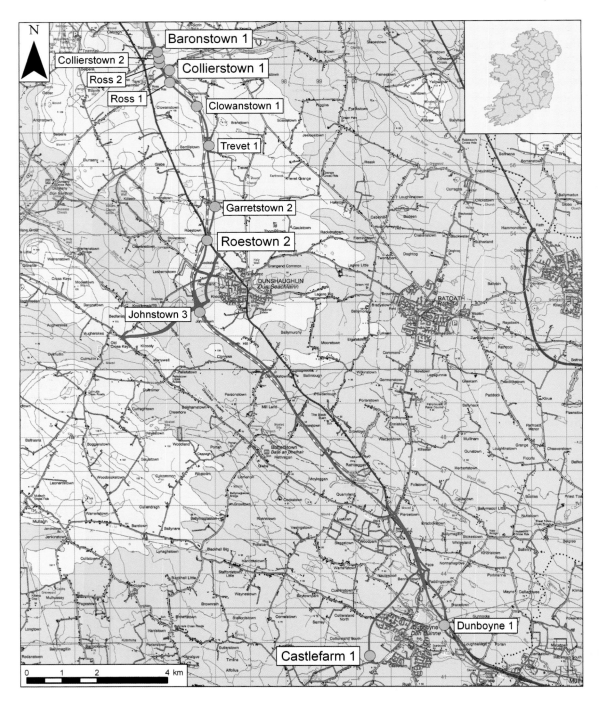

The route of the M3 Clonee–North of Kells motorway scheme northwards from its southern extent at Castlefarm 1, showing the locations of the principal excavated sites discussed. Opposite map follows route north of Baronstown 1 (based on the Ordnance Survey Ireland Discovery Series Map).

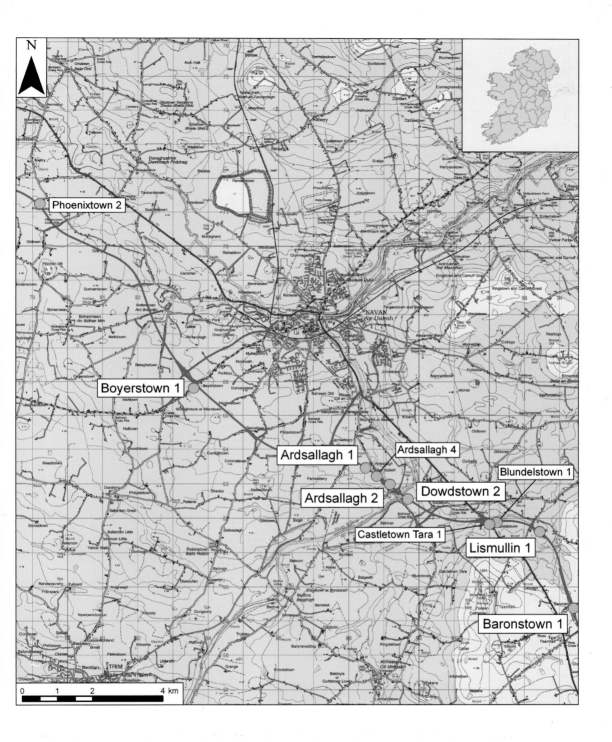

1

FROM FOCUS TO LOCUS: A WINDOW UPON THE DEVELOPMENT OF A FUNERARY LANDSCAPE

Linda Clarke and Neil Carlin

Focus: the centre of interest or activity
Locus: a particular position or place where something occurs or is situated

Two comparable funerary sites that were in use during the Early Bronze Age, Late Bronze Age, Middle Iron Age, Late Iron Age and early medieval period were recently excavated in the townland of Ardsallagh, Co. Meath. These are known as Ardsallagh 1 and Ardsallagh 2 and were situated almost 1 km apart in undulating countryside that gently slopes upwards from the River Boyne, which is immediately to the south (see site location map on page xv).[1] They were sited in prominent locations with clear views of the Hill of Tara (5 km) to the south-east.

Context of discovery

Ardsallagh 1 was originally identified as an anomaly of archaeological potential by a geophysical survey conducted by GSB Prospection Ltd along the route of the proposed M3 Clonee to North of Kells Motorway Scheme (Shiel et al. 2001). This interpretation was confirmed by archaeological testing in 2004 and the remains of a ring-ditch, possible cremation and inhumation burials, pits, and linear features were identified (Linnane 2004a). It was during these preliminary investigations that the remains of another circular ditched enclosure were discovered at Ardsallagh 2 (Linnane 2004b). The next phase of work (in spring 2006), which entailed the excavation of these features and a large area in the vicinity, resulted in the discovery of further archaeological features at both sites (Clarke & Carlin 2006a; 2006b). Additional inhumations were revealed to be enclosed by the ring-ditch at the former site, while it was revealed that the latter site consisted of three ring-ditches and scattered isolated pits, some of which contained cremation burials that formed an Early Bronze Age flat cemetery (Illus. 1.1). Centuries of agricultural activity such as ploughing have removed the uppermost levels of both sites, and thus only the deepest layers have survived.

The activity at Ardsallagh 2 was earlier than that at Ardsallagh 1 and shall therefore be discussed first.

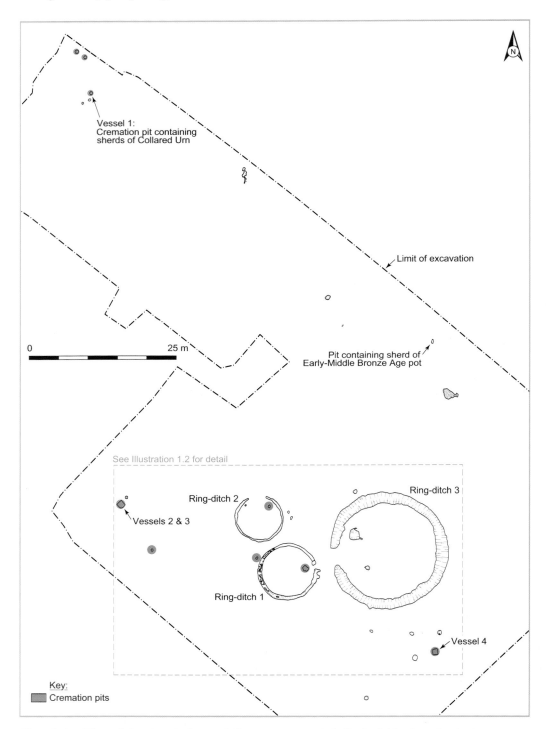

Illus. 1.1—Plan of the ring-ditches and flat cemetery at Ardsallagh 2 (Archaeological Consultancy Services Ltd).

Ardsallagh 2

Two small, Middle Iron Age ring-ditches (Ring-ditches 1 & 2) were located on the crest of a small rise (Illus. 1.2 & 1.3). Ring-ditch 1 was almost circular, with a diameter of 10.6 m, and was defined by a shallow penannular trench (0.63 m wide by 0.35 m deep) that contained a single deposit and had an eastern entrance. Apart from a single piece of flint, there were no other finds from this feature, although the remnants of timber planks of ash, hazel and alder were discovered within the ditch to the west and south (O'Donnell 2007). This timber was dated to 170 BC–AD 50 (Beta-237584; see Appendix 1 for details of radiocarbon dating results). Two shallow pits were present at the terminus of this ditch, one of which contained fruitwood, alder and willow charcoal (E OCarroll, pers. comm.) and returned a radiocarbon date of 2030–1870 BC (Beta-220121). A pit (0.82 m by 0.63 m by 0.35 m) located immediately inside the entrance contained fragmented cremated remains (that could not be confirmed as human) and hazel charcoal (ibid.), which produced a date of 2030–1750 BC (Beta-220122).

Ring-ditch 2 was located north-west of Ring-ditch 1 and consisted of a penannular ditch (0.45 m by 0.25 m) with an approximate diameter of 8.2 m and a northern entrance. The ditch contained a single fill, and the only artefact retrieved from it was a lump of flint. Internal features included a post-hole and a cremation pit (0.48 m by 0.4 m by 0.12 m) that were both situated immediately inside the entrance. Although as yet undated, its form and proximity to Ring-ditch 1 suggest that this also dates to the Middle Iron Age.

A third ring-ditch, Ring-ditch 3, dating from the Late Iron Age, was the largest of all the circular enclosures (1.7 m wide and 0.4–0.5 m deep), with an external diameter of 21 m. It was built on top of the natural rise that forms the highest point in this area, and the entrance was located directly opposite that of Ring-ditch 1 (Illus. 1.2). Two phases of activity were identified within the ditch fill. An almost continuous ring of stones lined the base, and these may have been arranged deliberately in this manner. It appears that the ditch was backfilled as part of an associated burial/ritual activity soon after construction. At a later stage the infilled ditch was partly re-dug to form a segmented enclosure composed of three separate curvilinear gullies. This was possible because the original ring-ditch would have been visible as a ringed depression caused by the gradual compaction of the ditch fill. The only finds from the fill of the original ditch were a few pieces of flint débitage and animal teeth (from the stone fill)—one of which returned a radiocarbon date of AD 450–640 (Beta-222060). A small iron rod and a flake from a broken, polished stone axehead were recovered from the fill of the re-cut ditch segments. Charcoal from this final layer was identified as blackthorn and ash (E OCarroll, pers. comm.) and was radiocarbon-dated to AD 650–770 (Beta-220124). One small concentration of cremated bone (probable human remains) found above the primary fill may represent a deliberate burial deposit. Tiny pieces of cremated bone (probable human remains) were also scattered throughout the primary ditch fill. The truncated remains of two pits in the ring-ditch interior produced no finds. A blue glass bead of probable early medieval date was found beside these during general site clearance.

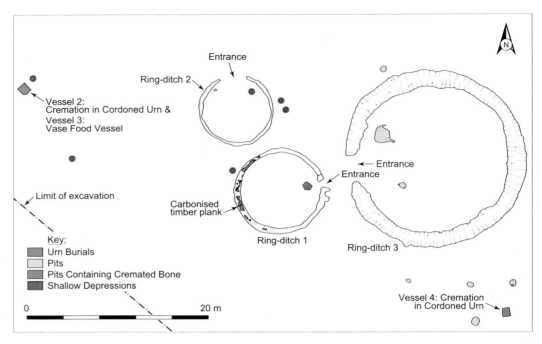

Illus. 1.2—Detailed plan of the Middle Iron Age ring-ditches and Late Iron Age ring-ditch at Ardsallagh 2 (Archaeological Consultancy Services Ltd).

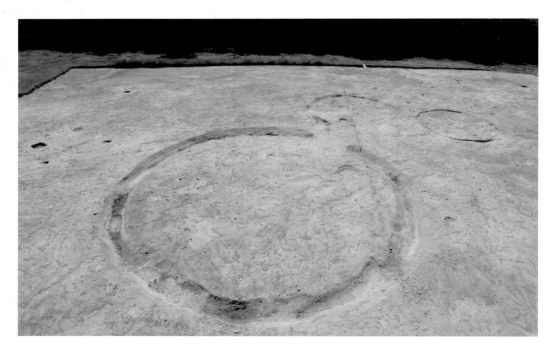

Illus. 1.3—Elevated view of Ardsallagh 2 post-excavation, showing largest ring-ditch in the foreground and adjacent ring-ditches in the background (Hawkeye).

In total 10 cremation pits were identified throughout this site (see Illus. 1.1). These features were not located in proximity to each other or to the ring-ditches, with the exception of the two cremation pits that were discovered within Ring-ditches 1 and 2. The pit enclosed by Ring-ditch 2 contained skull, tooth and mandible fragments of an adult human (O'Brien et al. 2007). Three of the cremations were accompanied by the remains of pots (Vessels 1–4). Sherds of a Collared Urn (Vessel 1) inverted over a few small fragments of cremated bone (probable human remains) were found within a pit situated in the north-western corner of the site. A cremation pit beside this was radiocarbon-dated to 1940–1740 BC (Beta-220126). Two of the pit-cremations consisted of cremated human bone (probably adults) contained within Cordoned Urns (Grogan & Roche 2007a). Both were deposited in an inverted position, and only the lowermost parts of the pots survived. One of the urns (Vessel 2) was located to the west of Ring-ditch 2 (Illus. 1.2 & 1.3) and contained the partial, but efficiently cremated, remains of an adult that gave a radiocarbon determination of 1950–1700 BC (Beta-221185), as well as sherds from a Vase Food Vessel (Vessel 3). The bones were highly fragmented, and thus it was not possible to identify further the age at death or the sex of this individual (Quinney 2006a). The second Cordoned Urn burial (Vessel 4) was situated south-east of Ring-ditch 1 (Illus. 1.2 & 1.3) and was radiocarbon-dated to 1870–1620 BC (Beta-221184). The bone recovered was efficiently cremated but was so highly fragmented that it could not be definitively identified as human (ibid.).

Other features included a number of isolated pits that were scattered throughout the site. Unburnt animal bone and tiny fragments of cremated human bone were recovered from most of these pits, one of which contained a compact body sherd/possible base sherd from a cinerary urn similar to Vessel 1 (Grogan & Roche 2007a). A pit discovered near the northern limits of the excavation contained a flint flake and charcoal fragments, which were dated to 1900–1690 BC (Beta-220123), while a similar pit further south returned a date of 2290–2010 BC (Beta-220127).

Discussion of Ardsallagh 2

This site appears to have become a focus of burial activity, with the deposition of the cremations in urns and isolated cremations in pits, forming a flat cemetery in the Early Bronze Age (c. 2000–1600 BC) (Illus. 1.4). There is a significant absence of evidence for subsequent activity in this location until the construction of Ring-ditches 1 and 2 in the Middle Iron Age. It is possible that the Early Bronze Age flat cemetery provided a focus for this activity, as is suggested by the fact that Ring-ditch 1 was constructed in the immediate vicinity of some of these cremation pits. Indeed the incorporation of one of these pits into the entrance and terminal of that monument may indicate that the position of these cremations was somehow still known c. 1,500 years later. Given the long duration separating these two phases of activity, it is equally plausible that their spatial association was entirely coincidental. There would seem to have been little or no activity here until the end of the Iron Age, when a larger replica of the existing ring-ditches was constructed deliberately in their immediate vicinity. The final phase of activity appears to be represented by the partial re-digging of the ring-ditch in the eighth century AD.

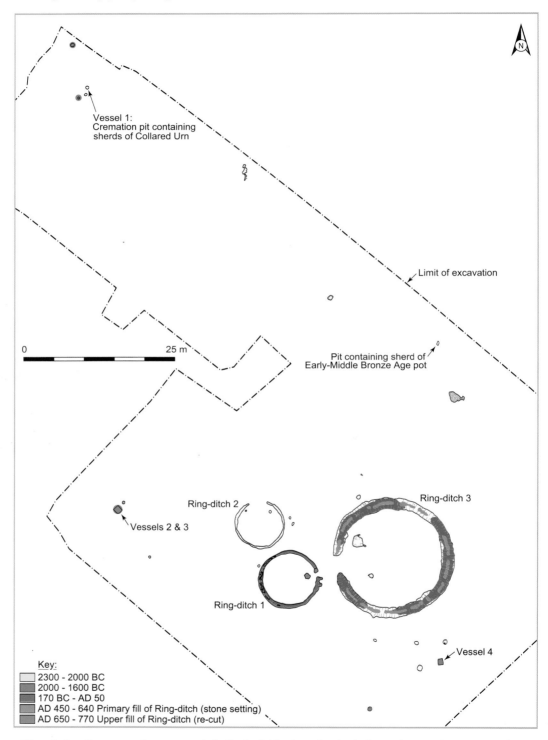

Illus. 1.4—Sequence of events at Ardsallagh 2 (Archaeological Consultancy Services Ltd).

The burial of cremated human remains in an inverted vessel within a pit became the dominant funerary rite towards the end of the Early Bronze Age (Grogan 2004). The radiocarbon dating of a number of the Ardsallagh cremation pits confirms that a flat cremation cemetery was established over the later part of the Early Bronze Age, between 2050 BC and 1700 BC. A concentration of Early Bronze Age activity in this locality is demonstrated by the re-use of the Mound of the Hostages passage tomb on the Hill of Tara (O'Sullivan 2005) as a cemetery from 2000 BC to 1600 BC and by the recent discovery of Beaker pottery at Ardsallagh 4 and Johnstown 3 on the M3.[2]

All three of the enclosures at Ardsallagh 2 represent ring-ditches—a form of monument that is thought to have fulfilled a burial, ceremonial or ritual function. This is a typically prehistoric site-type that originated in the Neolithic period and continued to be constructed, used and re-used up to early medieval times. They can range in diameter from 3 m to 90 m. Many such ring-ditches would originally have been encircled by an external bank, possibly with a low internal mound built up with the upcast material from the ditch. There was no evidence at this site for either feature, a situation paralleled at many other excavations.

The authors had previously speculated that the Middle Iron Age ring-ditches (1 and 2) were the remains of two Late Bronze Age domestic structures (Clarke & Carlin 2006a; 2006b), as these ditches seemed more like the slot-trenches of such buildings. The results of the radiocarbon analysis indicated a later date, and it may now be more appropriate to classify these as ring-ditches. However, a number of similar Middle Iron Age sites have been interpreted as structures, rather than as funerary monuments. These include three narrow and shallow circular ditches ranging in diameter from 3 m to 5 m (dated to 200 BC–AD 140) at Lislackagh, Co. Mayo (Walsh 1995), eight penannular and annular trenches with diameters varying from 4 m to 10 m dating from the first century AD at Cloongownagh, Co. Roscommon (Henry 2001), a penannular trench with a 4 m diameter and a north-eastern entrance at Magheraboy, Co. Sligo (Danaher 2007, 135), and a shallow circular ditch (8 m diameter) at Donaghmore, Co. Louth, dating to 170 BC–AD 60 (Ó Donnchadha 2002). It is possible that some of these sites have been misclassified; certainly the extant archaeological distinctions between the footprint of a structure and a ring-ditch are unclear. A paucity of synthesised data regarding ring-ditches has perhaps affected current understanding of these monument types.

Despite the uncertainty surrounding the classification of such Iron Age ditches as either ring-ditches or structures, the Ardsallagh examples may best be described as ring-ditches. They are remarkably similar to other Middle Iron Age ring-ditches that were definitely associated with funerary activity, such as Ferns, Co. Wexford (Ryan 2001), and Ballydowny, Co. Kerry, where a penannular monument with a north-eastern entrance and a diameter of c. 5 m was defined by a ditch 0.40–0.50 m wide and 0.16–0.20 m deep (Kiely 2004). The lack of cremated bone within Ring-ditches 1 and 2 does not completely contradict this interpretation, as many such monuments do not contain any evidence of human remains. A comparable Middle Iron Age ring-ditch that was associated with funerary activity but did not contain any burials was discovered also in County Meath, at Claristown 2 (Russell et al. 2002). What is perhaps most crucial in interpreting the Ardsallagh monuments as ring-ditches is their spatial association with both earlier and also later funerary activity.

The discovery of carbonised timber in the fill of Ring-ditch 1 at Ardsallagh is paralleled by its occurrence in the fills of similar Iron Age circular ditches such as Lislackagh, Magheraboy, Donaghmore, Ferns and Rathdooney Beg 2, Co. Sligo (Mount 1999). This may represent the remains of a timber lining, but the absence of evidence for *in situ* burning would suggest that this timber was burnt elsewhere before being deposited.

While similar in shape to the two smaller examples, Ring-ditch 3 at Ardsallagh 2 is much larger and was constructed over 600 years later, at the end of the Iron Age. The presence of cremated bone (probably human) in a context dating from AD 450–640 (Beta-222060) indicates a late date for the continuation of this burial rite. Although cremated human bone dating from AD 430–600 was excavated at Furness, Co. Kildare (Grogan 1984), it is highly unusual for cremation to have been practised as a burial rite beyond the fourth or fifth century AD (McGarry 2007, 10; in press). The contents of Ring-ditch 3 appear to be the product of a complex set of processes that may not have been of an exclusively funerary nature. This is suggested by the small amount and size of the bone fragments and the lack of accompanying charcoal, although this could also be interpreted as evidence that an effort was made to separate the pyre debris from the cremated remains, which were subsequently ground down before deposition. The re-cutting of this ring-ditch represents the continued use of this late prehistoric monument in the early medieval period—the digging of three long segments into the ditch may have been undertaken in order to redefine the ditch, but it may also have been an act imbued with meaning.

Evidence of a concern with the past on the part of Iron Age and early medieval people at Ardsallagh is suggested by the potentially deliberate re-use of the location of an Early Bronze Age cemetery in the Middle Iron Age (Ring-ditches 1 and 2) and the fact that the Late Iron Age/early medieval ring-ditch appears to have been positioned deliberately next to the pre-existing ring-ditches as part of an intentionally significant act. The entrance of Ring-ditch 3 faces directly into that of the Middle Iron Age Ring-ditch 1 and seems to replicate the earlier example. A parallel for such imitation was discovered at Rathdooney Beg, Co. Sligo, where a Neolithic bowl barrow was similarly replicated in the Iron Age (Mount 1999). The early medieval monument may represent an attempt to create a link between the past and the present (see Williams 1997).

Ardsallagh 1

The most notable feature of the excavations at Ardsallagh 1 was the discovery of 30 burials in association with a penannular ring-ditch that had an external diameter of 14 m and a western entranceway (Illus. 1.5). This enclosure was defined by a ditch (1.1–2 m wide and 0.17–0.5 m deep): it was shallower and narrower at the entrance and became deeper and wider as it progressed northwards and southwards.

Two main fills were identified, and these remained consistent throughout the ditch. The primary fill was visible as a narrow channel in the base and consisted of a layer of stones in a shallow silty matrix (Illus. 1.6). It looked like these stones were set deliberately within the base in

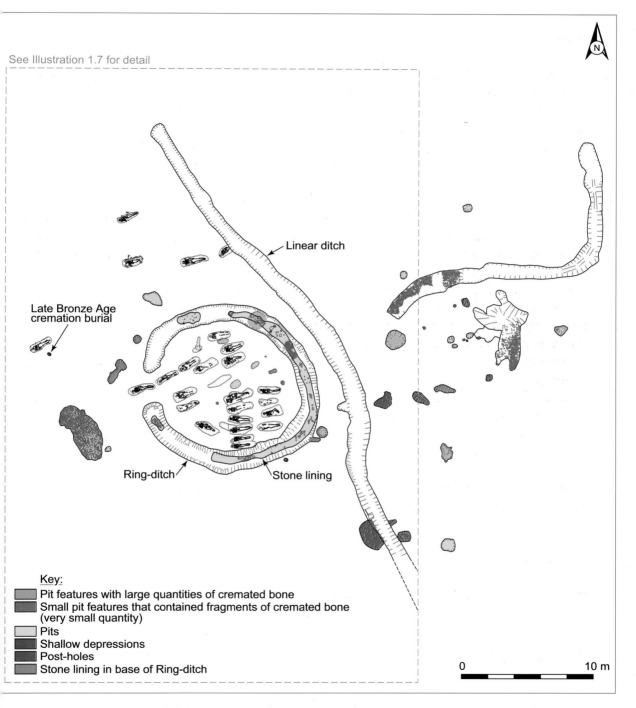

See Illustration 1.7 for detail

Linear ditch

Late Bronze Age
cremation burial

Ring-ditch

Stone lining

Key:
Pit features with large quantities of cremated bone
Small pit features that contained fragments of cremated bone
(very small quantity)
Pits
Shallow depressions
Post-holes
Stone lining in base of Ring-ditch

0   10 m

Illus. 1.5—Plan of the ring-ditch and associated features at Ardsallagh 1 (Archaeological Consultancy Services Ltd).

Illus. 1.6—The stone setting at the base of the Ardsallagh 1 ring-ditch (Archaeological Consultancy Services Ltd).

an attempt to form a kerb. This was particularly obvious in the north–eastern and south–western portions of the ditch and was identical to the base of the large ring-ditch at Ardsallagh 2. To the north-east, this stony layer, which was dated to AD 390–550 (Beta-222061), sealed a cremation deposit formed by a thin spread of blackened clay (0.85 m by 1.3 m) containing human skull, tooth and mandible (O'Brien et al. 2007). This spread was significantly earlier than the overlying stone kerb and was dated to AD 30–230 (Beta-233923). The main fill of the ditch consisted of a mid-brown, silty clay that appeared to have been deliberately deposited. Four fragments of flint (including a scraper, a flake, a piece of angular shatter and an unworked fragment) and a piece of coiled copper were recovered from this context. Two different radiocarbon determinations were obtained from cattle bones within this main fill: AD 370–540 (Beta-220128) and AD 440–640 (Beta-220129). At a later stage, the infilled ditch was partially re-dug to a depth of 0.4 m before being backfilled with a single deposit that contained a fragment of slag. Small amounts of cremated bone (human bone/probable human bone) and unburnt animal bone were scattered throughout all three fills of the ring-ditch, but no specific concentrations were identified. No evidence of an internal or external bank or of the slippage of bank material was identified during the excavation.

Inhumation burials

In the course of these excavations 30 poorly preserved inhumation burials were identified: 24 of these were enclosed by the ring-ditch; one (Burial No. 16) was located within the entranceway; and five were located outside the ring-ditch (Illus. 1.7). Four closely spaced external burials were located to the north, while the fifth occurred to the west. All the burials were extended inhumations aligned west–east (head to the west). They were tightly packed into simple, earth-cut graves, with the exception of Burial No. 8, which had slightly flexed legs (Illus. 1.8). Slight variations occurred in their alignment, and this is probably due to seasonal changes in the position of the sun. The neat and tight posture of the burials may suggest that the corpses were shrouded, although no evidence of this survived. Three double burials (Burial Nos 7 & 10, 11 & 15 and 14 & 26) were identified— all of these were contained within the area defined by the ring-ditch, and each consisted of an adult and a juvenile (Illus. 1.9). Burial Nos 1, 3, 4, 9, and 13 had a rough stone lining along the grave edges, and these were all located outside the ring-ditch. These graves were particularly shallow, and thus their linings were damaged by recent agricultural activity. Most of the burials appeared to be laid out in north–south rows—an obvious example of this is provided by those burials in the south-east extent of the enclosure. Those burials located in the western extent were more dispersed and not in clearly defined rows.

Grave goods were absent from most of the inhumations, but a copper-alloy object (Illus. 1.10), which lay above fragments of oak wood (E OCarroll, pers. comm.), was recovered from just above the left shoulder of Burial No. 29, and fragments of a copper-alloy pendant were found below the left jaw of Burial No. 20. Traces of oak timber were recovered from the fill surrounding Burial No. 1 and possibly also Burial No. 9, which may suggest the former presence of timber lining. Small fragments of cremated bone (probable human remains) were recovered from the fill of 11 graves (eight of which were located within the ring-ditch), and animal bone was found in seven graves (five of which were located within the ring-ditch). This probably represents residual material that pre-dates the interment of the inhumations. Other seemingly vestigial finds included a piece of flint, a small sherd of probably prehistoric pottery (Grogan & Roche 2007a), two pieces of slag and part of an iron knife, all of which were found in the upper fills of the grave cuts and were not directly associated with the burials.

Osteological analysis has revealed the demographic profile of the cemetery to be composed of five juveniles, five adolescents and 20 adults. Eleven of these were females/possible females (five of the 11 were identified as possibly female); five were males; and another four were of indeterminate sex (Quinney 2006b). Seven burials were dated and ranged from the fourth to the seventh centuries AD. Burial No. 4 was located to the north of the ring-ditch and dated from AD 370–540 (Beta-222015), and a date of AD 410–600 (Beta-222016) was obtained from Burial No. 16, which was located in the entranceway. Three of the seven burials were located within the ring-ditch. Burial No. 2 and Burial No. 29 were dated to the sixth–seventh centuries (AD 530–650 [Beta-222014] and AD 540–650 [Beta-237060]), while Burial No. 11 was dated to the fifth–seventh centuries (AD

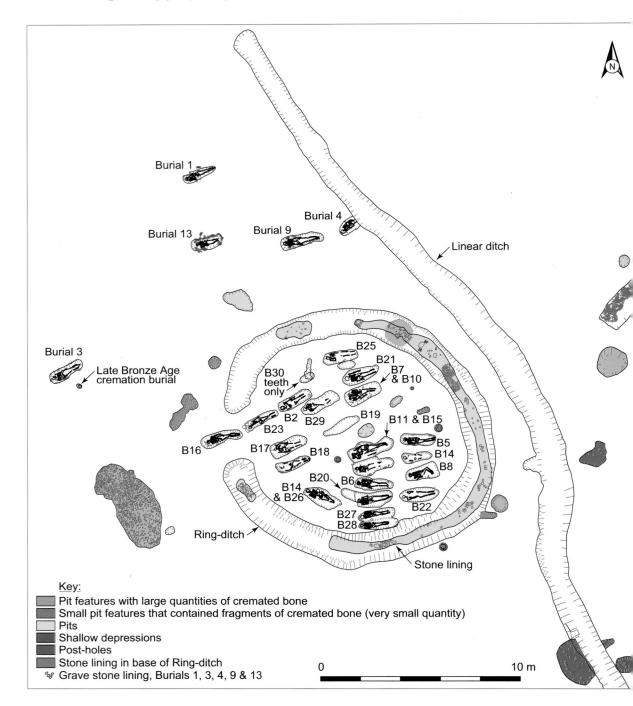

Burial 1

Burial 4

Burial 13

Burial 9

Linear ditch

Burial 3

Late Bronze Age
cremation burial

B25

B21

B30
teeth
only

B7
& B10

B2

B23

B29

B19

B11 & B15

B16

B17

B18

B5

B14

B8

B14
& B26

B20

B6

B27
B28

B22

Ring-ditch

Stone lining

Key:
Pit features with large quantities of cremated bone
Small pit features that contained fragments of cremated bone (very small quantity)
Pits
Shallow depressions
Post-holes
Stone lining in base of Ring-ditch
Grave stone lining, Burials 1, 3, 4, 9 & 13

0   10 m

Illus. 1.7—Plan of the inhumations associated with the ring-ditch at Ardsallagh 1 (Archaeological Consultancy Services Ltd).

Illus. 1.8 (above)—Inhumations being excavated at Ardsallagh 1. Burial No. 8, with slightly flexed legs, can be seen at the bottom left of the foreground (Archaeological Consultancy Services Ltd).

Illus. 1.9 (right)—A double burial at Ardsallagh 1 containing an adult female (Burial No. 10) and a juvenile (Burial No. 7) (Archaeological Consultancy Services Ltd).

Illus. 1.10—Copper-alloy object found in association with Burial No. 29 (Archaeological Consultancy Services Ltd).

450–640, Beta-237059). Burial No. 9 and Burial No. 13 were located outside the ring-ditch, to the north, and were also dated to the fifth–seventh centuries (AD 450–650 [Beta-237058] and AD 540–650 [Beta-227862]).

Other features associated with the ring-ditch

Aside from grave cuts, numerous features were identified within the ring-ditch. Six pits, four linear cuts, one shallow depression and three post-holes were present (Illus. 1.7). Three of the pits, the shallow depression and two of the linear cuts contained occasional and tiny fragments of cremated bone (probable human remains). One pit was centrally placed within the ring-ditch interior, and it may be significant that all of the burials appear to have respected it. Perhaps this feature may once have held a large stone or wooden marker, although evidence of such was not apparent. None of the post-holes were located in close proximity to each other, and they are unlikely to have been structurally related.

Illus. 1.11—A post-excavation view of Ardsallagh 1, facing north-west; the linear ditch can be seen curving outwards to avoid the ring-ditch (Archaeological Consultancy Services Ltd).

Features outside the ring-ditch

Nine pits, a linear cut and a small post-hole were also located immediately outside the ring–ditch (Illus. 1.5). One of these pits was located to the west/slightly north-west of its entrance and contained a cremation burial (human remains) within a Late Bronze Age coarse domestic vessel (Grogan & Roche 2007a). The pot had been deposited in an upright position, and only the base survived. The bones were identified as a single adult of indeterminate sex (Quinney 2006c) and were dated to 1060–880 BC (Beta-221186). Only a small amount of identifiable human bone fragments was recovered, including portions of the cranial vault and upper and lower skeleton. This may suggest a high degree of disturbance to the vessel following its deposition or that this represents a token burial deposit.

Six other pits also contained fragments of cremated bone (identified as human remains/probable human remains [O'Brien et al. 2007]). Two in particular contained high concentrations of cremated bone, and radiocarbon analysis placed these features in the Early Iron Age. The first was located immediately south-east of the ring-ditch and was dated to 380–160 BC (Beta-229294), and the second was dated to 350–40 BC (Beta-236026) and was located immediately west of the ring-ditch.

A ditch (74 m long by 1.5 m wide by 0.34 m deep) was located immediately east of the ring-ditch. This linear feature curved dramatically to avoid the ring-ditch, but it cut through the grave of Burial No. 4 (Illus. 1.7 & 1.11). A second area of activity was located east of this linear ditch and comprised a series of post-holes, shallow depressions, metalled stone surfaces and a curving ditch that may combine to represent the remains of a structural feature. One of these—a large irregular-shaped pit—was dated to 390–180 BC (Beta-229295) and is broadly contemporary with the above-mentioned Middle Iron Age cremation pits. It is likely, although not definite in the absence of datable artefacts or further radiocarbon analysis, that all of the features in this area can be attributed to this period.

Discussion of Ardsallagh 1

It appears that funerary activity began at this site with the deposition of a Late Bronze Age cremation in a domestic pottery vessel (Illus. 1.12); no other features have returned dates from this period, but it remains possible that some may be contemporaneous. The radiocarbon dates suggest that there was no further activity until the Middle Iron Age, which saw the deposition of cremated remains in pits. Two pits, located west and south-east of the ring-ditch, were dated to this period, and a large irregular-shaped feature, which may have been associated with some sort of structure and was located east of the ring-ditch, was also dated to this period (from the fourth to the first centuries BC). The next phase of activity was represented by the construction of the ring-ditch, which appears to have occurred between the first and third centuries AD, as indicated by the date of the cremation deposit in its base. At some stage in the fourth to the sixth century AD the ring-ditch was cleaned out and almost completely re-cut, except for the above-mentioned cremation deposit that was left in the base. Similar to the Late Iron Age ring-ditch at Ardsallagh 2, the occurrence of probable cremated human bone throughout the fills of this monument suggests that cremation practice may have been an enduring tradition.

Radiocarbon dates from Burial No. 4, located north of the monument, suggest that it was interred at around the same time that the monument was re-cut. Thus, it may be speculated that the ring-ditch initially provided a locus for these inhumations. Over time, burials began to be interred inside the ring-ditch, which indicates that it became the focus of burial activity. This movement of the funerary activity into the enclosure is suggested by the possibility that the entrance burial (No. 16) and Burial Nos 2, 11 and 29 seem to post-date Burial No. 4, as well as the first re-cutting and infilling of the ring-ditch. After this progression, burials were not confined to the interior of the ring-ditch; they also continued to be interred outside (e.g. Burial Nos 9 and 13) during the sixth to seventh centuries AD.

The layout of the five external burials did not appear to follow any pattern—four were located to the north and one to the west (adjacent to the urn burial). However, the layout of the internal burials seems to have been quite structured. The internal burials nearest the entrance were laid out from head to toe to form a line that extended eastwards into the monument. This contrasts greatly with the closely spaced inhumations in clearly defined rows running north–south in its eastern extent. It may be postulated that in general these rows represent the latest phase of burials as they

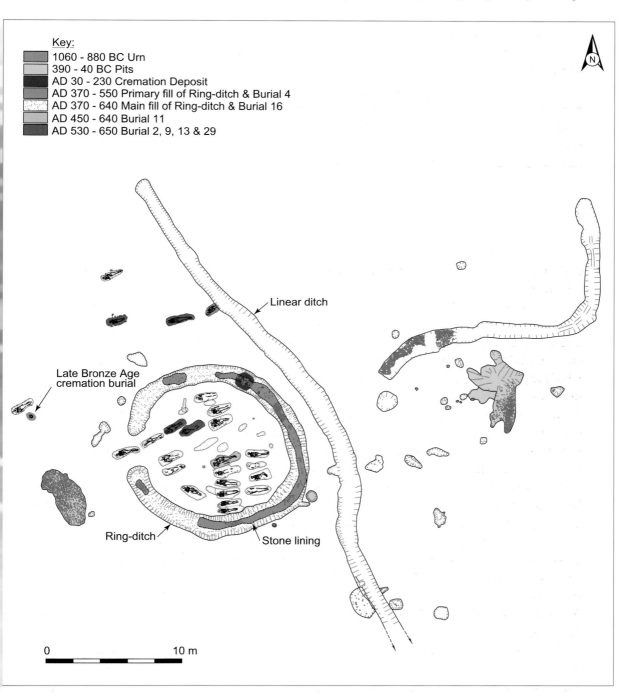

Key:
- 1060 - 880 BC Urn
- 390 - 40 BC Pits
- AD 30 - 230 Cremation Deposit
- AD 370 - 550 Primary fill of Ring-ditch & Burial 4
- AD 370 - 640 Main fill of Ring-ditch & Burial 16
- AD 450 - 640 Burial 11
- AD 530 - 650 Burial 2, 9, 13 & 29

Linear ditch

Late Bronze Age cremation burial

Ring-ditch

Stone lining

0   10 m

Illus. 1.12—Sequence of events at Ardsallagh 1 (Archaeological Consultancy Services Ltd).

are more ordered and space efficient. The highly patterned layout of the internal graves and the fact that all of these respect each other suggest that this cemetery was used for a relatively short period of time and/or that the position of each burial was known and clearly marked.

At some stage, probably during the use-life of the cemetery, the infilled ring-ditch was partially re-dug for the second time before being backfilled again. The ring-ditch continued to be visible for some time after this, as demonstrated by the fact that the linear ditch curves outwards to avoid it. This ditch cut into Burial No. 4, which confirms that it is later than the ring-ditch but also suggests that the location of the external burials had been long forgotten and therefore that this ditch may considerably post-date the funerary activity.

The cemetery does not appear to represent the remains of an entire community: the females and possible females heavily outnumber the males. Quinney (2006b) notes the absence of infants despite the fact that infant mortality rates would have been as high as 10–30 % in these centuries. The occurrence of grave goods with two burials may suggest that this cemetery contains the remains of people of considerable status. The dates from the ring-ditch (Appendix 1) show that it was constructed in the Middle Iron Age. It was re-dug in the Late Iron Age, and at least one burial (No. 4) was dated to this period.

There are clear parallels for the deposition of cremated human remains within and near similarly constructed ring-ditches in the Iron Age, including Darcytown and Glebe South, Co. Dublin (Carroll 2007; Ryan 2007), Ballybronoge South, Co. Limerick (Eogan & Finn 2000), and Ballydavis, Co. Laois (Keeley 1999). There is growing evidence for the re-use of pre-existing monuments such as these in the Late Iron Age and early medieval period as a locus or focus for inhumations, such as those recorded at Ballymacaward, Co. Donegal (O'Brien 1999), Kiltullagh, Co. Roscommon (McCormick et al. 1995; Robinson et al. 2000), and Lehinch, Co. Offaly, (Ó Floinn 1987–8).

Newly constructed penannular ring-ditches were also used to enclose cemeteries in the Late Iron Age and early medieval period. One such example was excavated at Raystown, Co. Meath (Seaver 2005b; 2006), which had a diameter of 20 m and was constructed in the fourth or fifth century AD. This was used as a focus for a cemetery of 93 extended inhumations, most of which were within the enclosure. This cemetery continued in use until the 10th century. A parallel is provided by the cemetery at Westreave, Co. Dublin (Gowen 1989a), which was focused upon a penannular enclosure (9.5 m in diameter) with a western entrance considered by Elizabeth O'Brien (2003) to date from the seventh or eighth century AD. Other possible parallels include Colp, Co. Meath (Gowen 1989b), Greenhills, Co. Kildare (Keeley 1991, 187), and Castleupton, Co. Antrim (Gahan 1998; see O'Brien 2003).

A significant aspect of many of these enclosures is that they functioned both as a locus and as a focus for funerary activity. The sequence of activity is not always clear, but in most cases the ring-ditch began as the focus of the cemetery and became a locus only after all available internal space was exhausted. It is in this regard that the Ardsallagh 1 site is particularly enigmatic. It may be speculated that the function of the ring-ditch was not primarily funerary initially but became so only over time.

The tradition of using enclosures to define burial places continued from the Iron Age into the early medieval period (O'Brien 1992, 133) and became Christianised. In this cemetery it is difficult to distinguish between pagans and Christians because the Romano-British tradition of west–east extended inhumations had become the predominant burial rite from the fifth century onwards (ibid., 131–2; McGarry 2007). Literary references suggest that Christians were being buried alongside pagans, as exemplified in Tirechan's description of Patrick discovering a cross that had been mistakenly placed over a pagan grave rather than the Christian grave beside it (see Bieler 1979, 155). The discovery of grave goods with two burials, as well as the occurrence of double burials, suggests that both pagans and Christians were buried at Ardsallagh 1. The abandonment of the cemetery appears to have occurred in the seventh or eighth century AD, and this may have been in accordance with the wishes of the Church, which at this time was encouraging people to abandon pagan burial practices and to bury their dead in Christian cemeteries (O'Brien 1992, 136).

Discussion of both sites

The location of the sites at Ardsallagh near the River Boyne and overlooked by the funerary complex on the nearby Hill of Tara, combined with the possibility of intervisibility between all of these places, suggests that these recently discovered sites had been strategically situated.

The uncovering of four Iron Age ring-ditches at Ardsallagh 1 and 2 makes an important contribution to our understanding of this monument type. Although the use of the ring-ditch at Ardsallagh 1 to enclose inhumation burials contrasts greatly with Ring-ditches 2 and 3 at Ardsallagh 2, where there was little direct evidence for funerary activity, it is clear that the ring-ditch at Ardsallagh 1 and Ring-ditch 3 at Ardsallagh 2 share many similarities. Both were in use at some time between the fifth and seventh centuries AD and bear much physical resemblance: both have western entrances and a ring of stones at their bases and display evidence of being re-cut. However, the Ardsallagh 1 ring-ditch was first constructed c. AD 30–230 and was lined with stone in the period AD 390–540, whereas the large ring-ditch at Ardsallagh 2 was constructed c. AD 450–640 and was re-cut as late as AD 650–770. Ring-ditch 1 and possibly Ring-ditch 2 at Ardsallagh 2 are also broadly contemporary with the first phase of use of the ring-ditch at Ardsallagh 1. These were constructed in the Middle Iron Age, although Ring-ditch 1 at Ardsallagh 2 (170 BC–AD 50) may be slightly earlier than that at Ardsallagh 1 (AD 30–230). This complex sequence of activity suggests that the pre-existing landscape was constantly being referred to in order to create new meanings.

Significantly, both sites share a spatial association with Bronze Age burials and seem to demonstrate a concern with and knowledge of past activity in the area. The re-use of prehistoric monuments appears to be a persistent aspect of the Iron Age and early medieval period in Ireland (O'Brien 2003). This interplay between the past and present is consistent with the character of the nearby Hill of Tara, where at least six monuments were integrated into the structure of newer ones (Newman 1998, 138), and this is typified by the long sequence of activity at the Rath of the Synods (see Grogan 2008).

People in the Late Iron Age and early medieval period existed in a pre-established landscape with extant monuments that would have had a direct and meaningful impact upon their land use. The re-use of ancient monuments was an integral aspect of early medieval social and political machinations in Britain (Williams 1997, 2; 1998, 91), and this may well have been the case in Ireland. The adaptation of earlier sites may indicate a conscious incorporation of the prehistoric landscape to construct new social identities and gain status through the deliberate manipulation of the past that must have been associated with these places (Donaghy & Grogan 1997, 26). It may simply have been the expression of loyalty to the ancestors in order to create or assert a long lineage (Fredengren 2002, 203). Alternatively, it may have been done to suit new purposes such as the forming of territorial boundaries or the legitimising of the sovereignty of a new group (Newman 1998; O'Brien 2003, 67).

The Hill of Tara saw intense activity during the three millennia that Ardsallagh 1 and 2 were being used. In a less elaborate fashion than that complex, Ardsallagh 1 and 2 were a focal location in the wider Tara hinterland and mirror this evidence of continuity in the context of funerary and perhaps associated ritual activity. These two recent excavations may have important implications for the Tara area, for they suggest that at least some of the ring-ditches at Tara may be Late Iron Age or early medieval replicas of earlier monuments while others may represent the re-use of pre-existing features at this time.

Notes

1. Ardsallagh 1: NGR 288482, 263460; height 55.86 m OD; excavation reg. no. E3088; Ministerial Direction no. A008/035; excavation director Linda Clarke.
   Ardsallagh 2: NGR 289171, 262980; height 50.97 m OD; excavation reg. no. E3087; Ministerial Direction no. A008/034; excavation director Linda Clarke.
2. Ardsallagh 4: NGR 288798, 263219; height 50.05 m OD; excavation reg. no. E3090; Ministerial Direction no. A008/037; excavation director Linda Clarke.
   Johnstown 3: NGR 295580, 251708; height 95.68 m OD; excavation reg. no. E3043; Ministerial Direction no. A017/021; excavation director Stuart Elder.

2
DIRECTOR'S FIRST FINDINGS FROM EXCAVATIONS AT LISMULLIN 1

Aidan O'Connell

Introduction

Archaeological excavations were undertaken at Lismullin 1 between February and December 2007.[1] The results of the excavations show that the site witnessed episodic use throughout the prehistoric period, which mainly comprised ritual and ceremonial activity. This activity culminated in the Early Iron Age with the construction of a large post-built ceremonial enclosure. In contrast, subsequent medieval settlement was more functional in nature. The series of discoveries at Lismullin made it one of the best-known and most talked about Irish archaeological sites in recent times. The preliminary results of the excavation are now presented against the background of the initial site discovery, the declaration of National Monument status and the subsequent use of a range of methodologies over the course of the excavations.

Lismullin 1 was located 850 m to the north-east of the existing N3, about halfway between Navan and Dunshaughlin (see site location map on page xv). It was 2.1 km north-east of the Hill of Tara and was bounded to the north-west by the River Gabhra. The site extended to the south-west from the River Gabhra through a natural saucer-shaped depression and occupied an area of 27,360 m².

Sequence of works and discovery

The first indication of the archaeological site at Lismullin was a range of pit and linear features at the northern corner of the site discovered during a geophysical survey carried out as part of the Environmental Impact Assessment (Shiel et al. 2001). A programme of test-trenching was subsequently undertaken in April 2004 by Archaeological Consultancy Services Ltd (ACS Ltd) and confirmed the presence of archaeological features in this northern portion of the site (Clarke 2004a). An area measuring approximately 130 m by 110 m was originally set aside for a full archaeological excavation. However, before excavation commenced, a topsoil assessment of the site was undertaken, consisting of a metal detection survey followed by the hand excavation of a series of test pits, 1 m² in size. This work was carried out over seven weeks from September to November 2006. Additional test pits 3 m² in size were then machine excavated and the spoil metal detected to provide fuller artefact recovery over two weeks in January 2007. The purpose of the topsoil assessment, which was carried out before each archaeological excavation on the Dunshaughlin–

Navan section of the M3, was to assess the potential for artefacts in the topsoil, which can in some instances be related to underlying archaeological features. However, at Lismullin, the majority of the 810 recovered objects were modern agricultural debris. Additionally, the relatively small number of late medieval artefacts recovered were most likely introduced to the topsoil by manuring.

Topsoil stripping in advance of excavation commenced on 25 January 2007 under archaeological supervision. On 7 February, an arc of post-holes was recorded at the south-west limit of the excavation cutting. The original excavation cutting was extended to uncover any additional archaeological features. The arc of post-holes was seen to extend from the western site boundary, forming a circular arrangement that was estimated at c. 70–80 m in diameter, but was still largely covered by topsoil. At this stage of the excavations the site was subjected to some heavy rainfall, which gathered at the base of a topographical hollow that coincided with the arc of stake-holes. Topsoil stripping in this area was temporarily halted to allow it to dry sufficiently. The combination of heavy rainfall and the relatively large size of the site presented major logistical problems for the topsoil stripping, which involved the removal of roughly 11,000 m³ of ploughsoil. The excavated soil was carried off site using multiple tracked mechanical excavators rather than risking damage to any underlying archaeology by wheeled vehicles sinking through the remaining saturated ploughsoil.

Topsoil stripping re-commenced at the arc of post-holes on 15 March. A circular arrangement of post-holes c. 16 m in diameter was noted towards the centre of the larger arc of post-holes over the next two days. Subsequently, the south and south-eastern sides of the larger (outer) enclosure were uncovered. A pre-excavation GPS (global positioning system) survey of the post-holes was then undertaken. The results of this preliminary survey, which became available in early April 2007, confirmed that the site consisted of an outer enclosure, 80 m in diameter, defined by a concentric double ring of post-holes, and a central inner enclosure, 16 m in diameter, defined by a single ring of closely spaced post-holes (Illus. 2.1). Both had east-aligned entrances. At this stage, it was realised that the best Irish parallels for the Lismullin enclosure were to be found in a series of later prehistoric ceremonial enclosures, or 'royal sites', at Navan Fort, Co. Armagh (Waterman 1997), Dún Áilinne, Co. Kildare (Johnston & Wailes 2007), Rathcroghan, Co. Roscommon (Waddell 1988), the Rath of the Synods, Tara (Newman 1997), and Raffin Fort, Co. Meath (Newman 1993a; 1993b). A brief description of the enclosure was sent to the Department of the Environment, Heritage and Local Government (DEHLG) and the National Museum of Ireland (NMI) on 3 April. Representatives from both bodies visited the site on 5 April and concurred that it was a potential National Monument. Nineteen post-holes were excavated on the south-eastern side of the outer enclosure in order to collect sufficient evidence for dating. The remainder of the enclosure was then covered with a layer of polythene to protect the archaeological layers from drying out. A formal report on the discovery of a National Monument was compiled by NRA Senior Archaeologist Mary Deevy and submitted to the DEHLG on 18 April.

In the meantime excavation of other areas of the site continued (outside the post enclosure), and a range of features dating to the Neolithic period, the Bronze Age, the early medieval period and the post-medieval/early modern period were identified.

Illus. 2.1—Post-excavation plan of Lismullin 1 (Archaeological Consultancy Services Ltd).

Background to excavation of enclosure

Ministerial Directions pertaining to the excavation of the post enclosure were issued on 12 June 2007. The Minister for the Environment, Heritage and Local Government appointed a committee of experts comprising representatives from the DEHLG; the NMI; the Department of Archaeology, NUI Galway; the School of Archaeology, UCD; and the NRA to advise on the excavations. Wet weather delayed commencement of excavation of the enclosure until August. In the meantime a series of additional geophysical surveys were carried out over the entire monument, both within and outside the road corridor. One of the primary concerns with respect to the geophysical survey related to an attempt to trace the line of the post enclosure outside the area affected by the motorway scheme. The technique of caesium vapour magnetometry, which is 1,000 times more sensitive than conventional fluxgate magnetometry, was initially employed, owing to its success in detecting later Neolithic timber palisade enclosures in North Wales (Gibson et al. 1999). The results from the caesium magnetometer survey at Lismullin were, however, disappointing as it failed to detect the remainder of the post enclosure, owing to the poor magnetic contrast between the ploughsoil and the underlying parent geology, which made it more difficult to differentiate between archaeological and geological features (Roseveare & Roseveare 2007, 6–7).

Subsequently, conventional fluxgate magnetometry was employed at the post enclosure, which also failed to detect unexposed post-holes (Bonsall & Gimson 2007, 9). However, a range of possible additional archaeological features were identified in both of these surveys, including a previously unknown ring-ditch outside the road corridor (Roseveare & Roseveare 2007, 8; Illus. 2.2). Magnetic susceptibility surveys were also undertaken over the stripped area and identified a number of zones of high magnetic activity.

A range of additional techniques were employed in tandem with the post enclosure excavations to ensure that the maximum amount of information was obtained; these included palaeoenvironmental and geoarchaeological studies and aerial photographic and topographical surveys.

A palaeoenvironmental assessment was carried out in a wet area adjacent to the River Gabhra to the north of the site. This identified a sequence of deposition and burning on the southern bank of a probable ancient lake bed, now the current eastern bank of the Gabhra river. A programme of pollen analysis and radiocarbon dating of the collected samples will establish the chronology of sediment deposition at this location and possibly help to place the excavated features on the site in their past environmental context (Geary & Hill 2007).

Geoarchaeological assessment was undertaken at the eastern and western excavation cutting sections to ascertain whether a greater depth of archaeological deposits may have been present in the interface between the modern ploughsoil and the archaeological deposits as visible and exposed on site. This concluded that only the overlying ploughsoil had been removed and that mechanical stripping had not removed additional archaeological deposits (S Lancaster, pers. comm.). A programme of systematic geoarchaeological sampling was also undertaken across the post enclosure. Specialist analysis will ascertain whether chemical signatures relating to the

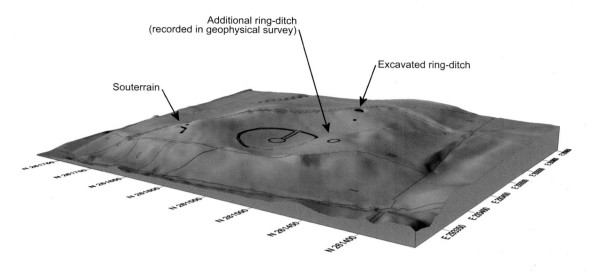

Illus. 2.2—Topographical survey of site (Multigraphic, based on data from aerial survey by BKS Surveys Ltd).

activities carried out at the site are present in the collected samples. If successful, this will greatly inform the interpretation of the excavation data.

A series of high-resolution aerial photographs were taken by BKS Surveys Ltd over the site and augmented by GPS survey undertaken by ACS Ltd. This enabled BKS to generate a set of topographical data, which was subsequently rendered into a topographical model by Multigraphic for ACS Ltd (Illus. 2.2). Further elevated photographs were taken of the site in the course of the excavations.

Excavation results

Although post-excavation analysis is, at the time of writing, at a very early stage, a preliminary broad chronological overview of various phases of activity across the whole site from the early prehistoric to the late medieval period is presented below. This includes early prehistoric activity, a ring-ditch, a field system, the post enclosure, a souterrain, kilns and miscellaneous medieval features.

Early prehistoric activity
A sequence of prehistoric pits (Phases I–IV) was excavated at the south-east of the site, 58 m from the eastern side of the post enclosure (Illus. 2.1). The three earliest phases consisted of a range of

pits of varying size with largely sterile fills. Owing to the probable absence of dating material from the fills of these pits, tube samples of soil were collected for optically stimulated luminescence (OSL) dating (for a concise description of the scientific principles behind this dating technique see Rathbone 2007, 56). Using this method, the fill of a large pit from the third phase of this sequence was dated to 9200–7600 BC (Burbidge & Sanderson 2008, 35). This is an exceptionally early date for a feature from an Irish archaeological site and is being treated with caution at this early stage of analysis. Furthermore, the specialists who conducted the dating programme speculated that the dating results may have overestimated the time since the pit fills had accumulated (ibid.). However, it should be noted that a cremation pit associated with two burnt flint microliths at Hermitage, Co. Limerick, was dated to 7550–7290 BC (Collins & Coyne 2003, 25). Additionally, Waddell (1998, 23) speculates that an earlier Irish lithic industry may await discovery, based on perceived differences between Irish and British Early Mesolithic stone industries. It may be possible to obtain a radiocarbon date to test the validity of the OSL results if sufficient quantities of charcoal can be obtained from the earlier pit fills in the course of post-excavation analysis. It should also be noted that, although Mesolithic settlement is rare in County Meath, significant Mesolithic assemblages have come to light in the course of the M3 excavations on sites at Clowanstown 1 (O'Connor 2008) and Blundelstown 1 (Danaher 2008).[2]

The fourth phase consisted of four pits, the largest of which was crescent shaped and associated with the deposition of three sherds of Middle Neolithic broad bowl pottery (3500–3000 BC) and four small fragments of adult human skull (Coughlan 2007a, 6). A second, smaller pit from this level was associated with a deposit of burnt bone. The burnt bone fragments are currently awaiting specialist analysis, but if they are positively identified as human they may represent a token cremation deposit.

The fifth phase in this sequence was represented by four further pits, which may have supported wooden posts, possibly forming a four-post structure. This structure was subsequently dismantled and the post(?) pits were filled with dark, silty clay fills and decayed stones. Three of the pits were cut through the large crescent-shaped pit from the earlier phase. One of these pits contained two separate deposits of burnt, possibly cremated, bones. The fourth pit from this phase cut one of the smaller Phase IV pits and contained 31 fragments of Early Neolithic Carinated Bowl (3850–3700 BC). The deposition of Early Neolithic pottery in this context (Middle Neolithic broad bowl pottery was collected from an earlier phase) is noteworthy. Although this pottery was manufactured in the Early Neolithic period, its deposition within the post cavity may have taken place considerably later.

The final pit (Phase VI) contained further burnt bone deposits, which were associated with Beaker pottery, a macehead of Bronze Age type (Illus. 2.3) and some further sherds of Early Neolithic pottery. The macehead was undoubtedly an item of some prestige and appears to have been deliberately deposited with the pottery sherds and the burnt bone. Future specialist analysis will determine if the burnt bones represent another human token cremation deposit. The Early Neolithic pottery from this context may provide further evidence for the curation and deliberate deposition of ritually charged material. However, it is also possible that the Early Neolithic pottery sherds were simply found in the course of digging the pit and re-deposited with the pit backfill.

Illus. 2.3—Bronze Age macehead (John Sunderland).

All of these features were sealed by a thin layer of soil with large stones, fragments of cremated bone and a final sherd of Middle Neolithic pottery.

The overwhelming impression of these pits is that they are of a ritual nature. The location of this activity is at a point in the landscape that would have had a clear line of sight to the passage tomb known as the Mound of the Hostages on the Hill of Tara. Interestingly, at the Mound of the Hostages, one of the perimeter features (Pit B, Burial 1) consisted of a cremation deposit in the upper levels of a pit that also contained one sherd from an Early Neolithic Carinated Bowl and a sherd of possible Grooved Ware pottery (later Neolithic) (O'Sullivan 2005, 31–3, 42). Although the Neolithic activity at Lismullin may be somewhat earlier than the perimeter burial at the Mound of the Hostages, both features had small token burial deposits associated with sherds of Neolithic pottery that were considerably earlier than the burials. This may be an indication of culturally similar, small-scale ritual activity. The Neolithic pits at Lismullin are, however, broadly contemporary with the use of the passage tomb, which would have been a significant visual reference. A passage tomb may have been situated in the immediate vicinity of the Lismullin complex. This can be inferred from the re-use of a decorated passage tomb kerbstone in the souterrain located 186 m to the north-west (see below). The Neolithic activities at Lismullin may therefore have been small-scale, sporadic, ritual actions carried out in the shadow of two passage tombs.

Further final Neolithic/Early Bronze Age activity at Lismullin consisted of a small pit at the northern corner of the site that contained 204 sherds of domestic Beaker pottery. This comprised a significant proportion of a large vessel with a perforation towards the base of the neck (Grogan & Roche 2007b, 7). Similar perforations have been noted on later Bronze Age vessels, and proposed functions include the ventilation of food-storage and cooking vessels and the securing of lids on vessels (Grogan 2005, 317). However, on the basis of the perceived association of Beaker pottery with the consumption of alcohol (see O'Flaherty 1999), it might be possible to speculate that the large Lismullin pot acted as a fermentation vessel. In this context, the purpose of the perforation may have been to facilitate the release of carbon dioxide during the fermentation process. Future specialist analysis on the pottery may identify the contents of the vessel to aid in the interpretation of its function and the circumstances of its deposition.

Ring-ditch

A small ring-ditch was recorded at the south-east of the site, c. 88 m from the post enclosure and 30 m east of the Neolithic pits (Illus. 2.1 & 2.4). A ring-ditch in its simplest form is a circular or penannular ditch of uncertain function that may date to any period from prehistoric to modern times. In archaeological terms, ring-ditches are frequently associated with barrows (circular burial monuments usually associated with a mound or bank that were created by the excavation of an enclosing ditch). These can date from the Neolithic to the early medieval period and usually range from 6 m to 15 m in diameter (Newman 1997, 155–7).

The Lismullin ring-ditch was 10–11 m in external diameter and c. 7–8 m in internal diameter. The ditch had a U-shaped profile and was 2.9 m wide and 1.05 m deep. Although the dimensions of the ditch indicate that the soil generated would have formed a low internal mound or an external bank, there was no surviving above-ground earthwork evident before the excavation. There was, however, evidence for at least two re-cuts from the fills of the ditch, indicating three separate phases of use. No datable artefacts associated with the use of the ring-ditch were recovered, and no cremated bone was positively identified during the excavations. Significantly, the ring-ditch was located on the brow of a north-facing ridge of high ground at the southern end of the site. A second possible ring-ditch identified during geophysical investigations was situated 126 m to the south-west and on the brow of the same ridge (Illus. 2.2; Roseveare & Roseveare 2007, 8). As there is no definite evidence for a funerary function for the excavated ring-ditch, the location of two similar sites aligned on a slightly prominent position may be significant.

Both sites may originally have been associated with earthworks that were visible above the ground surface (i.e. banks and low mounds). The siting of these earthworks in relatively prominent positions would indicate that they were intended to be seen or viewed from a wider area in the

Illus. 2.4—View of Lismullin 1 from the south-east, with ring-ditch in foreground and post enclosure in background (Archaeological Consultancy Services Ltd).

landscape. Cooney and Grogan (1999, 131–2) have noted that Middle Bronze Age barrow cemeteries in the North Munster region were located on the periphery of territories where people in this period would have had a strong localised sense of identity. Additionally, Pryor (2001, 162–6) has stated how the landscape at Fengate and West Deeping (Cambridgeshire, England) was divided into family territories (farms?) mainly demarcated by natural features, but with barrows acting as permanent markers at strategic points. In this way the landscape was controlled through the power of the ancestors. Perhaps the Lismullin ring-ditches can be seen in a similar light, marking the boundary of a family territory while commemorating deceased prominent individuals from the area (Daly & Grogan 1993, 60) as a means of legitimising claims to the land. In the absence of secure dating evidence, a preliminary broad date range spanning the Bronze Age and Iron Age to the early phases of the early medieval period is proposed.

Field system

Two roughly north-east/south-west-aligned field ditches were recorded at the site (Illus. 2.1). As they are broadly parallel, they are interpreted as forming a field system. The southern ditch was cut by (and so is earlier than) the Iron Age post enclosure, and the northern ditch was cut by an early medieval figure-of-eight-shaped cereal-drying kiln. This field system therefore pre-dates the Early Iron Age. A programme of luminescence sampling at both of these ditches has confirmed that they are contemporaneous. They were initially cut before 1500 BC and filled with archaeological sediments until at least 700–500 BC (Burbidge & Sanderson 2008, 36).

Post enclosure

The post enclosure occupied a natural saucer-shaped depression at the west of the site, surrounded on all sides by a ridge of higher ground (Illus. 2.5 & 2.6). Both the enclosure and this high ridge extend beyond the south-western site boundary. There are three surviving enclosure elements: an outer enclosure defined by a concentric double ring of post-holes, a central inner enclosure defined by a single ring of closely spaced post-holes and an eastern entrance.

Outer enclosure

The outer enclosure was 80 m in diameter and defined by a concentric double ring of post-holes. The two outer enclosing rings were 1.5–2.5 m apart, and the individual post-holes were arranged at 0.4–1 m intervals (averaging 0.6 m). In total, 215 post-holes associated with the outer enclosure were recorded in the course of the excavation: 131 on the inner ring, and 84 on the outer ring. The excavated post-holes from the outer enclosure average 0.15–0.23 m in diameter by 0.15–0.23 m deep but range from smaller examples less than 0.15 m in diameter to larger post-holes up to 0.29 m in diameter. Charcoal from post-pipes associated with two of the post-holes on the southern side of the outer enclosure has been dated to 520–380 BC (Beta-230460; see Appendix 1 for details) and 490–370 BC (Beta-230461), placing the site in an Early Iron Age context.

Entrance

The enclosure entrance was located at the east and was defined by a gap in the outer enclosure. This gap coincided with a rectangular arrangement of four large post-holes enclosing a space measuring approximately 6 m east–west by 4 m north–south. Two were located 2.5 m beyond the external ring of the outer enclosure, while the other two were c. 1 m inside the inner ring. On excavation, two of the post-holes had clear post-pipes, all had vertical sides and all had some element of stone packing. They were between 0.75 m and 0.9 m in diameter but varied significantly in depth: the two on the southern side of the entrance were 0.6 m deep while the two on the northern side were much shallower, 0.36 m and 0.2 m deep.

Currently, there is no dating evidence available for this four-post structure. However, the fact that its location coincides with a break in the outer enclosure indicates that it may be contemporary with it. Additionally, the four-post structure is aligned with an apparent avenue that runs from the gap in the outer enclosure to the inner enclosure. The entrance avenue consisted of two parallel lines of stake-holes with dimensions of 0.08–0.1 m in diameter by 0.08–0.1 m deep. The rows of stake-holes were approximately 4 m apart, with individual stake-holes 2.5–3 m apart. There were 10 stake-holes on the northern row and 11 on the southern row.

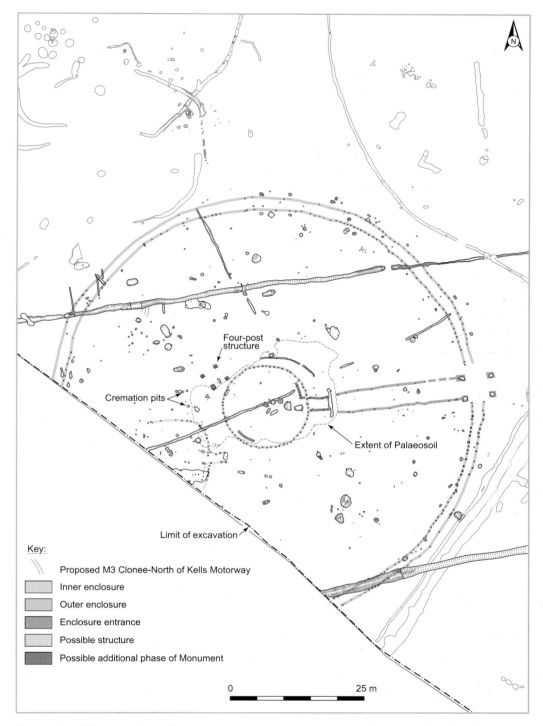

Illus. 2.5—Schematic plan of post enclosure showing main structural elements (Archaeological Consultancy Services Ltd).

Illus. 2.6—Elevated view of site from the south-east, showing extent of outer enclosure (John Sunderland).

Inner enclosure

The inner enclosure was located at the centre of the site and at the lowest point of a pronounced topographical hollow. It had a diameter of 16 m and consisted of 62 closely spaced post-holes with dimensions of 0.15–0.29 m in diameter by 0.18–0.29 m deep. These post-holes were more substantial than those on the outer enclosure. This may be due to the fact that less material was truncated from the top of these post-holes than the outer enclosure post-holes as they were located at the lowest point of the site. However, the construction of the inner enclosure was more regular than the two outer rings: the spacing between the posts was closer, and there were fewer gaps between posts.

Significantly, the inner enclosure posts were driven through a layer of ancient soil (palaeosoil) that partially survived at the base of the topographical hollow (Illus. 2.5). This palaeosoil may contain chemical signatures of activities that took place in the interior. Geoarchaeological samples have been collected on a grid interval of 2 m from this soil and, on specialist examination, may inform us of the nature of activities that were carried out at the site.

A range of features were recorded in the interior of the inner enclosure. Two shallow pits were recorded inside the entrance. Both contained charcoal and burnt bone fragments, possibly

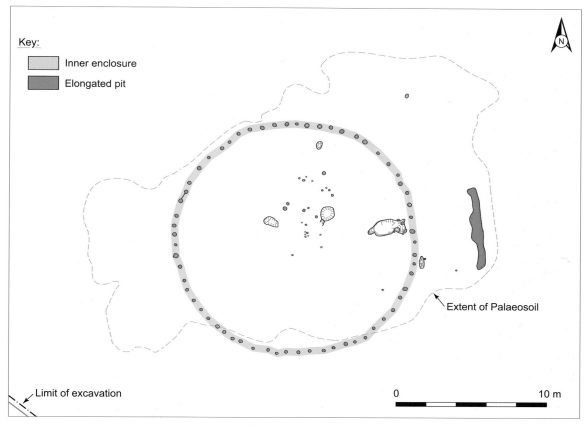

Illus. 2.7—Post-excavation plan of inner enclosure showing extent of palaeosoil and features below palaeosoil (Archaeological Consultancy Services Ltd).

representing token cremation deposits. Additionally, seven post-holes and seven pits that have been provisionally grouped into three separate phases of activity were recorded to the west of the entrance. The third and final phase of these features appears to be contemporary with the two pits located at the entrance. Additional pits, post-holes and stake-holes were also recorded in the space occupied by the inner enclosure, but below the palaeosoil, indicating a possible earlier phase of activity (Illus. 2.7).

Short arcs of small and shallow stake-holes were recorded in two areas, internally, along the south-western and along the north-eastern side, close to the enclosure (Illus. 2.5). These may indicate a separate phase of enclosure construction (see below).

Features between the outer and inner enclosures
A range of features were recorded between the inner and outer enclosures. These included pits, post-holes, hearths and assorted linear features (Illus. 2.5). Nine of the pits produced later Bronze

Age pottery, and an additional pit located between the two outer enclosure rings contained 18 sherds of Middle Bronze Age pottery (Grogan & Roche 2007b, 4). These features may indicate earlier phases of activity at the site, before the construction of the Early Iron Age post enclosure.

Before the excavations a linear feature was recorded across the entrance avenue at a distance of 4 m from the inner enclosure. This was provisionally interpreted as the remains of a slot-trench that supported a wooden or wattle screen restricting both the movement and the view of people into the inner enclosure (O'Connell 2007a, 12). Excavation of this feature has not revealed any structural components (e.g. post-holes or stone packing) associated with it. The fill contained large quantities of charcoal in addition to burnt and unburnt bone fragments. This feature may constitute another burial deposit. If it proves to be contemporary with the inner enclosure, its function may have been symbolically to close off the inner enclosure after it had gone out of use. Alternatively, it may belong to a different phase of activity.

Two rows of post-holes extended from the western side of the elongated pit and into the inner enclosure. These post-holes were larger than the stake-holes on the entrance avenue. Additionally, the southern line of post-holes did not line up with the southern row of stake-holes on the entrance avenue. Finally, the northern row of post-holes was aligned with the north-eastern arc of internal post-holes within the inner enclosure. These factors may suggest that the double row of post-holes located between the entrance avenue and the inner enclosure may belong to a separate phase of activity. Perhaps this could be viewed as a separate phase of formal monument construction (Illus. 2.5).

A possible rectangular structure was recorded to the south-west of the inner enclosure. It was formed by two perpendicular lines of post-holes (12 m east–west by 12 m north–south) and a double row of deep post-holes aligned east–west forming an entrance feature. There were no finds of a domestic nature and no internal hearth. In addition, at the east of the possible structure, four of the post-holes cut the palaeosoil that extends across the inner enclosure. However, it should be noted that the structure and, in particular, the entrance post-holes do not appear to be aligned towards the inner enclosure.

At the north-west of and adjacent to the inner enclosure a second discrete area of activity has been recorded. This consists of four large post-pits forming a square structure (c. 3 m long by 3 m wide; Illus. 2.5 & 2.8). There were definite signs of stone packing at the base and lower sides of the pits. There were, however, no post-pipes associated with them, which may indicate that this structure was deliberately dismantled. A cremation pit was recorded 4 m to the south-west of the four-post structure. Fragments of burnt bone were found in association with a sherd of later Bronze Age Coarse Ware pottery, and the base of the pit was lined with a single flat stone. The upper surface of the lining stone had been ground before its deposition. A similar pit, also lined at the base, was located 2 m east of this but contained no pottery or burnt bone.

Post enclosure in context

The Lismullin excavations have afforded an opportunity to examine a rare site-type from a perceived dark age in Irish prehistory (Cooney & Grogan 1999, 173). However, this rarity has led to an initial problem in site classification. In classifying sites, archaeologists try to use terms that

Illus. 2.8—Elevated view of site showing four-post structure at north-west of inner enclosure (John Sunderland).

convey their physical form and general date. The terms timber circle and henge are usually suggestive of a range of site-types defined by earth and/or timber boundaries associated with ceremonial activity in the later Neolithic period (2900–2500 BC). Although there has been considerable debate surrounding the later survival or 'reincarnation' of the concepts of these sites in the Irish Iron Age (Gibson 2000; 2005, 78–80; Collis 1977; Wailes 1982; Warner 2000), the descriptive term 'post enclosure' has been preferred for Lismullin to differentiate it from the Neolithic henge/timber circle tradition and to underline both the structural and the locational differences between it and comparable Iron Age sites (see below).

The post enclosure is interpreted as being ceremonial owing to the lack of recorded domestic artefacts and the lack of suitability for domestic settlement in the poorly drained topographical hollow. However, the exact nature of the activities carried out at this location is not currently known. It is anticipated that the programme of geoarchaeological study being undertaken may inform us about these activities. It can be stated that cremation rites played a role in the Lismullin Iron Age ceremonies as cremated bones have been recorded in two pits located at the inner enclosure entrance and in the elongated pit at the end of the entrance avenue. Additionally, the eastern entrance may have been aligned towards the sunrise on the autumn equinox, raising the possibility that there may have been an astronomical significance attached to the site.

The best comparisons for the Lismullin post enclosure are to be found at a range of ritual and ceremonial sites in the Middle Iron Age that are generally referred to as 'royal sites'. These include Sites A and B, Navan Fort, Co. Armagh (Waterman 1997), Dún Áilinne, Co. Kildare (Johnston & Wailes 2007), Raffin, Co. Meath (Newman 1993a; 1993b), and the Rath of the Synods, Tara, Co. Meath (Newman 1997). The Rath of the Synods may be of particular importance owing to its proximity to Lismullin: the second phase of activity here comprised three apparently successive circular timber palisade enclosures (25 m, 20 m and 30 m in diameter) that have very general similarities to the inner enclosure at Lismullin (ibid., 178). Additionally, a probable further timber palisade enclosure with dimensions of 210 m north–south by 175 m east–west ('the ditched pit circle') has been recorded externally to and concentric with the Rath of the Synods by geophysical survey (Fenwick & Newman 2002). If this were contemporary with the three smaller enclosures, it would provide a significant parallel to the Lismullin enclosure, albeit with a substantial ditch between the outer rings of posts.

There are, however, significant differences between these sites and the Lismullin post enclosure. The Lismullin enclosure occupied a discrete, sheltered position, with the surrounding higher ground giving the effect of an amphitheatre. Topographical survey at the site has demonstrated that the inner enclosure occupies the lowest point in this natural hollow rather than its exact centre. This suggests that the activities taking place within the enclosure could be viewed from the outside. This location, which appears to have been deliberately chosen, contrasts with the siting of other Iron Age ceremonial enclosures on prominent hilltops.

The form and construction of the Lismullin post enclosure also differ from other Iron Age ceremonial enclosures. The rings of posts at Lismullin appear to have been free standing. There was no indication from the excavations of a slot-trench between them that would have supported a timber or wattle facing. Additionally, the use of large numbers of relatively small posts and their close spacing suggest that there would have been no need to define further the enclosed area or its circular manifestation. Although there were irregularities apparent in the spacing and location of the outer enclosure posts, the overall impression of a perfectly circular construction would have been apparent when viewed from the external ridge of higher ground. We can therefore begin to imagine an extensive unroofed structure, simply constructed with a large number of relatively small posts and taking advantage of the unusual local topography, which would have afforded a natural elevated viewing platform into the site (Illus. 2.9). In contrast, other prominent Irish Iron Age sites are characterised by the use of much larger timbers in association with slot-trenches and enclosed by large earthworks. Additionally, the excavated evidence at Navan Fort suggests that the Phase 4 multi-ring structure ('the forty metre structure') would have supported a substantial roof and a light external wall (Waddell 1998, 341), while at Dún Áilinne both the Rose and the Mauve phase site reconstructions depict timber faces or walls on the excavated structures (Johnston & Wailes 2007, 16, 18).

Initially, the Lismullin post enclosure was seen to represent a single phase of construction and a short period of use (O'Connell 2007a, 12). However, the excavation of the site has raised the

Illus. 2.9—Conjectural reconstruction of post enclosure inside road corridor based on excavation data (Archaeological Consultancy Services Ltd).

possibility that it saw more prolonged and/or phased activity. A number of internal pits were found to contain Bronze Age pottery. Additionally, the clustering of pits, post-holes and stake-holes in the area defined by the inner enclosure, but below the palaeosoil, is further evidence for earlier activity. Additional undated features include the four-post structure to the west of the inner enclosure and the possible rectangular structure to the south-west of the inner enclosure. However, although these individual features point to additional activity in the space occupied by the post enclosure, the alignment of post-holes at the west of the elongated pit with the internal arc of post-holes inside the inner enclosure may be of the most significance in pointing to a distinct and separate phase of formal monument construction. It is also possible that some of the internal features associated with the inner enclosure may belong to this phase.

The Lismullin post enclosure represents an additional focus of ceremonial activity in the Tara landscape. The form and construction of the enclosure and its siting in a discrete, sheltered position mark the Lismullin site as distinctive from other excavated Irish Iron Age ceremonial enclosures. However, on examination of these 'royal sites', it is clear that they are characterised by their location in larger archaeological complexes with a high number of additional ritual monuments

(Newman 1997; Warner 1994; Waddell 1988). Lismullin may represent one of these outlying additional ritual monuments in the Tara complex.

Souterrain

A souterrain was located at the brow of the north-west-facing slope overlooking the River Gabhra (Illus. 2.1 & 2.2). This drystone-built underground structure was entered from the south-east on the brow of the hill and consisted of two passages with a complex of inbuilt ramps, turns and trapdoors terminating with a chamber or room at the end of each passage. The first passage extended approximately 20 m from the entrance and was constructed from a mixture of limestone, sandstone and shale angular stones. Chamber 1 was located at the northern extremity of the souterrain and consisted of an irregular, four-sided structure measuring 1.6 m north–south by 1.85 m east–west, with a simple lintelled roof. The disarticulated skeletal remains of an adult female human were deposited in a pit north of and adjacent to the souterrain entrance at Passage 1. Two separate deposits of skeletal material were recorded in the pit, which on specialist examination were found to represent the remains of a single individual (Coughlan 2007a, 2–3). It is therefore possible that a formal burial at Lismullin was disturbed by the construction of the souterrain and was subsequently re-interred in the adjacent pit.

A second passage, approximately 25 m long, extended to the south-west of Passage 1, terminating at a large, beehive-shaped, corbelled chamber c. 3.5 m in diameter (Illus. 2.10). A large sandstone boulder, 1.7 m long, 0.7 m high and 0.8 m wide, acted as a capstone. The capstone was in turn partially covered by rounded limestone packing stones that were sealed by a layer of yellow clay. A sample of articulated cattle bone collected from the packing material built up around the capstone has been dated to AD 980–1150 (Beta-237057). On removal of this packing material around the capstone, decoration was noted on one side of the stone and proved to be megalithic art (Illus. 2.11). This consisted of a series of concentric circles and a nest of arcs incorporated into one motif. In addition, a double row of zig-zags was located above these. The surface of the stone was ground to give a smoother texture around the concentric circles and the zig-zags. Additionally, a number of naturally eroded indentations were accentuated to give the impression of cupmarks on the opposite side of the same face of the stone.

Although the nearest recorded megalithic art to the site is located at the Mound of the Hostages, Tara, the Lismullin art appears to have closer affinities with the passage tomb art at Knowth (M O'Sullivan & G Eogan, pers. comm.). It is probable that this stone is derived from a passage tomb kerbstone that was split in half and was originally located in close proximity to the site before it was re-used.

Kilns

Fourteen earth-cut kilns have been recorded across the site (Illus. 2.1). Some have the classic figure-of-eight-shaped cut associated with cereal-drying kilns of early medieval date. These consist of two conjoined pits (with one end wider and deeper) attached by a short flue. Monk (1981, 217) has suggested that the main functions for these kilns are the drying of cereals before threshing

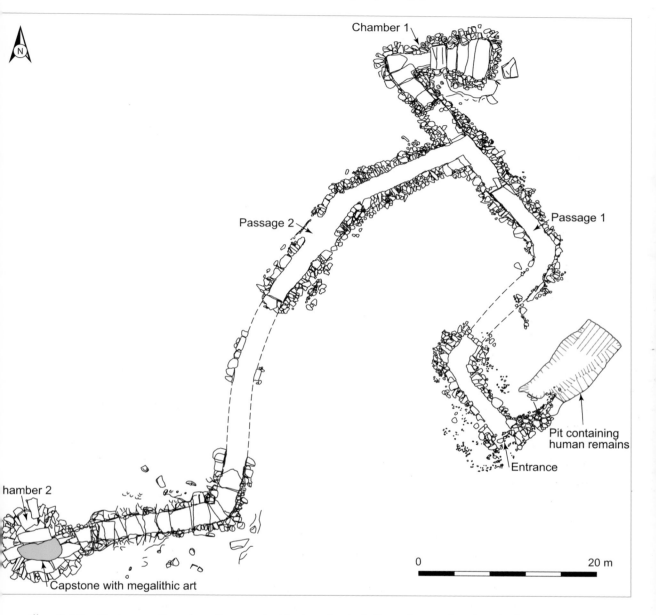

Chamber 1

Passage 2

Passage 1

Pit containing
human remains

Entrance

hamber 2

0   20 m

Capstone with megalithic art

Illus. 2.10—Post-excavation plan of souterrain (Archaeological Consultancy Services Ltd).

following a damp harvest or a short growing season, and the hardening of grain to allow effective milling. This was achieved by lighting a fire in the wider and deeper pit (fire-pit) from where the resultant heat travelled up the flue and into the shallower pit (drying chamber). Cereal grains would have been placed on a mesh of organic material in the drying chamber (Kelly 1997, 241).

Illus. 2.11—Souterrain capstone with megalithic art (John Sunderland).

Monk and Kelleher (2005, 105–6) suggest that the figure-of-eight kilns date to the early medieval period. However, a projecting ring-headed pin of Late Iron Age date came from the backfill of an elongated kiln adjacent to the north side of the post enclosure (O'Connor 2007; Illus. 2.12). Additionally, the burial of a dog dated to AD 1020–1210 (Beta-233921) was recorded in a crescent-shaped kiln to the south-east of the enclosure (see below). The Lismullin kilns are therefore characterised by a certain variety in both form and date. When post-excavation analysis has been completed, this variety may also become apparent in their function.

Miscellaneous medieval activity

The articulated remains of a dog were recovered c. 70 m south-east of the post enclosure (Illus. 2.1 & 2.12). The dog was recorded in the backfill of a crescent-shaped, earth-cut kiln. The kiln consisted of a fire-pit (1.48 m long, 0.88 m wide and 0.89 m deep) attached by a short flue to a drying chamber (1.06 m long, 1.12 m wide and 0.37 m deep). The earth at the base of the kiln was fire reddened or oxidised. There were no fills associated with the primary use of the kiln,

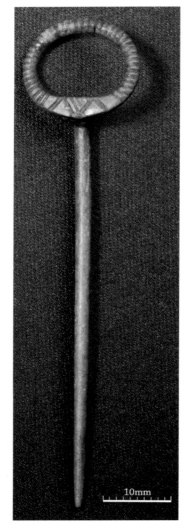

Illus. 2.12—Ring-headed pin from elongated kiln (John Sunderland).

10mm

Illus. 2.12—Dog burial in crescent-shaped kiln (Archaeological Consultancy Services Ltd).

which was backfilled with a single layer of dark clay. The dog was recovered from this backfill layer in the fire pit on the south-eastern side of the kiln. It would appear that the dog was deposited deliberately within the backfill after the kiln had gone out of use. It is of medium size and may be most closely paralleled to a modern boxer in terms of size/build (Sloane 2007a, 1). A sample of bone from the dog burial was dated to AD 1020–1210.

The disarticulated remains of another animal were found deposited in a pit on the northern side and outside of the enclosure (Illus. 2.3). Excavation revealed the presence of the partial remains of a single cow, and specialist analysis revealed an estimated shoulder height of 111.6 cm and an estimated age of 42–48 months (Sloane 2007b, 1–2). A sample of bone from the cow has been dated to AD 990–1160 (Beta-233922). As the bone was disarticulated and the skeletal remains incomplete, this feature is interpreted as a refuse pit. The radiocarbon date is suggestive of the later stages of the early medieval period. Additional medieval activity was recorded at the southern and south-eastern end of the site in the form of a range of linear field boundary ditches.

Conclusions

Perhaps the most significant aspect of the Lismullin excavations is the identification and examination of a sequence of prolonged, if somewhat episodic, activity stretching from at least the Middle Neolithic through the medieval period. The vast majority of this activity appears to have been of a ritual or ceremonial nature in the prehistoric period (notwithstanding the field system). Additionally, the location of the site appears to have been carefully chosen and may have been viewed as having a deep symbolic significance by the prehistoric inhabitants of the Gabhra Valley.

By the early medieval period the nature of activity at the site was more functional and included the exploitation of local tillage resources and their processing in the various cereal-drying kilns. The souterrain may have been used to store the dried grain and to safeguard it and the local landowners in times of danger and attack.

Thus far, the Lismullin excavations have offered us a tantalising glimpse of the archaeology and early history of the site, which will be greatly expanded on completion of the post-excavation analysis and full publication of the final results.

Notes

1. Lismullin 1: NGR 293437, 261602; height 77 m OD; excavation reg. no. E3074; Ministerial Direction nos A008/021 & A042; excavation director Aidan O'Connell.
2. Clowanstown 1: NGR 295518, 257771; height 118 m OD; excavation reg. no. E3064; Ministerial Direction no. A008/011; excavation director Matt Mossop.
   Blundelstown 1: NGR 292218, 261875; height 70 m OD; excavation reg. no. E3075; Ministerial Direction no. A008/022; excavation director Ed Danaher.

3
EXCAVATIONS AT CASTLEFARM—DIRECTOR'S FIRST FINDINGS

Aidan O'Connell

Introduction

The site at Castlefarm, Co. Meath, was located a short distance south-west of Dunboyne town on the R157 Dunboyne–Maynooth road, on the proposed M3 Dunboyne Link Road South (see site location map on page xiv).[1] It occupied a slightly elevated ridge in an area of gently undulating pastureland drained by the River Tolka. In the fifth century AD this ridge was chosen as the site for a relatively high-status settlement. A succession of ditched enclosures dating to the medieval period was subsequently located here and suggests a sequence of continuous settlement between the fifth and 13th centuries AD (Illus. 3.1 & 3.2).

A full archaeological excavation was carried out at the site from November 2005 to October 2006. A large assemblage of animal bones (in excess of 700 kg) was preserved in the fills of the enclosure ditches and other features, which when analysed will provide important information on the economy and diet of the inhabitants of the site. In addition, a wide range of artefacts including objects of copper, iron, bronze, glass, wood, antler, bone, pottery and stone were also recovered. The excavations have therefore provided us with an opportunity to examine the development of an early medieval settlement of some considerable wealth and to speculate on the nature of the interaction between these native inhabitants and the succeeding Anglo-Normans.

Neolithic period

At the north-west of the excavated area, between two later enclosure ditches, a scatter of 27 stake-holes, six post-holes and two pits were excavated. Unfortunately, it has not been possible to discern the outline of a structure from the pattern of post-holes and stake-holes in this area. However, a flint arrowhead, of a type known as *petit tranchet* derivative, recovered from the fill of one of the post-holes can be dated to the Late Neolithic period at 3000–2500 BC. Although the practice of collecting and depositing prehistoric objects at early medieval sites is well attested (O'Sullivan 2006), the possibility remains that this artefact may indicate the earliest datable activity at the site.

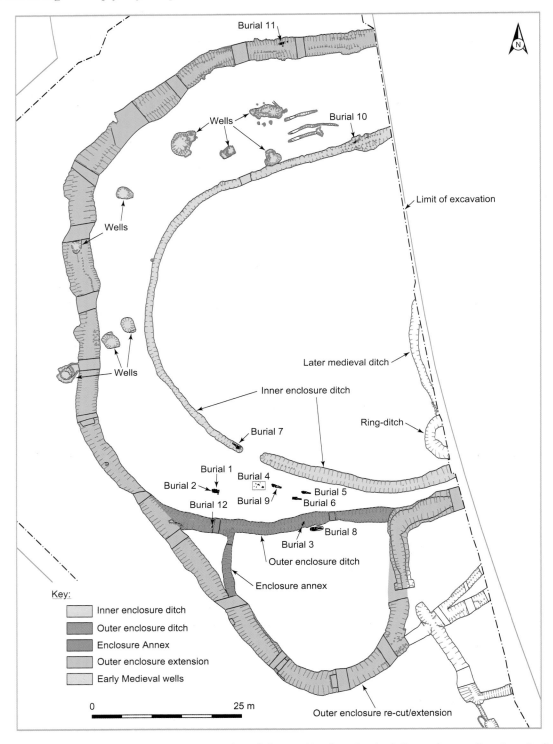

Illus. 3.1—Simplified post-excavation plan of the site (Archaeological Consultancy Services Ltd).

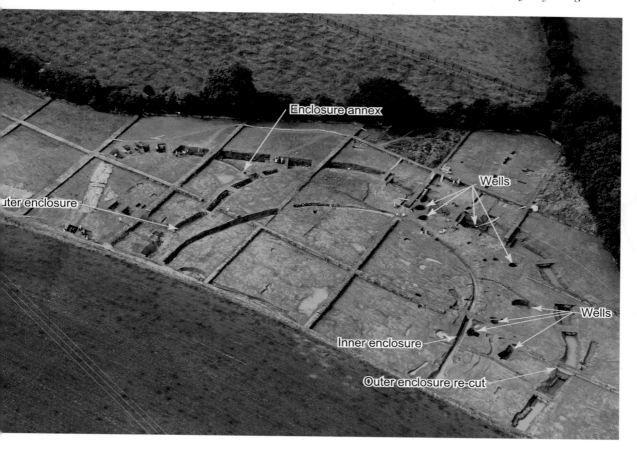

Illus. 3.2—Aerial view of the site, from the north-east (Archaeological Consultancy Services Ltd based on a photograph by Studio Lab).

Bronze Age

Three linear features of unknown function were recorded c. 40 m east of the above-mentioned post-holes and stake-holes (Illus. 3.1). These east–west-aligned features were roughly parallel and ran perpendicular to the natural gradient in this area of the site. A bronze disc-headed pin was collected from the fill of the central feature; such disc-headed pins can be ascribed to the Dowris phase of the later Bronze Age in Ireland (c. 1000–800 BC). All three features were filled with a grey, marl-like material, and the absence of stone packing, charcoal, associated post-holes and perpendicular returns would suggest that they are not structural. Their alignment against the natural gradient suggests that they are not drains. In addition, their depth and an absence of further similar features suggest that they are not prehistoric plough marks. The presence of the disc-headed pin, however, provides further evidence of prehistoric activity at the site.

Outer enclosure ditch

Inner enclosure ditch

Later medieval ditch

Ring-ditch

Illus. 3.3—Annotated elevated view of the site post-excavation, from the east (Archaeological Consultancy Services Ltd based on a photograph by Hawkeye).

Iron Age

The final area of possible prehistoric activity was a ring-ditch located at the east of the site (Illus. 3.1 & 3.3). This consisted of a circular ditch c. 7 m in diameter, 2 m in width and 0.7–0.8 m in depth. Five separate fills were recorded in the ditch. Two fragments of corroded iron were recovered from the middle fill of the ditch and the site has therefore been ascribed a provisional Iron Age date. In addition, some small fragments of burnt bone (as yet unidentified) came from two of the fills, suggesting a token cremation deposit. There was no trace of an external bank or an internal mound; these features, if present originally, may have been ploughed away by modern agricultural activity.

Medieval enclosure complex

The site at Castlefarm occupied a low natural ridge that extended east–west across the proposed road corridor. This elevated area was initially chosen as the site of an enclosed settlement between the mid-fifth and the mid-seventh century AD and occupied between this time and the 13th century. Four successive elements to the early medieval enclosure complex were recorded during the excavations: an inner enclosure ditch, an outer enclosure ditch, a southern enclosure annex and an outer enclosure re-cut/extension (Illus. 3.1–3.3). As the site has been subjected to extensive ploughing in post-medieval and modern times, no internal banks associated with the enclosure ditches survived. Additionally, no direct evidence of internal occupation (i.e. structures or dwellings) was recorded during the excavation. In effect, what remained on site were the lower fills of the enclosure ditches. To the east of the site an additional geophysical survey, undertaken outside the road corridor during the excavations in order to determine the full extent of the site, recorded the remainder of the enclosure and some additional associated linear features/ditches (Illus. 3.4; Nicholls & Shiel 2006).

Inner enclosure ditch

The inner enclosure ditch (Illus. 3.1–3.3) followed the brow of the elevated ridge. It was a D-shaped feature measuring 90 m east–west by 60–70 m north–south. Roughly half of this ditch (c. 123 m along its circumference) lay within the road corridor. A causewayed entrance was situated at the south-west. In contrast, entrances to early medieval enclosures in Ireland are usually aligned to the east and south-east. It has been suggested that this location derives from a concern to gain protection from prevailing winds and to orient entrances towards the rising sun (Stout 1997, 18–19). It is also possible that these orientations are a cultural continuity stretching back into prehistory.

To the east of the causewayed entrance the inner ditch was 2 m wide and 1.35 m deep. The basal fills of the ditch in this area indicate that it was allowed to silt up. The finds recovered from throughout the ditch in this area included various metal dress fasteners in the form of ringed pins (Illus. 3.5), bone pins made from pig fibulae, iron knife blades and various pieces of worked antler, including a knife handle with ring and dot decoration. The main form of ringed pin represented in the inner ditch was the spiral-ringed, looped-headed pin. This class of ringed pin has parallels at pre-Viking Age ringfort and crannog sites in Ireland and can be dated to the fourth to eighth centuries AD (Fanning 1994, 14–15). In addition, the ring and dot decoration on the antler knife handle is also suggestive of a pre-Viking origin. Cattle bone from the primary fill of this ditch has been radiocarbon-dated to AD 450–640 (Beta-220131; see Appendix 1 for details of radiocarbon dating results), confirming that it was constructed towards the beginning of the early medieval period.

At the west of the causewayed entrance, the inner ditch was significantly narrower and shallower (1–1.4 m wide by 0.4–0.8 m deep). This may be explained by the fact that it was cut through compact, stony boulder clay in this area. The south-western section of the inner ditch was re-cut in the later medieval period, but to the north, north-west and west the recovered artefacts from the inner ditch were overwhelmingly early medieval in date. The northern segment of the inner ditch would have been waterlogged when in use, and successive re-cuts recorded in this area indicate the need for periodic cleaning of the ditch in this wetter area.

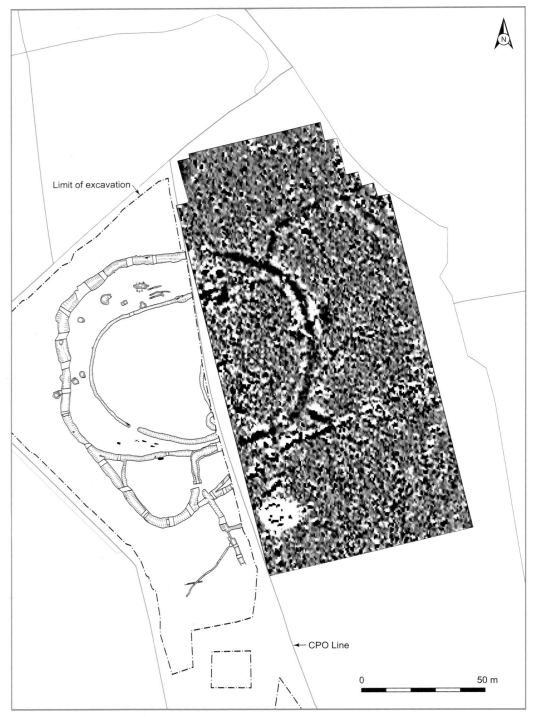

Limit of excavation

CPO Line

0   50 m

Illus. 3.4—Post-excavation plan of the site combined with a greyscale image of the geophysical survey results from outside the road corridor (Archaeological Consultancy Services Ltd based on an image by Target Archaeological Geophysics).

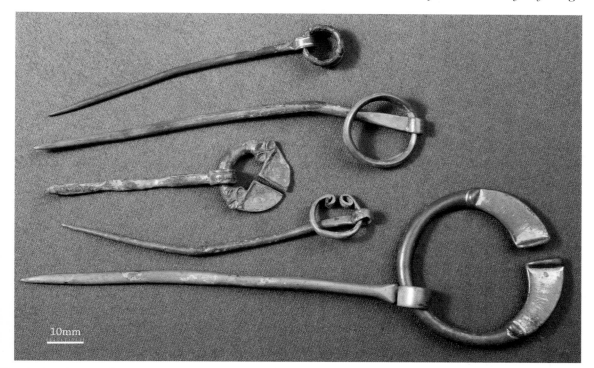

Illus. 3.5—Copper-alloy pins recovered at Castlefarm: (top to bottom) ring-pin, double spiral ring-pin, penannular brooch, scroll-headed pin and penannular brooch with tinning (John Sunderland).

Illus. 3.6—Close-up view of copper-alloy penannular brooch (John Sunderland).

Burials

A total of 12 burials have also been recorded at the site. Four of these are from the upper levels of various ditches, and one is an infant burial that may be significantly later than the other archaeological activity on the site. The remaining examples were recorded at the south-west of the site in the vicinity of the entrance to the inner enclosure. These seven burials (three male, two female, two unknown) were laid on their backs in simple earth-cut graves. The bodies were orientated west–east, with the head at the west. In some cases the burial posture suggests that they were buried in a shroud; however, no associated bone or metal pins or other grave goods were recovered. One of the seven burials (Burial 1) has been dated to AD 410–580 (Beta-229298), which indicates that this group may be associated with the primary occupation of the early medieval inner enclosure. They were located adjacent to, but outside, the causewayed entrance at the south-west of the inner enclosure. These seven burials may therefore belong to the kin group who inhabited the Castlefarm enclosure complex in the early phase of its occupation. While they ascribed to the relatively new Christian belief system, they retained a tradition of burial on family lands. O'Brien (in press) has suggested that burial in monastic cemeteries was reserved for clerics, patrons and high-status individuals until the late seventh/early eighth century.

Another burial (Burial 7) at the south-west of the site was also associated with the first phase of occupation. The remains of a young adult male (age at death estimated at 28–34 years) were found in the south-western ditch terminal at the causewayed entrance to the inner enclosure ditch and have been dated to AD 420–610 (Beta-229299). The skull was missing, and two of the vertebrae showed signs of trauma, possibly caused by sudden impact (Coughlan 2007b, 1–6), suggesting that the lives of the inhabitants were not always entirely peaceful.

Outer enclosure

The enclosure complex was later augmented by the construction of an outer enclosure ditch that was roughly concentric with the inner enclosure. This outer enclosure would have affected a considerable expansion to the north and west of the site at a later stage in the early medieval phase of occupation (see below), enclosing an area measuring 110 m east–west by 90 m north–south. The ditch was re-cut later in the early medieval period except for a section to the south, which was c. 47 m long, 2.20 m wide and 1 m deep (Illus. 3.1–3.3). Numerous early medieval artefacts, including glass beads, a spindle whorl, pig fibula pins and a baluster-headed, spiral-ringed pin, were recorded from the fills of this ditch. In addition, cattle bone from this feature has been dated to AD 770–980 (Beta-220132), a later stage in the early medieval occupation.

The construction of this outer enclosure ditch suggests an expansion of the complex between the eighth and the 10th century. At the east, the geophysical survey suggests that the inner enclosure was re-cut, as the two features cannot be differentiated (Illus. 3.4). In addition, breaks visible in the ditch in the geophysical survey results suggest that the enclosure entrance was re-located either to the north or to the south-east. Two rubbish pits, containing lignite bracelets, iron knives, a spindle whorl and a bone pin, were cut into the top of the surviving early medieval section of the outer enclosure ditch, indicating that this section went out of use in the early medieval period.

Enclosure annex

An annex was added to the south of the outer enclosure. This was formed by a curving ditch that survived partially at the south-west of the enclosure (Illus. 3.1 & 3.2). The majority of the annex ditch was cut away by a later extension to the outer enclosure (see below), and it is therefore currently dated to the early medieval period. The former extent of the annex can be surmised from the line of the outer enclosure extension. It is likely to have measured some 30 m east–west by 20–25 m north–south and may have functioned as a livestock enclosure. The surviving portion of the annex ditch was orientated roughly north–south, had a V-shaped profile and was 9 m long, 1.3–1.75 m wide and 0.65–0.82 m deep. No datable artefacts or other materials were recovered from the ditch fills. In addition, compounding this lack of datable material, the direct relationship between this annex ditch and the outer enclosure to the north could not be ascertained as the point where they originally joined had been cut away by a later pit.

Outer enclosure extension

The outer enclosure ditch was later re-cut, widened and deepened at the north and west (Illus. 3.2) and was extended through the southern enclosure annex, incorporating it into the main body of the newly extended outer enclosure. The dimensions of the extended outer enclosure were 120 m north–south by 100 m east–west.

Three phases of activity have been recorded in this ditch extension. The two initial phases were early medieval in date. The third phase occurred in the later medieval period (see below). In the primary phase, the recovered artefacts included a bone stick-pin of seventh- to ninth-century date, which can be paralleled with a similar pin from the Period II occupation at Lagore crannog (Hencken 1950, 192–3; Kinsella 2006a, 14), and wooden items including numerous bucket fragments. A sample of a sheep horn core from the primary fill of this ditch has been dated to AD 780–980 (Beta-220133). Finds from the second phase of this ditch included an omega pin dating from the seventh to 10th centuries (Ó Floinn 1999, 77) and a decorated copper-alloy mount with a perforated wooden insert.

Wells

A series of nine earth-cut wells were located at the site (Illus. 3.1 & 3.2). They varied in depth from 1.60 m to 2.50 m and were unlined. The bases of these features were below the water table, resulting in good preservation of environmental remains, worked leather fragments and wooden items such as bucket staves (Illus. 3.7). The size and quantity of the wells indicate that they may have been used in a semi-industrial context. Numerous metal needles were recovered from some of the ditch fills on the site, as well as spindle whorls and a loom beater pin, suggesting that textile production may have been carried out at the enclosure complex.

It is unlikely that all nine wells were in use at the same time. It is more probable that they span the entire timeframe of the early medieval site occupation. Two of the wells were cut by the early medieval outer enclosure re-cut/extension, indicating that they are associated with the earlier phase of site occupation relating to the inner enclosure ditch. A later date is indicated for a large

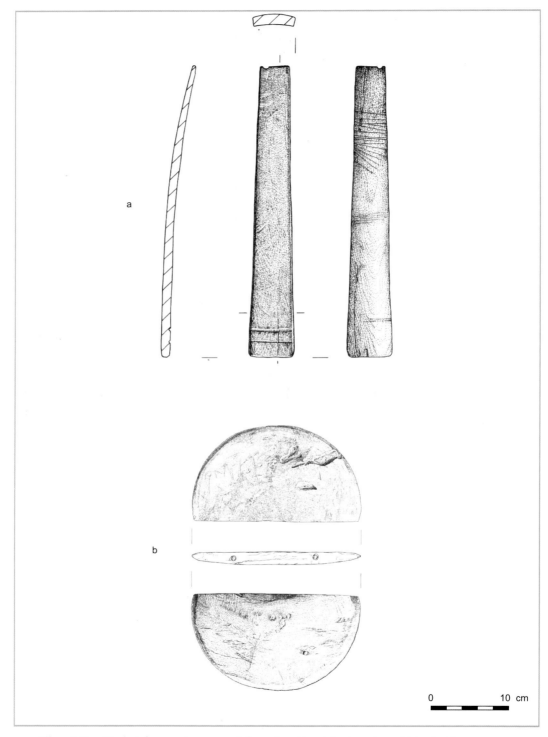

Illus. 3.7—Bucket fragments recovered from the site: a) bucket stave; b) bucket base (Archaeological Consultancy Services Ltd).

well located at the north of the site, which cut a pit containing a tinned copper-alloy penannular brooch (Illus. 3.5). A similar brooch was found in the early 11th-century levels at Ballinderry crannog no. 1 (Hencken 1936, 155; fig. 24, D; Kinsella 2006a, 15).

Later medieval occupation

Substantial later medieval activity was also recorded at the site. This was confined to the space previously occupied by the early medieval inner and outer enclosures. The entire circuit of the extended outer enclosure ditch was once again re-cut in this period. Additionally, a portion of the inner enclosure ditch at the west of the causeway was also re-cut.

The final phase of the outer enclosure ditch (incorporating the enclosure annex) had numerous later medieval finds including sherds of medieval pottery and metal stick pins. This activity points to a continuity of use of the enclosure into the medieval period. Significantly, some of the stick pins, such as the club-headed variety, can be dated to the mid-11th to the mid-13th century (Scully 1997), suggesting an overlap between the early and late medieval periods.

The early medieval inner enclosure ditch was also re-cut to the west of the causewayed entrance. This later section of re-cut ditch produced large quantities of ironworking waste, suggesting industrial activities in this area. The re-use of the apparently obsolete outer enclosure ditch was evidenced by a medieval kiln that was cut into the ditch.

An additional enclosure was located within the inner enclosure, north of the ring-ditch. This was represented by a shallow curving ditch, 0.35 m deep, containing numerous sherds of late medieval pottery, fragments of iron pins and a fragment of a bone comb. Only the western side of this ditch (c. 18 m along its circumference) was located within the proposed road corridor; however, evidence from the geophysical survey suggests that its diameter may be 20 m.

Early modern period

At the southern side of the enclosure complex, a field boundary ditch depicted on the first-edition Ordnance Survey six-inch map (1836) was recorded during the excavation. Numerous modern finds including pottery, glass, metal fragments and a clay pipe were recovered from its fill. In addition, limited evidence for modern drainage and cultivation practices was recorded during the excavations.

Discussion

The earliest activity on the site is suggested by the Neolithic arrowhead associated with the post-hole and the Late Bronze Age disc-headed pin associated with the linear features. Neither is indicative of any large-scale or permanent settlement. The ring-ditch has been ascribed a provisional Iron Age date on the basis of the corroded iron recovered from the ditch fill; however, the possibility that it was constructed or continued in use into the early medieval period cannot be discounted.

Four broad phases of activity can be recognised at the early medieval enclosure. The first phase involved the construction of the D-shaped inner enclosure ditch between the fifth and seventh centuries. This was a substantial feature with dimensions of 90 m east–west by 70 m north–south. A rich artefact assemblage from this phase included iron blades, worked antler, bone comb fragments, copper-alloy needles, pig fibula pins, a lignite bracelet and ringed pins. This material is indicative of a relatively high-status settlement of the early medieval period. Large quantities of animal bones in the ditch fills suggest that livestock played an important role in the economy of the site. In addition, the needles and a highly polished bone artefact possibly used in association with a loom are suggestive of textile production. The two wells cut by the outer enclosure ditch probably belong to the earlier inner enclosure phase, as did seven burials at the south-west of this.

The enclosure complex was extended, probably in the later eighth to the early ninth century, by the construction of the outer enclosure ditch. This extension involved a re-cut of the inner enclosure ditch at the east (outside the road corridor; see Illus. 3.4) and a substantial expansion of the enclosed area at the north, west and south of the site. A similar finds assemblage to the inner enclosure was recovered from this feature. The intention of the expansion would appear to have been to include formally the industrial activity centred on the wells to the north and west of the inner enclosure.

The next phase of activity saw the addition of an annex at the south of the outer enclosure. This may have functioned as a livestock pen and was possibly an attempt to separate industrial activities from agricultural ones. The final early medieval phase saw a further southern extension of the enclosure complex to incorporate the southern annex. This extension was initially carried out between the late ninth and the early 10th century.

The continued wealth and prosperity of the inhabitants of the site can be seen in the appearance of new dress ornaments like omega- and scroll-headed pins and two penannular brooches. The penannular brooches in particular would have been highly prized dress ornaments. Both were associated with wells. One was deposited deliberately with an omega pin in a small pit cut by a later well. It may have been deposited for safe keeping. The second was a decorated miniature copper-alloy brooch of late eighth- to ninth-century date (M Ryan, pers. comm.) collected from the backfill of a well at the west of the site.

From the available evidence it appears that the early medieval enclosure complex was inhabited by a family unit of some wealth and status who could draw upon local labour resources for the construction and extension of the enclosure and probably to carry out industrial activities requiring numerous wells. The bases of two bowl furnaces and metallurgical waste in refuse pits were also recorded at the site but currently await dating. They may, however, indicate that limited metalworking was carried out at the site in this period, although the relatively small scale of this activity suggests that metalworking was not central to the economy of the early medieval occupants of Castlefarm.

The wealth of the site's inhabitants is also indicated by the rich artefactual and faunal assemblages (in excess of 700 kg of animal bone was recovered during the excavations). This wealth is particularly emphasised by the high incidence of dress ornaments, including ringed pins, pig fibula pins, penannular brooches, omega pins, and lignite bracelets. Mytum (1992, 136) has proposed that individuals displayed their place in society by what they wore. As such, one would expect to find a much lower incidence of dress ornaments on a site of lesser status. Unfortunately, no evidence of any dwellings or other structures related to the enclosure was recorded. It is probable that these were destroyed by deep ploughing associated with modern agricultural activity. Alternatively, structures and/or dwellings from the early medieval period may survive at the east of the site, beyond the road corridor.

The archaeological evidence at Castlefarm would appear to suggest a continuity of settlement from the early medieval period into the early stages of the later medieval period. Medieval activity consisted of the re-cut in the outer enclosure ditch and limited localised industrial activity carried out within the inner and outer enclosure ditches, and the later medieval activity on the site was confined within the spaces previously occupied by the early medieval enclosures. These existing ditches and the morphology of the site were not altered significantly. This is an interesting situation that contrasts with the excavated evidence at other multi-period sites. For example, at Rathmullan, Co. Down, an early medieval raised rath was heightened in the later medieval period by the Anglo-Normans for use as a motte (Lynn 1988, 48); at Duneight, Co. Down, another early medieval enclosed settlement was converted to a motte and bailey and at Beal Boru, Co. Clare, a ringfort was possibly converted to a ringwork (O'Keeffe 2001, 21, 29). Ó Drisceoil (2002, 189–94), in examining the excavated evidence from 15 motte castles, found that six originated as ringforts and a further two were associated with underlying souterrains. The reasons cited for the conversion of existing sites are the convenience of using a readymade foundation for a new fortification and the symbolism inherent in the replacement of the existing owners with a new political authority (O'Keeffe 2001, 29; Ó Drisceoil 2002, 189). A contrasting continuity in the settlement pattern at the Castlefarm enclosure would therefore suggest that the Anglo-Normans, while taking control over the area, did not need to assert their claim to the lands by occupying an existing enclosure. They instead appear to have chosen an adjacent site to build their ringwork.

In the later medieval period, Dunboyne was an important manorial centre and attained the status of one of Meath's second-stratum borough settlements after the Anglo-Norman colonisation (Murphy 2006a, 11). The earliest mention of the castle at Dunboyne is in a charter of William Petit concerning the church at Dunboyne in 1205–1210 (ibid., 7). The castle in question may be the ringwork recently excavated by Claire Cotter (pers. comm.) before the construction of the Dunboyne Castle Hotel and located at a short distance from the early medieval enclosure at Castlefarm.

The early stages of the later medieval period appear to have remained largely peaceful in the Meath region (Murphy 2006a, 18). Perhaps this enabled the descendants of the early medieval occupants of the Castlefarm enclosure complex to retain their lands despite the success of the new ruling Anglo-Norman class who undoubtedly exercised control over the wealth and resources in the region. Alternatively, the existing occupants may have been replaced by a new community or family unit of Gaelic Irish betaghs (from the Irish *biatach*, meaning food provider) subject to

Norman control. Either way, the economy and status of the site appear to have declined in this period. This can be seen in the relatively sparse later medieval faunal remains and artefacts. The occurrence of Dublin-type cooking wares suggests that the later medieval occupation can be dated to the 12th and 13th centuries.

In the 15th century the area around Dunboyne experienced an increase in warfare and lawlessness (ibid., 18). In 1475 the castle was rebuilt by Edmond Butler and the demesne lands may have been reorganised (ibid., 12–13), perhaps incorporating the Castlefarm enclosure complex. The site was probably taken into direct Anglo-Norman control at this time and subsequently functioned as grange or an out-farm to the castle for the remainder of the later medieval period. The agricultural nature of the site subsequently remained unchanged until recent times.

Note

1. Castlefarm 1: NGR 300394, 241605; height 73 m OD; excavation reg. no. E3023; Ministerial Direction no. A017/001; excavation director Aidan O'Connell.

4
EARLY MEDIEVAL SETTLEMENT AT ROESTOWN 2

Robert O'Hara

Introduction

Sometime during the sixth century AD, a slight rise overlooking a small marsh north-east of Dunshaughlin, Co. Meath, was chosen as a site that would remain a focus for settlement for the following five or six hundred years. During this time the surrounding landscape was enclosed and farmed, the settlement developed, and fortunes made and undoubtedly lost. Settlement at the site continued into the 13th century, but after this time it was abandoned, its location, history and name eventually forgotten until the excavation of the site in 2005–6. The site was Roestown 2 (see site location map on page xiv).[1] Previous papers dealing with the archaeological investigations here have focused on the findings of a geophysical survey of the site and the provisional excavation results (Deevy 2005, 85–6; O'Hara 2007). The summary below presents a further update on the preliminary findings of the excavation.

Townlands may sometimes reflect, with some compensation for subsequent alterations, the farm holdings of pre-Norman Ireland. Townland names in Meath suffixed by -town are generally held to be of medieval origin as they are frequently compounded with personal names of Norman origin. This perhaps led antiquarian John O'Donovan (1836) to list the Irish name for the townland as *Baile an Róidh*, suggesting that *Róidh* was derived from such a family (Roe or Rowe). In south-east Meath, a study of the distribution of Gaelic and English townland names revealed that many of the historical parish centres (including Ratoath, Trevet and Skreen) remained surrounded by strongly Gaelic-named areas (Murphy 2006b). O'Donovan's translation is almost certainly incorrect, the scholar probably intending *Baile an Roidh*, 'the settlement/place of/near/at the red mire' (Dineen 1927), a location that must refer to the former marsh, now the townland of Redbog immediately east of Roestown. The modern townland name thus developed from an Anglicisation ('Raweston') of an existing Gaelic name, although the *baile* prefix may not pre-date the 11th century AD on etymological grounds (Toner 2004, 27).

However, O'Donovan's notes also mentioned that locals occasionally referred to the townland as *Raiste*. Although its meaning had been lost by the early 19th century, the prefix *Ra-* is a common diminution of *rath* ('earthen rampart'), the Irish equivalent of the modern term ringfort, an early medieval enclosed settlement. Stout (2005, 145) has highlighted that there is rarely more than one ringfort in each townland unit. On this evidence, *Baile an Roidh* and *Raiste* could preserve pre-Norman names of the area, and probably associated with the settlement under discussion.

A medieval extent compiled in the 14th century recorded a holding of two carucates at Raweston at the manor of Dunshaughlin (Murphy 2006b). Two carucates represented 240 medieval acres, or between 500 and 600 statute acres (between 2–2.5 km²). The 14th-century holding may thus have consisted of the modern townlands of Roestown and Redbog (398 and 209 statute acres respectively). Bhreathnach (1999) has argued that land grants of the Anglo-Normans were, in some cases, predetermined by existing divisions and that, on entering the territory of the ancient kingdom of Southern Brega, they exploited the established pattern of territorial division and settlement. There are no contemporaneous records that give the acreage of farm holdings in this period, but we may consider that the pre-Norman holding associated with Roestown 2 was not vastly different from that of the 14th century, in the region of 500–600 statute acres.

Before the introduction of modern drainage systems, much of the surrounding landscape would probably have been quite damp, and perhaps seasonally waterlogged. A small stream that was significantly widened and deepened in the 1950s passes to the south of the site, forming a natural boundary between the townlands of Roestown and Cooksland. The stream continues into Dunshaughlin, through the former lake at Lagore (now reclaimed), where it would have merged with the Broadmeadow river system, thus linking it to the famous crannog that was excavated at Lagore (Hencken 1950) and onward to the recently excavated mill/settlement site at Raystown (Seaver 2006). Rivers and streams were convenient boundary indicators and often used to delimit territory (Kelly 1997, 409).

Perhaps Roestown 2 was close to a fording point across this stream. It was also located along the modern boundary between the baronies of Ratoath and Skreen, while the barony of Deece lay a short distance to the west. Stout (1997, 123) outlined legal references to grades of noblemen whose duty was to protect the borders of a kingdom (*aire forgill*) or to carry out raids or do battle in neighbouring *tuatha* (*aire deso*) and who consequently would have had their residences close to a territory's border. Perhaps Roestown 2 served such a purpose. Arguably, it was intentionally sited and developed in relation to the chief settlements based around Dunshaughlin and Lagore crannog, perhaps acting as an intermediate between client and king, receiving tribute and food rent from outlying clients and ultimately forming a protective ring around the seat of royal power of the Clann Chernaig Sotail, a family of the southern Uí Néill dynasty.

Archaeological excavation

The site was divided into two distinct areas of excavation on the east (Area A) and west (Area B) side of the existing N3. The site was previously unrecorded until the advance geophysical survey in 2000–1 (Illus. 4.1). Both areas of excavation had separate stratigraphical sequences that could not be comprehensively integrated owing to the truncation of the site by the N3 (Illus. 4.2). A broad sequence of development for the site is suggested below (date ranges are approximate):

Phase 1A: Sixth century. Construction of main settlement enclosure (Enclosure 1), including Structures A–C and ancillary field systems/enclosures (Enclosures 2, 5–7 and 11 and ditch F935).

Illus. 4.1—Greyscale geophysical image of the site at Roestown 2 showing how the existing N3 has split the site into two areas, Area A (to the east) and Area B (to the west) (Archaeological Consultancy Services Ltd based on the geophysical image produced by GSB Prospection Ltd).

Illus. 4.2—Post-excavation aerial view of Roestown 2, from the west (Studio Lab).

Phase 1B: Seventh century. Construction of Enclosures 12 and 13 (and perhaps F1315). Re-cuts to Enclosure 11. Creation of Enclosure 10 from F935. Structure D.

Phase 1C: Seventh century. Extension of Enclosure 13.

Phase 2A: Eighth century. Construction of Enclosures 3, 8 and 14 and possibly souterrain. Re-cut of Enclosure 1, with internal subdivisions.

Phase 2B: Eighth–ninth century. Construction of Enclosure 9 and ditch F933. Re-cuts to Enclosure 3.

Phase 2C: Ninth–10th century. Construction of Enclosures 15 and 16. Re-cuts to Enclosures 3 and 9. Partial backfilling of Enclosure 1 with associated alterations to Enclosure 3, F933, and ditch F252.

Phase 3: 10th century. Re-cut of Enclosure 1. Western partition ditches.

Phase 4: 11th century. Shallow ditches F403 and F841 define former extent of Enclosure 1. Large refuse pits F411 and F1301. Backfilling of souterrain.

Phase 5: 13th century. Enclosure 4 and pit F176.

No features of certain prehistoric date were recorded in the site, although a number of earlier artefacts were recovered in unstratified or chronologically later deposits, including a lozenge-shaped arrowhead and two hollow-based arrowheads, probably of Late Neolithic date. These could have been dropped or lost while hunting along the prehistoric lakeshore situated immediately east of the site (Redbog), although O'Sullivan (2006) has argued for the possibility that certain prehistoric items, such as arrowheads or stone axeheads, were actively sought out by early medieval people as talismans or charms. In addition to these arrowheads, a quantity of flint and chert flakes and blades was recovered from stratified early medieval deposits. Worked or struck flint occurs frequently in such contexts (Ó Ríordáin 1949; Cleary 2006; Comber 2002), some of which may be residual prehistoric artefacts, but some crude flint objects found in the early medieval deposits may be strike-a-lights, which, when used in conjunction with fire-steels and suitable tinder, for example wheat chaff (Kelly 1997, 242), could be used to start a fire. A fine example of an early medieval fire-steel was found at Roestown 2 (Illus. 4.3). This triangular piece of iron with turned-in ends is similar to objects from Garryduff I ringfort, Co. Cork (O'Kelly 1963, 51, fig. 7, nos 381, 297), and closely resembles more decorative types found at Viking Age sites across Scandinavia and the Baltic region (Petersen 1951, 433–8). An object described as a belt runner from Ballinderry No. 1 crannog, Co. Westmeath, would also appear to be a fire-steel (Hencken 1936, 167, fig. 31, A).

Phase 1A

The D-shape of the principal enclosure (Enclosure 1; Illus. 4.4), approximately one-fifth of which was beyond the western limit of excavation, was formed during the initial construction of the settlement and was largely retained, with little alteration, through two subsequent re-cuts. The original ditch had a U-shaped profile (2.2 m wide by 1.30 m deep), enclosed an area with maximum internal dimensions of 76 m by 53 m and was a completely excavated circuit, although a stepped inner slope indicated a likely entry point, facing north-east. A bridge was thus required to gain access to the interior of the settlement, perhaps a similar arrangement as recorded at

Illus. 4.3—Group of finds from Roestown 2 including (clockwise from lower left) iron fire-steel, stone pin sharpener, whetstone, stone ingot mould, crucible fragment and iron slotted punch (John Sunderland).

Baronstown 1 (A008/017), where a bridge formed by split tree trunks spanned the ditch (Linnane & Kinsella, chapter 6; Linnane & Kinsella 2007). This ditch at Roestown 2 contained bone motif or trial pieces, an iron knife, a bone pin, a copper-alloy ringed pin, fragments of iron and copper-alloy objects, and struck flint. Significant amounts of animal bone survived, and a fragment of cattle bone provided a radiocarbon date of AD 530–650 (Beta-220115; see Appendix 1 for details of radiocarbon dating results). Lesser quantities of burnt bone, charcoal, slag and seashell were recovered, as well as grasses and brushwood where preservation allowed.

Within the interior of Enclosure 1, three potential structures were identified as belonging to Phase 1A (Illus. 4.4). Structure A was formed by a curving drip gully and associated post-holes enclosing a roughly circular area approximately 6.5 m in diameter. Structure B comprised a semicircular drip gully enclosing an area approximately 4 m in diameter. Surrounding this structure were a number of shallow gullies, perhaps the remains of small pens abutting the Phase 1 bank. They may also be associated with Structure C, a series of segmented drip gullies forming a roughly square

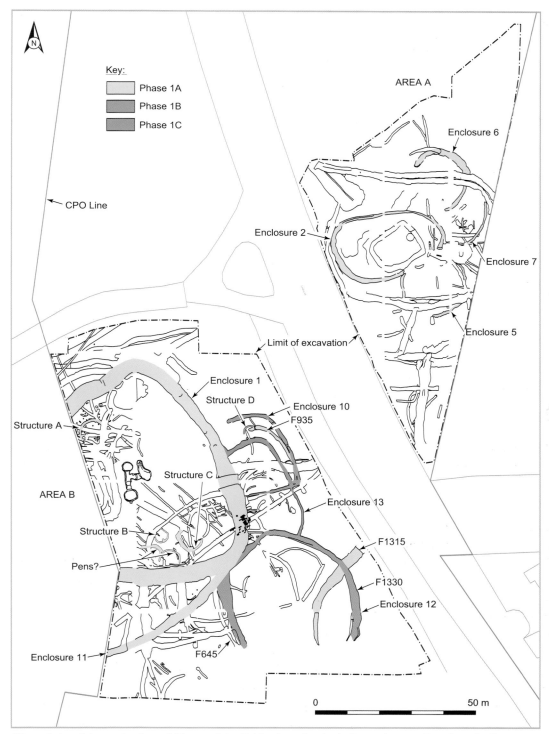

Illus. 4.4—Schematic plan of Phases 1A–C (Archaeological Consultancy Services Ltd).

structure (7 m by 6.5 m). Separating Structures B and C were extensively disturbed metalled pathways that represent the truncated remains of former stone paths.

Five bone motif pieces were excavated at Roestown 2, each bearing one or more motif panels, as well as etched but unfinished patterns (Illus. 4.5). Motif pieces were scraps of portable material, usually bone or stone, but also wood and possibly leather, carved or incised with discrete positive patterns and are believed to be connected with fine metalworking (Comber 1997; O'Meadhra 1987).

The closest parallels for the Roestown 2 pieces, both geographically and stylistically, can be found at Lagore (Hencken 1950, 182–3, figs 95, 96). The available radiocarbon dates for Enclosure 1 suggest a late sixth- or seventh-century date for some of these pieces, one of which came from a primary deposit within the initial cut for Enclosure 1 (F405). Hencken (1950, 138) had no doubt that the Lagore motif pieces were from the same hand or workshop and that this group of craftsmen tested a variety of chip-carved designs on bone before manufacturing objects, including the 'Dunshaughlin brooch', a penannular brooch recovered from the Dunshaughlin area in the 19th century, and saw parallels between the Lagore motif pieces and decorative motifs on this brooch. It seems reasonable to suggest that craftsmen from the same tradition or background practising at Lagore also produced the motifs on the Roestown 2 pieces. There are clear chronological and stylistic parallels between the metalworking assemblages of Roestown 2 and Lagore, with Lagore perhaps one element (albeit an important one) in a wider network of sites producing or involved in specialised metalwork in the period (late sixth to early seventh century AD). It is important,

Illus. 4.5—Bone motif pieces from Roestown 2 (John Sunderland).

however, to highlight that a marginally greater number of motif pieces were identified at Roestown 2, suggesting perhaps that the site enjoyed a role in the concept and design of the motifs found at Lagore.

From the beginning of the settlement at Roestown 2, the surrounding landscape was in a constant state of change as successive annexes and field systems developed in tandem with Enclosure 1. The area immediately south of Enclosure 1 was enclosed by a multi-phase ditch (Enclosure 11) that extended beyond the limit of excavation. It was a long, deep ditch that was re-cut on a number of occasions. It is possible that this ditch continued west for some distance beyond the road corridor before returning to rejoin Enclosure 1. Immediately beyond the entrance to Enclosure 1 was a short arcuate ditch (F935) that developed into Enclosure 10 at a later stage. Further east (in Area A) a penannular ditched enclosure (Enclosure 2) bounded an area measuring approximately 35 m by 20 m and was the focus for its own annex ditches, including Enclosure 5 (approximately 20 m diameter), Enclosure 6 (10 m by 17 m) and Enclosure 7, a curving ditch that probably linked Enclosures 5 and 6. An articulated skeleton of a dog (*Canis familiaris*) found within the ditch of Enclosure 6 (O'Hara 2007, illus. 5) was radiocarbon-dated to AD 630–710 (Beta-219003). The burial did not appear to cut into the overlying ditch fill but rather was carefully placed on the base of the ditch, suggesting that the burial of the dog closely followed the excavation of the ditch.

Two sherds of E-ware were recovered from Enclosure 2, with further examples found within Enclosure 1, albeit as residual inclusions in stratigraphically later deposits. E-ware is a coarse, unglazed, wheel-thrown pottery with an increasing distribution among sixth- and seventh-century contexts in Ireland. It was probably used for domestic purposes as it consisted in the main of kitchen and table wares. The native ceramic tradition in this period was a coarse handmade fabric, most suited to storage of foodstuffs or cooking (Ryan 1973, 620–3). Wooding (1996, 82) has argued that stratification in early medieval society could have manifested itself in the use of vessels appropriate to rank. E-ware on archaeological sites has traditionally been understood as an indicator of status and also as evidence of external trading contacts in the period, probably having accompanied shipments of wine from north-central or western France (Thomas 1976; 1981; 1990; Wooding 1996, 81). A brief review of sites in Meath producing E-ware indicates its extensive distribution during this period. Sherds have been identified at Lagore (Hencken 1950), Moynagh Lough (Bradley 1991; 1993; 1995; 1996), Ninch (Eogan & Reid 2001; McConway 2003; 2004), Colp West (Gowen 1989b; Clarke & Murphy 2001), Painestown (O'Hara 2008a), Smithstown (Gowen 1989c), and elsewhere along the M3 at Garretstown 2 (S Rathbone, pers. comm.) and Castletown Tara 1 (S Elder, pers. comm.).[2]

A curvilinear ditch (F1315) located south-east of Enclosure 1 was recorded for only a short distance within the limit of excavation. It extended eastwards beneath the N3, while to the south it had been removed by modern disturbance. It was largely devoid of archaeological material but appeared to have been re-cut before being backfilled and cut by later features. It could potentially pre-date Enclosure 1; however, in the absence of definite dating material and unambiguous pre-sixth-century features, this ditch is currently interpreted as being broadly contemporary with Enclosure 1 (see below for further discussion).

Phase 1B

The two subsequent subdivisions of Phase 1 are defined by extensions or re-cutting of existing features and the creation of new annexes. Enclosure 2 was re-cut, and re-cuts of Enclosure 11 probably occurred in this period also. The ditch F935 was replaced with Enclosure 10 (25 m by 17 m), which was probably associated with Structure D, which survived as two curving gullies forming a circular structure approximately 4 m in diameter. It possibly functioned as a metallurgy workshop as it produced a crucible fragment, while further artefacts relating to fine metalworking, including an ingot mould (Illus. 4.3) and bone motif pieces, were found in backfilled Enclosure 1 ditch deposits immediately west of the structure. Enclosure 12 was a complex multi-phase enclosure that, in its later stages, was certainly sub-circular (approximately 35 m in diameter). It abutted Enclosure 1 to the south-east and was formed by two curving ditches (F645 to the west, F1250 to the east). F1330 continued the same alignment as F1250 but was separated by a thick outcrop of bedrock, and it could not be determined whether they were contemporaneous features. The enclosure continued to be used into Phase 2 and was re-cut on several occasions.

The relationship between the curvilinear ditch F1315 and Enclosure 12 has important implications for the overall phasing of the site. F1315 pre-dated a possible addition to Enclosure 12, but it was not clear if it pre-dated the original ditch (F1250). It may be the case that F1330 belongs to a secondary re-cut phase, and thus Enclosure 12 may have assumed its circular form only at a later stage, perhaps originating as a short arcuate ditch linking Enclosure 1 and F1315. Finally in this phase, Enclosure 13 began as a small enclosure (12 m by 15 m) created by a shallow ditch connecting Enclosures 10 and 12. It was expanded in the following phase.

Phase 1C

Enclosure 13 was extended northwards (28 m by 15 m) through the ditch of Enclosure 10, which had been backfilled at this time. It extended up to and drained into Enclosure 1 (F405).

Phase 2A

This phase was initiated by a re-cut (F404) of Enclosure 1 (Illus. 4.6), which was excavated within the limits of its predecessor and thus had a slightly reduced internal area (70 m by 57 m). This enclosure ditch adopted a causewayed entrance in the same location as the previous F405 entrance. The causeway was approximately 2 m wide and was consolidated by a layer of tightly packed stones secured within a revetment of large, angular, limestone boulders. This ditch also contained large amounts of animal bone, some charcoal and slag. Further bone motif pieces were found, along with a stone ingot mould (Illus. 4.3) (these items could possibly be residual artefacts from Phase 1B activity associated with Structure D), glass beads (Illus. 4.7), a tinned copper-alloy stud, an iron knife and pin, an antler weaving tool, fragments of unidentified copper-alloy and bone objects, and yet more struck flint. A radiocarbon date of AD 710–960 (Beta-220114) from an articulated skeleton of a dog (*Canis familiaris*) indicates a broad range from the early eighth to the early 10th century for this phase, with an earlier date in this range probably more likely, based on an interpretation of the ditch stratigraphy and radiocarbon dates for later phases. At the time of

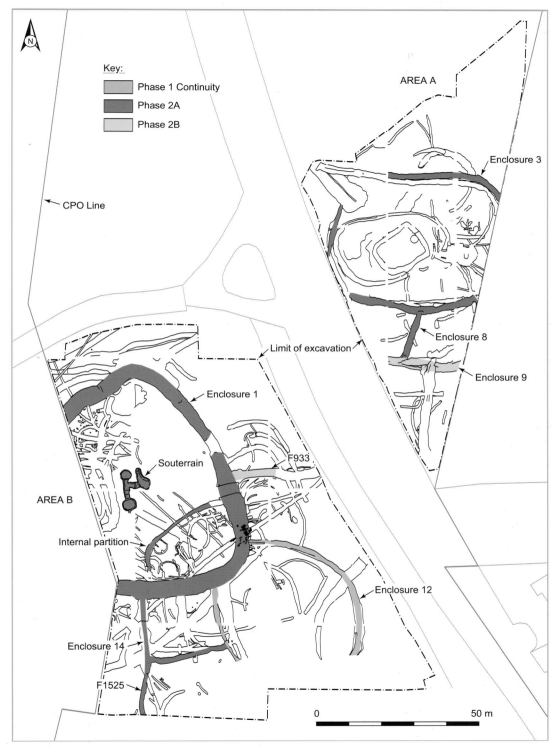

Illus. 4.6—Schematic plan of Phases 2A & 2B (Archaeological Consultancy Services Ltd).

writing, the re-cutting of Enclosure 1, perhaps in the late seventh or early eighth century AD, has been interpreted as heralding a series of major changes to several other features in the site.

The south-east corner of Enclosure 1 was partitioned by a series of curvilinear ditches in what seemed to be a deliberate effort to segregate the remainder of the enclosure from probable agricultural activities based around cereal drying. The earliest phases of activity in this area, small structures or workshops surrounded by metalled surfaces (see above), were truncated by successive curvilinear ditches, each of which respected the inner edge of Enclosure 1 (F404), stopping approximately 5 m west of it, which suggested that these ditches had extended up to the bank associated with the second phase of Enclosure 1. These ditches abounded in artefacts, including interlocking copper-alloy rings, iron ringed pins, E-ware pottery, bone pins (Illus. 4.8), assorted iron objects, lignite bracelet fragments (Illus. 4.9), glass beads (Illus. 4.7) and a crucible fragment (Illus. 4.3).

A drystone-built souterrain (Illus. 4.10) was situated centrally within Enclosure 1 and comprised three beehive-shaped chambers (Chambers 1–3), interconnected by three short passages (Passages

Illus. 4.7—Glass beads and amber bead fragment from Roestown 2 (John Sunderland).

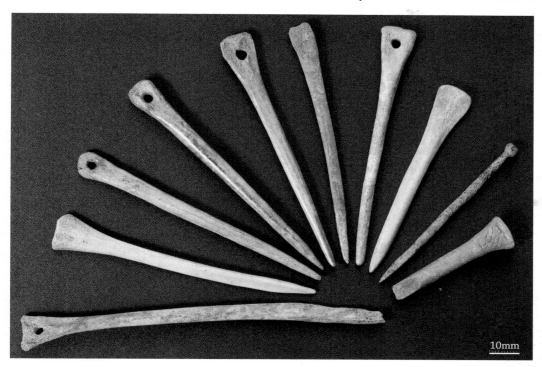

Illus. 4.8—Bone pins from Roestown 2 (John Sunderland).

Illus. 4.9—Lignite bracelet fragments from Roestown 2 (John Sunderland).

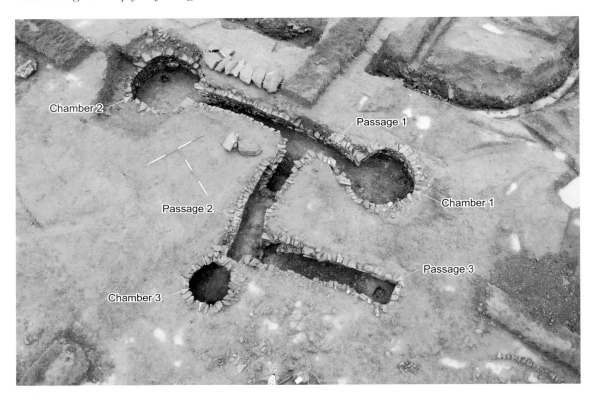

Illus. 4.10—Mid-excavation elevated view of souterrain at Roestown 2 (Hawkeye).

1–3). Souterrains occur in large numbers across Ireland (upwards of 3,500 recorded sites) with notable concentrations in counties Antrim, Cork, Galway and Louth (Clinton 2001, 20). A broadly similar but significantly larger example was excavated at Lismullin 1 (O'Connell, chapter 2; 2007b). The Roestown 2 structure was set within a deep cut that the builders purposely undercut in places to receive the corbelled walls. Many of the capstones had been deliberately removed, probably before the 12th century AD when much of the structure was backfilled. A metal stick-pin, of a type popular during the 11th century (O'Rahilly 1998), and a perforated piece of slate that may once have been part of stone roof were included within these deposits. Similar material was recorded within the backfill of souterrains at Ballycatteen, Co. Cork (Ó Ríordáin & Hartnett 1943, 34, fig. 11).

Incorporated within the structure were a series of defensive measures centred on Passage 2 and its junctions with Passages 1 and 3. A step at the end of Passage 1 was accompanied by a width and height constriction, forcing entrants into a prone position that had to be sustained through Passage 2, which had a low roof height leading to the trapdoor at the junction with Passage 1. It appears that entry to the souterrain was gained through a hole in the roof at the north end of Passage 3.

Passage restriction was a simple and common defensive feature of souterrains, although more elaborate security measures were also used: for example, slabs placed horizontally across passages or compartments hidden above a passage, which were known as 'murder holes', from where an intruder could be dealt an unexpected, and doubtless mortal, blow. Another method was to incorporate a trapdoor or a sudden change of level, and such a feature existed here at Roestown 2. These unusual and ambiguous features have been the subject of a number of theories, whether they were defensive features, temperature regulators or for securing areas of the souterrain to lock in valuable items, as opposed to locking out intruders (Clinton 2001, 123–33).

Each chamber in the Roestown 2 souterrain had a pit cut into its base, possibly for drainage or storage. A single cubbyhole was found close to the floor of the entrance passage. An air vent incorporated into the wall provided ventilation into Chamber 3, although each chamber may originally have had one. The floors consisted of unpaved, compacted earth covered in a thin layer of dark soil containing charcoal and fragments of burnt bone, material potentially relating to the period of occupation. The bones of small rodents were numerous at this level and may be contemporary with these floor deposits; however, it is not uncommon for some species, such as mouse, rat or indeed badger, to inhabit these structures in more recent times.

It is possible that the interior of Enclosure 1 was raised, in the fashion of a raised or platform rath. The evidence for this is not compelling but includes the absence of a significant portion of the roof of Chamber 1 in the souterrain, perhaps as much as 0.5 m (see above). Furthermore, there is currently a dearth of recognisable habitation features after Phase 1. Even the overwhelming survival of Phase 1 features may be a result of their burial beneath a raised deposit, into which later features were cut and which was gradually denuded. This theory will be explored more fully in a future publication as dating evidence and specialist reports are received.

The surrounding annexes and enclosures were also in a state of flux. Enclosures 2, 5, 6 and 7 in Area A were replaced by the multi-phase enclosure designated Enclosure 3 (42 m by 45 m). This was roughly square, recorded in the excavation as two east–west ditches that extended beyond the eastern limit of excavation; however, the geophysical survey results clearly showed a north–south element further east (Illus. 4.1). The western equivalent was recorded, but any direct relationship between this and the other elements of Enclosure 3 was removed by a modern quarry and the current N3. A large quantity of animal bone and an array of artefacts were recovered, including a stone-incised game board, a bone pin and a hone stone. An articulated chicken skeleton (*Gallus gallus*) from a primary deposit in Enclosure 3 was radiocarbon-dated to AD 650–780 (Beta-219002).

The game board was one of three found at the site (Illus. 4.11). Similar boards have been found in other early medieval contexts, usually on stone or, where preservation allows its recovery, on wood. A possibly unfinished example was uncovered in an unstratified deposit at Lagore (Hencken 1950, 176–7), which the excavator classified as a miscellaneous stone object. The crude nature of its design fits well with the hand-carved designs on two of the Roestown 2 boards, although their closest parallels were from eighth-century deposits at Garryduff I (O'Kelly 1963, 88–9, 91) and Borris-in-Ossory, Co. Laois (M Ó Droma, pers. comm.). The pattern in each of these examples was crudely executed with squares of varying size and shape. These examples most likely represent a common early medieval game known as *hnefatafl*, a Norse word meaning 'the king's table'. The game may ultimately have originated in Scandinavia, but variations of it developed in Scotland,

Illus. 4.11—Stone game board from Roestown 2 (John Sunderland).

Wales and Ireland, where it was called *ard-rí*, *tawlbyund* and *fidchell* respectively. *Fidchell* may describe board games in general (MacWhite 1945) and is referenced in a number of medieval texts or glosses: for example, *Cormac's Glossary* and earlier texts such as the *Táin Bó Fraích* or *Táin Bó Cuailnge*. In these texts the game was played exclusively by noble or *nemed* (privileged) classes, often associating the playing of board games with the expression of status, where the accoutrements of these games were objects of value and display, such as the pieces of precious stone, gold and silver or boards of tinned bronze and gold, as are mentioned in the *Táin Bó Fraích*.

An intricately decorated wooden board recovered from 10th-century levels in Ballinderry No. 1 crannog, Co. Westmeath (Hencken 1936, 175–90), would appear to be a high-status board, but the greater number of identified game boards more closely resemble the Roestown 2 or Garryduff incised stone types and were probably the boards of lower classes, perhaps the half-free or slaves, a theory supported perhaps by the location of two boards within a livestock enclosure.

Two of the Roestown 2 *hnefatafl* boards came from stratified mid–late seventh-century deposits (AD 650–780, Beta-219002; AD 620–690, Beta-219005), indicating the presence of the game in Ireland more than a century before the first recorded Viking attacks in the late eighth century AD. If these game boards are variants of *hnefatafl*, and ultimately of Scandinavian origin, the most likely method of introduction was via trading links with settlements in Scotland and the Northern Isles and onwards with Scandinavia. Irish hermits were apparently on the Faroe Islands by AD 725 (Ó Corráin 2001, 17), and there is evidence for trade between Norway and Ireland/Britain from the mid-eighth century (Ambrosiani 1998), as suggested by the use of reindeer antler for comb making by Picts (Myhre 1998, 7–8) and instances of *hnefatafl* games in pre-Viking deposits in Pictish settlements on the Northern Isles off Scotland (Hall, undated).

A second type of game known as merels was also represented on site. It was from a late deposit sealing the Enclosure 1 ditches but is identical to an example (E141:5149) from ninth-century deposits at Fishamble Street, Dublin, and currently on display at the National Museum of Ireland. Both games were in fashion at the same time, as evidenced by the occurrence of double-sided boards containing both games, such as that from the Gokstad ship burial in Norway (Nicolaysen 1882, 46–7; Hencken 1936, 175–90). No gaming pieces, such as those identified from Knowth, Co. Meath, or Ballinderry 2, Co. Offaly (Eogan 1968, 372; Hencken 1942, 54), were associated with the Roestown boards or recovered from the site generally, but it is unlikely that these boards used specially crafted pieces. Small pebbles, bones, shells or twigs could have served as counters, all of which would have been readily available in the site and which would be impossible to distinguish archaeologically.

A deep curved ditch (Enclosure 8) was a contemporaneous feature formed by a V-shaped ditch running south-west from Enclosure 3, and Enclosure 14 in Area B was a new annex that cut through the backfilled Enclosure 11 ditch. It was a complex series of re-cut ditches that formed a rectangular enclosure (approximately 25 m by 18 m) off the southern side of Enclosure 1 and abutted the western side of Enclosure 12, indicating that it remained in use for a time at the beginning of Phase 2. There was some suggestion of further enclosures (F1525) to the south of Enclosure 14; however, this area was extensively disturbed by land reclamation in the mid-20th century.

An unusual copper-alloy mount in the shape of a ringed cross (60 mm in diameter; Illus. 4.12) was found within one of the Enclosure 14 ditch fills. The centre of the cross was squared, while the terminals were expanded into a rectangle. The back of the object had a slight rim along its circumference with a lug, each with a central perforation, behind each of the expanded cross terminals. Stylistically, this motif resembles cross symbols on ninth-century croziers from County Antrim and Clongowes Wood, Co. Kildare (Henry 1967, 124–5; Bourke 1987, 166–8). The closest parallel for this object is perhaps an item (NMI W1) found during turf cutting in a bog close to Castle Kelly, Co. Roscommon, in the mid-19th century (Wilde 1861, 576–7) and sketched by Worsaae (see item #11 on drawing 4 at 'Retracing Ireland's Lost Archaeology' at http://publish.ucc.ie/doi/worsaae?section= N112D7). There is some similarity to objects, possibly brooches, worn by the ecclesiastical figures gracing a reliquary known as the Corp Naomh (Henry 1967, 124–5; Johnson 2005) and on a stone carving at Invergowrie, Scotland (Boyle 1937–8;

Illus. 4.12—Group of copper-alloy and iron finds from Roestown 2 including copper-alloy ringed cross (John Sunderland).

McRoberts 1960–1). These recurring iconographic motifs may be evidence of an ecclesiastical connection to the site during the eighth or ninth century AD.

Phase 2B

Phase 2B represents a brief period that witnessed alterations to the arrangement of divisions in Area A. Ditches belonging to Enclosure 3 were re-cut, and the deposits within these produced a range of artefacts, including the second stone-incised game board, further bone pins, a bone comb fragment, iron knives and unidentified iron objects. An articulated pig (*Sus* sp.) foot bone from one of these deposits was dated to AD 620–690 (Beta-219005). Elsewhere, Enclosure 8 was replaced by Enclosure 9, a sub-rectangular enclosure (15 m by 34 m), while in Area B a new sequence of ditches replaced Enclosure 13, beginning with ditch F933.

Phase 2C

A further re-cut to Enclosure 3 (Illus. 4.13) enclosed a slightly larger area (42 m by 52 m). Finds included an iron knife, iron objects, struck flints, a fragment of lignite, a stone lamp, bone pins, a broken bone whittle flute, a fragment of tinned copper alloy, a decorated copper-alloy strip and crudely shaped bone objects. Crucially, the western arm of Enclosure 3 was not re-cut at this time, which may be interpreted as evidence for the amalgamation of previously separate entities from the eastern and western areas of the site. A possible square subdivision of the north-east corner of Enclosure 3 may have been added in this stage. Elsewhere, Enclosure 9 was re-cut while, in Area B, Enclosures 15 (30 m by 10 m) and 16 (8 m by 15 m) replaced Enclosures 12 and 14.

This was an important phase in the overall development of the site. There was a partial backfilling of the Enclosure 1 ditch south of the entrance (perhaps also to the north, but this was not implicit), which was probably accompanied by an extension (F1531) of F933 towards Area A, possibly extending up to F252, a ditch annexed to Enclosure 9. The alterations to Enclosure 1 required some maintenance to its internal partition, whereby the eastern terminal was extended up to the edge of Enclosure 1. This extension could have been excavated only when the bank associated with Enclosure 1 had been removed and before a subsequent re-cut in Phase 3.

Phase 3

The third phase of activity was also related to a re-cut of Enclosure 1 (Illus. 4.14). This second and final re-cut began approximately 15 m north-east and 10 m south-west of the Phase 2 entrance, which had already become obsolete by Phase 2C. An entrance to the settlement during Phase 3 was not identified in the area of excavation. A third articulated dog skeleton (*Canis familiaris*) from the site, which was buried within a waterlogged deposit close to the base of the Enclosure 1 ditch, was radiocarbon-dated to AD 770–980 (Beta-220116). Artefacts recovered included assorted unidentified iron objects, a whetstone, lignite bracelet fragments, iron knives, wooden staves, a horseshoe fragment, struck flint, copper-alloy objects, a stone spindle whorl, and fragments of medieval pottery from later backfill deposits. Animal bone was abundant, with lesser quantities of slag, charcoal and organic material such as brushwood. There was limited evidence for an internal bank (approximately 2.4 m wide) in the north-west interior of Enclosure 1. It was probably associated with either re-cut phase of Enclosure 1. The south-east partition was also re-cut (F571) to enclose a smaller space and in doing so cut through a cereal-drying kiln. No significant change in the surrounding annexes was noticeable in this period, but there were further additions to the F1531 ditch sequence, and perhaps new ditches extending towards Area A. If the surrounding enclosures from Phase 2 were extant during this phase, the site at this developed stage would have been unrecognisable as a typical ringfort settlement.

Possibly also belonging to this phase is a sequence of ditches in the western interior of Enclosure 1 (F550 etc.). Further radiocarbon dates (pending) are required to finalise the position of these features in the sequence. The sequence, however, pre-dates a pit feature that is assigned to Phase 4.

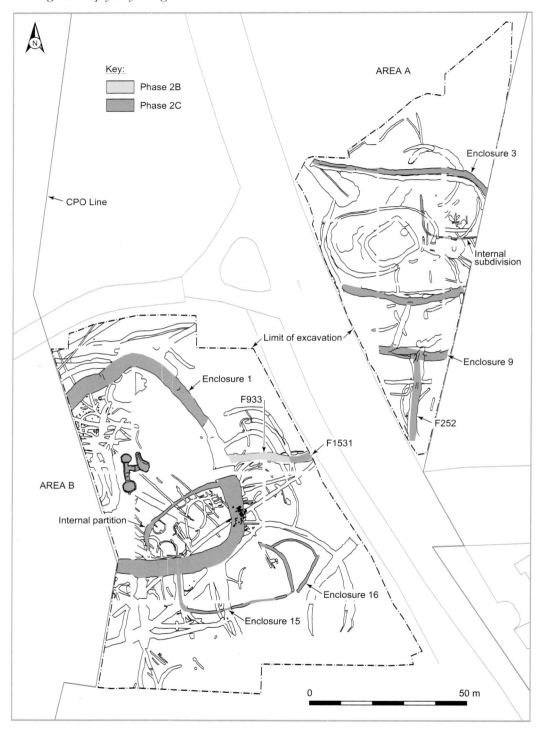

Illus. 4.13—Schematic plan of Phases 2B & 2C (Archaeological Consultancy Services Ltd).

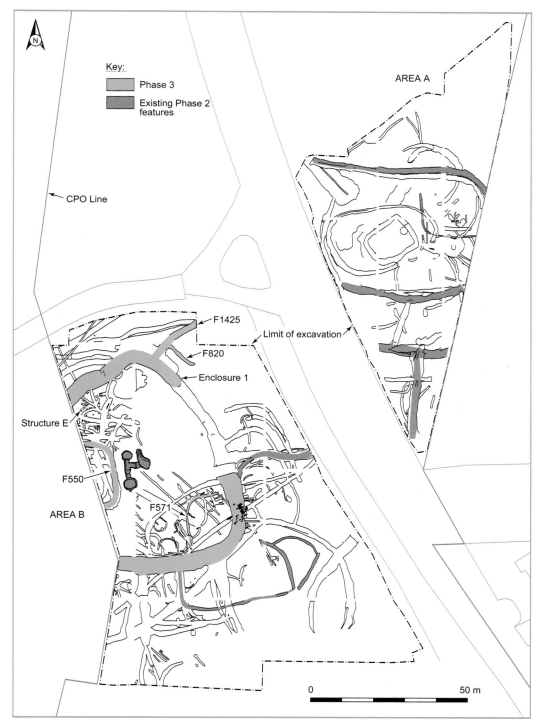

Illus. 4.14—Schematic plan of Phase 3 (Archaeological Consultancy Services Ltd).

Phase 4

In this phase, Enclosure 1 had been largely backfilled and partially sealed to the south-east beneath a stone path (Illus. 4.15). Two shallow ditches (F403 & F841) that corresponded to the extent of the final re-cut of Enclosure 1 retained the enclosure shape of previous phases; however, these ditches cannot have been anything more than boundary markers delimiting a large field. The souterrain was possibly backfilled during this period, and two large refuse pits (F411 & F1301) are also assigned to this phase. The nature of settlement in this phase is unclear. The next definite settlement evidence was not until the 13th century and then confined to a small area in Area A.

Phase 5

In the medieval period, probably during the mid-13th century AD, a rectangular enclosure (13 m by 10 m; Illus. 4.15), designated Enclosure 4, was positioned centrally within Enclosure 3, suggesting that this enclosure may have remained visible for some time. A sub-circular pit was the sole surviving feature within this enclosure; further remains were most likely ploughed out in later periods. These features produced bone pins, an iron spearhead (Illus. 4.16) and Dublin-type Ware, a coarse, wheel-thrown, glazed pottery that took a number of forms—for example, jugs, bowls, pipkins, moneyboxes and storage vessels. The name implies its widespread distribution in the Dublin region, but no production site or kiln exists in the archaeological record of this area, and recent studies have suggested a mid-13th century AD date for this material (McCutcheon 2006).

Anglo-Norman colonists frequently used existing earthwork sites for their own needs, and a number of excavated sites have revealed early medieval horizons sealed beneath ostensibly medieval structures (for a recent summary of such sites, see Ó Drisceoil 2002). Enclosure 4 may have surrounded a small domestic structure, perhaps belonging to the peasant classes, and the small number of late medieval pottery sherds from the site certainly suggests a short-lived occupation. There is currently little archaeological evidence for dispersed peasant settlement within Irish manors (O'Conor 1998, 57).

Human remains

Two poorly preserved inhumation burials were located within Enclosure 3 but could not be dated or assigned to a particular phase. They had been extensively truncated by post-medieval ploughing. A partial grave cut survived around one burial, and both appeared to have been laid on a lightly metalled surface. One burial was identifiable as a juvenile (approximately 10–12 years old) of indeterminate sex orientated west–east. It consisted of a number of skull fragments, including portions of the frontal lobe and mandible. Fragments of the left humerus were also present. The second burial, an adult of undetermined sex, comprised skull fragments and bones from the left hand (metacarpals and phalanges) and right hand (a phalanx). The poor preservation of the remains limited the pathological analysis that could be undertaken; however, both burials presented evidence of iron-deficient anaemia (Coughlan 2006), a condition that can be caused by a diet insufficient in iron or by blood loss. The preservation of bone in both burials was too poor to permit radiocarbon dating.

N

Phase 4

Phase 5

AREA A

CPO Line

Enclosure 4

Limit of excavation

Pit F411

F403

AREA B

F841

Path F492

0   50 m

Illus. 4.15—Schematic plan of Phases 4 & 5 (Archaeological Consultancy Services Ltd).

Illus. 4.16—Iron spearhead from Roestown 2 (John Sunderland).

There was no further evidence of formal human burial in the remaining excavated portion of the site, although disarticulated fragments were found in a number of contexts across the site, most notably a human cranium fragment within the souterrain. These instances of disarticulated human remains may reflect any number of bloody instances that the settlement undoubtedly witnessed during its long occupation. Contemporaneous records of violent attacks on neighbouring sites reflect a region subjected to periodic terror, and it is not implausible to suggest that a prominent site such as Roestown 2 also suffered, for example, from the attack on the church of Trevet in AD 848 that left 260 people dead or the attack on Lagore in AD 850 (Cogan 1874; Price 1950).

Conclusions

The floruit of the site was between the mid-sixth and the 13th century AD. This has largely been borne out by radiocarbon dating (see Appendix 1), continuing artefact research and comparative studies. This was certainly a period of continuous occupation. The dearth of domestic structures after Phase 1 may perhaps be explained by the artificial raising of the interior of the site during Phase 2. The evidence to date indicates the site originated in the mid-sixth century as a wealthy settlement in which fine metalworking was undertaken and which had access to imported goods (E-ware). The economy of the site was no doubt supported by rent, in the form of food, raw materials and labour services, from clients and tenants.

It seems likely that a dynasty known as the Déisi, who controlled the area around Roestown 2 before the mid-seventh century (Bhreathnach 1999), was probably responsible for the earliest phase of activity at the site. The second and third phases probably occurred during the time when a branch of the Southern Uí Néill, the Síl nÁedo Sláine and in particular the Uí Chernaig faction, was establishing dominance in the kingdom of Brega. Although this political change may not have manifested itself at a domestic level, substantial changes to the morphology of the site in Phase 2 occurred in this historical period. The final phases of activity may well have occurred at a time when the Déisi or others were reclaiming former territory, although these were largely impotent in the wider political machinations of the 11th century as a second Southern Uí Néill dynasty, Clann Cholmáin, extended its control directly over the kingdom, Brega thus becoming known as 'East Mide' (ibid.).

Agriculture formed the backbone of the economy. Animal husbandry was the most important activity (Table 4.1), but there was also strong evidence of arable farming across each of the phases, primarily through cereal-drying kilns; however, there was also evidence of plough marks, and a poorly preserved plough fragment was recovered. Some craft activity was carried out, textile weaving and bone working most obviously, but not on an industrial scale. Carpentry and ironmongery must have been part of daily life, but conclusive evidence for fine metalworking was not forthcoming after Phase 1. A significant number of artefacts were recovered: knives were very common (over 30 examples), as were ringed pins (approximately 32 in copper alloy and iron), bone pins (25, almost exclusively of the pig fibula type), glass beads (11 and also a single amber bead fragment) and lignite bracelets (7 fragments). Four partially complete bone combs were also found, all bearing incised decoration (Illus. 4.17). At the time of writing, post-excavation analysis is still under way, with some additional radiocarbon dates being processed that should confirm the sequence suggested above.

Table 4.1—Recorded faunal specimens across all phases at Roestown 2.

Species	Number of specimens	% of total
Cattle	5,985	57.78%
Sheep/goat	1,787	17.25%
Pig	1,447	13.97%
Horse	453	4.37%
Sheep	309	2.98%
Dog	281	2.71%
Cat	69	0.67%
Mouse	21	0.20%
Red deer	4	0.04%
Rat	3	0.03%

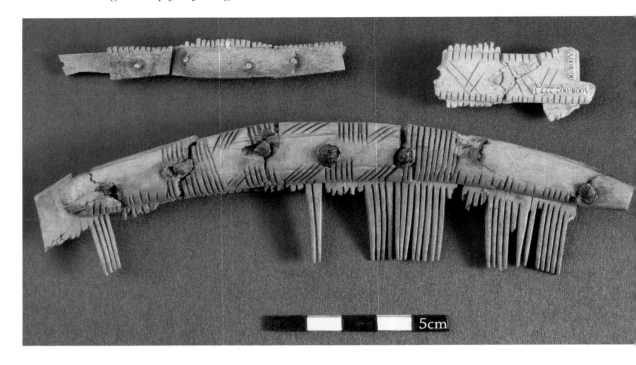

Illus. 4.17—Bone combs from Roestown 2 (John Sunderland).

Notes

1. Roestown 2: NGR 295793, 253824; height 106 m OD; excavation reg. no. E3055; Ministerial Direction no. A008/002; excavation director Robert O'Hara.
2. Garretstown 2: NGR 296021, 254807; height 120 m OD; excavation reg. no. E3061; Ministerial Direction no. A008/008; excavation director Stuart Rathbone.
   Castletown Tara 1: NGR 292003, 261818; height 63 m OD; excavation reg. no. E3078; Ministerial Direction no. A008/025; excavation director Stuart Elder.

5
COLLIERSTOWN 1: A LATE IRON AGE– EARLY MEDIEVAL ENCLOSED CEMETERY

Robert O'Hara

Sometime near the end of prehistory a slight ridge east of the Gabhra River in the townland of Collierstown, Co. Meath, was chosen as the site for a burial mound (see site location map on page xiv).[1] An adult female was placed lying on her back in a dug grave. Around her a segmented ring-ditch was excavated, the material from which was used to create a low mound sealing the burial beneath. This event probably occurred between the first and the fourth century AD, based on comparisons with excavated sites at Claristown, Co. Meath (Russell et al. 2002), and Pollacorragune, Tuam, Co. Galway (Riley 1936–7; O'Sullivan & Harney 2008), both of which had later Iron Age inhumation burials sealed beneath a low mound. The site subsequently developed as a cemetery in the fifth and sixth centuries AD; however, the date at which interments in the cemetery ceased is unclear. Radiocarbon dates are in preparation at the time of writing.

The site at Collierstown 1 was identified during advance test-trenching in 2004, which highlighted the existence of inhumations possibly associated with two earthen mounds (Illus. 5.1).

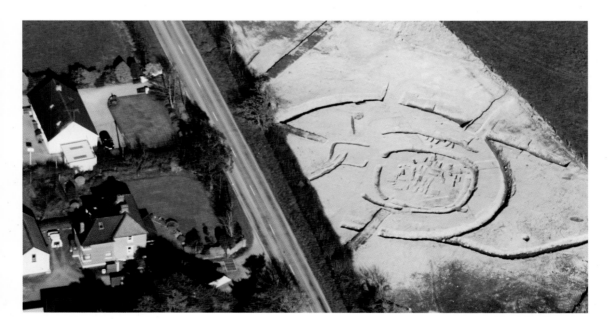

Illus. 5.1—Post-excavation aerial view of Collierstown 1, from the north-east (Studio Lab).

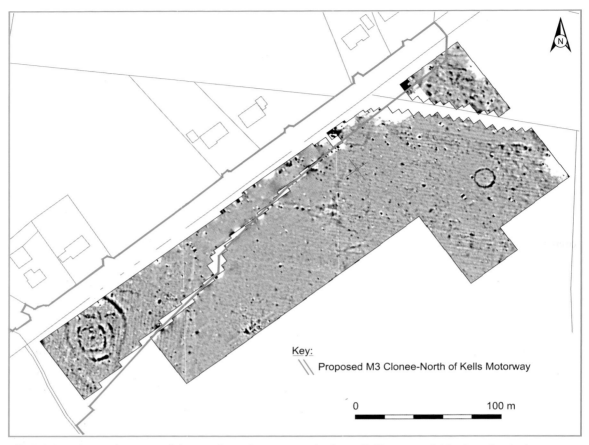

Illus. 5.2—Greyscale image of the geophysical survey results from Collierstown 1 (Archaeological Consultancy Services Ltd based on a geophysical image produced by Target Archaeological Geophysics).

A thorough geophysical investigation of the site and the surrounding area was undertaken in 2005 and 2006 (Illus. 5.2), which recorded two sub-circular enclosures, the outer one measuring approximately 50 m in diameter and the inner one measuring approximately 20 m in diameter (Nicholls & Shiel 2006, 14–15). An anomaly interpreted as a possible pit was identified at the centre of the inner enclosure. Excavation took place between September 2006 and April 2007.

Archaeological excavation

The earthen mounds that signalled possible archaeological remains at this location were proven during excavation to be modern features, probably the result of upcast from the ditch flanking the road immediately to the north-west. These mounds contained modern pottery and sealed post-medieval ridge and furrow features that were clearly visible in the geophysical image as north-east–south–west linear anomalies crossing the site. The placing of a mound within the medieval enclosures may be entirely coincidental; however, it is also possible that the site was recognised as a burial ground, when bone was disturbed through ploughing, and the mounds may have been intended to mark the burial site. The preliminary findings of the excavation suggest a four-phase development of the site (Illus. 5.3), during which a minimum of 61 people were buried in four broad stages (Illus. 5.4 & 5.5). The site was extensively ploughed in the post-medieval period, and some burials showed evidence of this disturbance. It is possible, therefore, that other burials were removed completely before excavation.

Phase 1

The earliest stratified activity in the site was a series of segmented ditches (Enclosure 1; 15 m by 17 m), which were extensively truncated by later features (Illus. 5.3). These ditches contained small quantities of animal bone and trace inclusions of charcoal and burnt bone. A single struck flint and a sherd of an imported pottery vessel, Bii Ware, were the only artefacts recovered. Bii Ware belongs to a type of ribbed amphora that is believed to have been manufactured in northern Syria/south-west Turkey during the late fifth–early sixth century AD (Kelly 2008a). The pottery was in a late backfill deposit and conceivably intrusive. The enclosure was perhaps penannular and open to the north, as no evidence for a contemporaneous enclosing feature was found there, but such a feature may have been removed by ditches associated with Phase 2 (see below). An inhumation burial (Burial 48), centrally placed within this enclosure, contained the remains of a young adult female orientated west–east in a partially stone-lined grave (Illus. 5.4 & 5.6). This form of burial is considered to be a significant change in mortuary ritual from native Iron Age practices (i.e. cremation, with or without grave goods, placed on the ground surface or in small pits and generally covered by a low mound, enclosed by a ditch and bank arrangement, or inserted in existing burial monuments). O'Brien (1992; in press) argues for the re-introduction of inhumation, initially crouched or flexed, around the first century AD, most likely through contact with Britain and burial practice in the later Roman world. Before radiocarbon dating, it seems appropriate that the primary burial at Collierstown is placed within this milieu of change. The form of the burial is not dissimilar from the primary burial at Claristown, Co. Meath (Russell et al. 2002), where the remains of an adult male dated to AD 60–420 were inhumed beneath a low earthen mound enclosed by a shallow ditch. This became the focus for later burials in the early medieval period.

Burial 48 contained a deposit of burnt clay and charred plant remains covering the pelvis of the dead woman. The practice of depositing burnt grain with burials was a widespread custom among Anglo-Saxon communities in England (O'Brien 2003; O'Sullivan & Harney 2008), and there are some instances in Ireland, at Levitstown, Co. Kildare (ibid.), and at a fifth–seventh century AD burial at Ballygarraun West, Co. Galway (Quinney 2007).

A further eight inhumations (which, together with Burial 48, formed Group 1; see below) were placed centrally within Enclosure 1. The relative depth of Burial 48 compared to surrounding Group 1 burials (it was approximately 20 cm deeper) suggested that these later burials had been inserted from a higher level, most likely through a low mound formed by the upcast from the ditches of Enclosure 1. The span of time between the initial burial and the subsequent interments

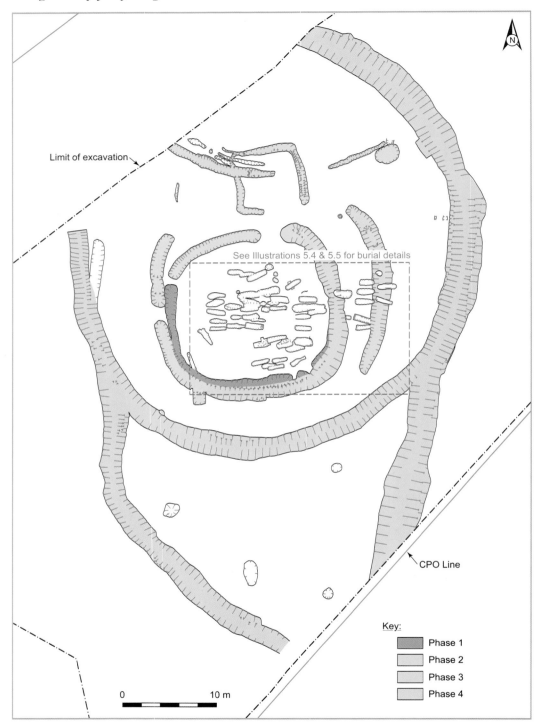

Limit of excavation

See Illustrations 5.4 & 5.5 for burial details

CPO Line

Key:

▨	Phase 1
▨	Phase 2
▨	Phase 3
▨	Phase 4

0   10 m

Illus. 5.3—Schematic plan showing probable phases of Collierstown 1 (Archaeological Consultancy Services Ltd).

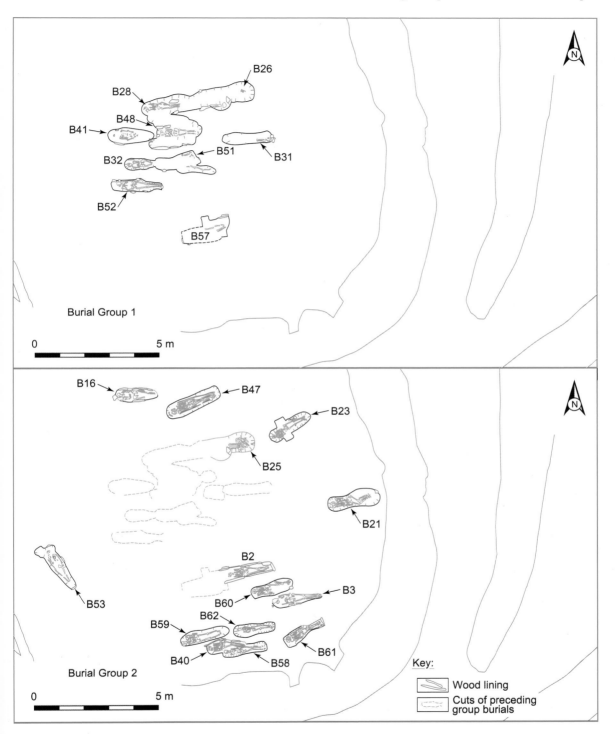

Illus. 5.4—Burial Groups 1–2 (Archaeological Consultancy Services Ltd).

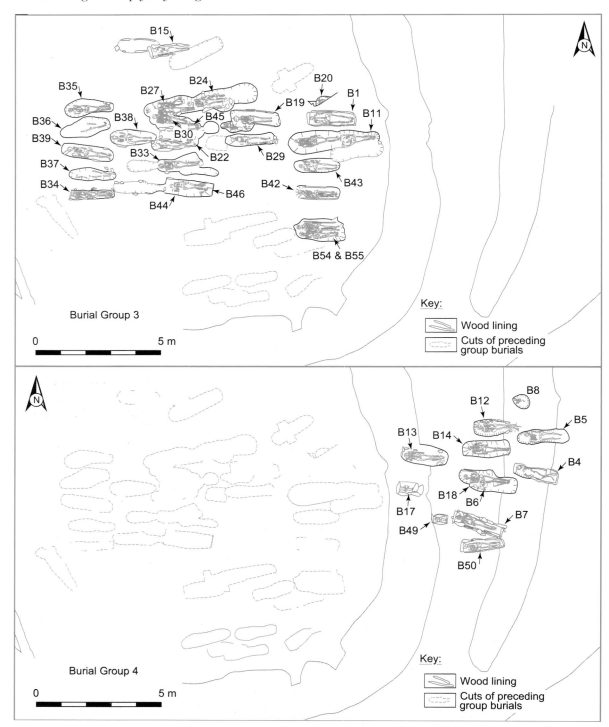

Illus. 5.5—Burial Groups 3–4 (Archaeological Consultancy Services Ltd).

is currently unknown. Where determinable, the division between the sexes was equal—two male, two female (including Burial 48) and five unsexed (Coughlan 2008). Also the absence of infants and children suggests that it was not a familial plot but may have been reserved for adult members of the community.

The layout of the subsequent burial group (Group 2) suggests that they post-date Group 1 (Illus. 5.4). There were just two instances of truncation of outlying elements of the earlier group; otherwise the Group 2 burials appeared to avoid the central area of the cemetery while still contained within the Enclosure 1 ditch. Indeed, the excellent preservation of some of these remains in comparison with the Group 3 burials may have resulted from their being sealed beneath an internal bank associated with Enclosure 2 (see below). Where determinable, the 14 burials were biased towards females—seven female, four male and three unsexed (ibid.)—and they were buried in a mix of unlined and stone- and wood-lined graves.

Illus. 5.6—(far left) Burial 48, the primary burial at Collierstown 1 (Archaeological Consultancy Services Ltd).

Illus. 5.7—(left) Burial 47, showing oversized grave and wood lining (Archaeological Consultancy Services Ltd).

An interesting phenomenon in this group concerned Burial 47, a young adult male in an oversized wood-lined grave (Illus. 5.4 & 5.7). It has been suggested that such a large grave may have been dug to accommodate organic goods that accompanied the burial (E O'Brien, pers. comm.). Similar graves in the cemetery may include Burial 13 and Burial 17 (both belonging to Group 4), the latter an infant burial in a wood-lined stone cist (Illus. 5.5). A broadly contemporaneous inhumation (AD 420–650; O'Brien, in press) beneath an earthen mound at Ninch, Co. Meath (Sweetman 1983), was associated with a deposit of fern and bracken beside the body, which the excavator believed may have been wrapped around the burial. Hughes (1966, 142) considered that burial fees paid to churches in the seventh or eighth century AD, which included 'the clothing and trappings of the dead man', might reflect the kind of possessions buried with earlier pagan burials, and they are precisely the type of material that would not be detectable archaeologically.

Phase 2

The second phase of activity at the cemetery probably commenced with the infilling of the Enclosure 1 ditches, followed by the excavation of a series of multi-phase curvilinear ditches (Enclosure 2) that were cut into the earlier ditches, fossilising the extent and shape of the previous phase (Illus. 5.3). The homogeneity of deposits and associated finds within these lengths of segmented ditches, particularly the presence of Bii Ware, implied that they were broadly contemporaneous, although the arrangement of the ditches suggested that some features were chronologically later than others. A number of re-cuts were obvious within these ditches. Finds from this phase included bone and antler items (Illus. 5.8), struck flint, unidentified iron objects including slag, five sherds of Bii Ware and a single sherd of Phocaean Red Slipped Ware (PRSW) (Illus. 5.9). The PRSW sherd belongs to a large class of dish characterised by a vertical thickened rim and known as Form 3 (Kelly 2008a; 2008b). A sherd of E-ware was found in the same deposit as this sherd of PRSW. The association of the two forms suggests a deposition date of AD 550 (I Doyle, pers. comm.).

So few sherds of PRSW have been found in Ireland that its identification at Collierstown is highly significant. The Bii Ware sherds belong to a type of ribbed amphora that is believed to have been manufactured in the broader Antioch region (i.e. northern Syria/south-west Turkey), or generally within the eastern Mediterranean, and was important throughout the Mediterranean world, especially in the fifth and sixth centuries (Kelly 2008a). The most logical explanation for the presence of Bii Ware amphorae in Ireland is a demand for eastern Mediterranean wine or oil by the secular élite. In north-western Europe, Bii Ware is dated mainly through its association with PRSW, and, as both Bii Ware and PRSW have been found in Phase 2 levels at Collierstown, we can consequently date this phase to the late fifth or early sixth century AD. Though quite rare, these amphorae are found at a greater number of sites than PRSW, and other find spots in County Meath include Colp West and Randalstown (ibid.). The overall distribution of this ware may reflect coastal trade routes from the Continent, and the identification of this pottery at Colp West may signify movement along the eastern coast, as well as river trade along the Boyne towards Tara, incorporating sites such as Collierstown and Randalstown (1 km from the Boyne) en route (ibid.). In Britain, Bii Ware enjoys a wide circulation, mainly in the south-east, particularly Cornwall,

Illus. 5.8—Bone and antler items from Collierstown 1: (top to bottom) whale bone sword hilt, decorated antler connecting plate from a comb and antler fish gorge used to retain a fishing line (John Sunderland).

Illus. 5.9—Sherds of Phocaean Red Slipped Ware (left) and Bii Ware from Collierstown 1 (John Sunderland).

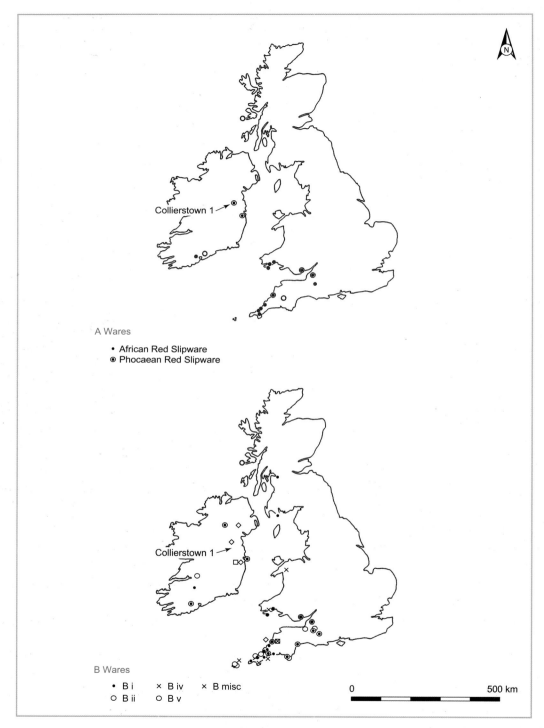

Illus. 5.10—Distribution map of Phocaean Red Slip Ware and North African Slip Ware pottery in Britain and Ireland (after Edwards 1990).

Illus. 5.11 (left)—Example of attention given to the reburial of disarticulated bone. In this case leg bones from Burial 16 disturbed by a later burial (Burial 15) have been placed back in the grave just below the pelvis (Archaeological Consultancy Services Ltd).

Illus. 5.12 (below)—Double burial (Burials 54 & 55). Note the preserved wood lining flanking the remains (Archaeological Consultancy Services Ltd).

Devon and Somerset (Illus. 5.10). This distribution suggests that the Bii trade in Britain was concentrated on the tin industry. What was exchanged in Ireland is not so visible archaeologically, although the main items for exchange were animals and farm products (Doherty 1980; Laing & Laing 1995; Kelly 2008a). The presence of the pottery in areas beyond south-west Britain may indicate secondary trade to those areas (Edwards 1990).

A third group of burials (Group 3) was placed centrally within Enclosure 2 (Illus. 5.5) and was probably mainly associated with this phase. It constituted the largest number of burials (perhaps 26 individuals) in the site, with the remains formally laid out in four rows of approximately five burials each. The burials were placed without regard to earlier burials, leading to a significant amount of disturbance. The disarticulated remains of the preceding inhumations were reburied, in the original grave, in charnel pits or as lining in later graves (Illus. 5.11). There were some instances of the re-use of existing grave cuts and one example of a double burial (Burials 54/55), with both bodies placed side by side in a wide grave (Illus. 5.12). The demographic pattern of the cemetery continued to be exclusively adult (five male, 12 female, nine unsexed), which suggested that the cemetery continued to be used in this period for individuals of high status, which may also be inferred from the recovery of rare imported pottery in the surrounding ditches.

Two L-shaped ditches formed a possible square enclosure (with internal dimensions of 6 m by 6 m) immediately north of Enclosure 2, and the positioning of a possible opening on its southern side suggested that it may have been accessible from the enclosure (Illus. 5.1 & 5.3). Artefacts included an iron knife fragment, B-ware and a twisted copper-alloy (?necklace) fragment (Illus. 5.13). There was no surviving evidence for internal features, and the exact nature of this square enclosure is unclear. It perhaps functioned as a small earthen shrine in the cemetery. Although it could be queried how readily we can identify pagans or Christians through their burials during this period, it is assumed here that this was probably the period in which the cemetery was Christianised. A number of post-holes, one of which cut into the fill of Group 2 burials, perhaps represent wooden crosses erected in the site at this point (Illus. 5.4).

What may be considered as pagan rites were still occurring at this stage; for instance, Burial 39 was buried with an antler tine placed by its left hand, a deliberate deposition that can be paralleled at Ballygarraun West (Quinney 2007) and Lehinch, Co. Offaly (Ó Floinn 1987–8). The practice may have an Iron Age precedent from a site at Bellinstown, Co. Dublin, where a deer antler was found in potential association with a segmented ring-ditch that contained a discrete deposit of cremated human bone. This site became a focus for at least nine later inhumations (Lynch 2004).

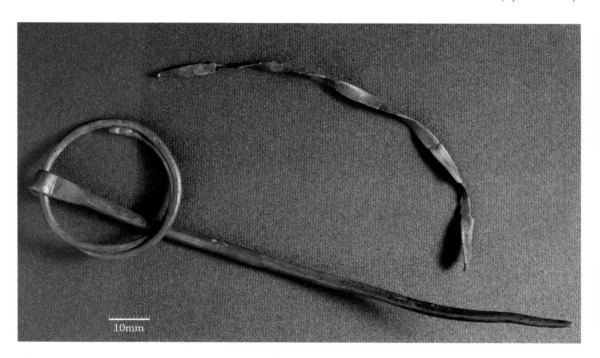

Illus. 5.13—Twisted copper-alloy (?necklace) fragment (from Phase 2) and copper-alloy, spiral-headed ring-pin (Phase 4) (John Sunderland).

The occurrence of mixed religious practices in the cemetery highlights the continuity of traditional beliefs in a society becoming increasingly Christian. Such practices presumably imply a strong bond to past rituals, which probably offered a tangible connection to the community's ancestors, a further expression of identity beyond the burial at an ancestral cemetery. A recent synopsis of early medieval burials (O'Sullivan & Harney 2008) has highlighted the growing body of evidence for the prolonged continuation of pagan practices and, consequently, a slower adoption of Christian belief than previously thought.

Phase 3

The segmented ditches of Enclosure 2 were probably succeeded by a circular enclosure (Enclosure 3) that was represented by a partially surviving ditch (Illus. 5.3 & 5.14), the remainder

Illus. 5.14—Excavation progressing on Enclosure 3 ditch (Archaeological Consultancy Services Ltd).

of which was extensively truncated during Phase 4 (see Illus. 5.3). A diameter of 40 m is estimated for Enclosure 3. The space created by this enclosure was significantly greater than required for the purposes of burial and certainly in excess of the area needed to accommodate the Group 4 burials—if they are proven to be contemporaneous. The northern half of this enclosure may have been partitioned by an internal ditched division that cut the earlier square structure (Illus. 5.3). If this enclosure was used for purposes other than burial in this period—for example, domestic or industrial activity—it was not immediately obvious from the archaeological remains.

At the time of writing, the final group of 12 burials (Group 4) are interpreted as having been associated with this phase; however, this has yet to be determined by radiocarbon dates. This group could be a late extension of Group 3 that spread beyond the limits of a late phase of Enclosure 2, after the final Phase 2 ditch at this location was backfilled. It is likely, however, that they represent a later group of interments, not only because they post-date Enclosure 2 but also because their age profile was strikingly different from earlier groups, including three infants (the first non-adult or non-adolescent burials recorded in the cemetery). The age profile is perhaps appropriate for a cemetery used by an extended family for a generation or so. In addition to the three infants was an adult population comprising three males, two possible males, three females and one unsexed adult, all aged 17–35 years old. In demographic terms, this contrasts sharply with the profiles of Groups 1–3. If Group 4 and Enclosure 3 were contemporaneous, it is a matter for consideration that the final group associated with such a large expansion of the site had the lowest number of individuals; perhaps further burials were intended but did not transpire for some reason. Hughes (1966) and O'Brien (1992; 2003; in press) have made important contributions to understanding the role of the Church in seeking to formalise burial of Christians in consecrated sites from the seventh century AD onwards. Certainly, growing numbers were attracted to ecclesiastical burial grounds from this period at the expense of traditional sites. The full enclosing of the cemetery during Phase 3 may reflect these developments; the delimiting of the site could suggest that, although it did not develop as an ecclesiastical site, it was nonetheless recognised as consecrated ground, perhaps having received the bodies of high-ranking Christians.

Phase 4

Enclosure 4 was the final phase of enclosure at the site. It appeared to be a re-cut of Enclosure 3, which also incorporated a substantial extension on its south side. The enclosure in this phase would have been trapezoidal in plan (Illus. 5.3). As with the previous phase, the function of the enclosure in this period was difficult to determine. Animal bone was less common in this phase; its presence may indicate that some activity was undertaken at the site in this period, but the possibility of the bone being residual from an earlier period cannot be overlooked. Finds included a copper-alloy, spiral-headed ring-pin (Illus. 5.13), a further sherd of Bii Ware, and wooden objects including a stave fragment. The final deposits sealing this enclosure ditch contained a medieval iron spur fragment and medieval and post-medieval pottery, indicating the period during which it remained open and the relatively late date at which it was finally fully backfilled. Perhaps some sign of this enclosure was still visible when the earthen mounds were created within it in the modern era.

Discussion

The cemetery was situated immediately north-east of the Gabhra River, which forms the townland boundary between Collierstown and Ross. Rivers had a special significance as boundaries during the prehistoric period and continued to have importance during the medieval period. That they were imbued with symbolic or religious significance is demonstrated by the repeated deposition of prestigious objects at such places from the Neolithic onwards (Dowling 2007). Natural features repeatedly influenced the location of certain types of monuments throughout prehistory, particularly sites of highly ritualised activity: for example, megalithic tombs or ring-ditches/barrows.

Along the route of the M3, such activity was identified at Dunboyne 1, where two small cremation pits (?Late Bronze Age) were excavated beside the River Tolka, and at Ardsallagh 2 a multi-period cemetery developed immediately north of the River Boyne (Clarke & Carlin, chapter 1; 2006a; 2006b).[2] The tendency for barrows in the Lough Gur region of County Limerick to be situated on valley floors, on opposing river banks, perhaps marking the periphery of small territories stretching back from the valley floor (Cooney & Grogan 1999, 133), may also be identified within the landscape of the River Gabhra, where ring-ditches were found flanking the river at Collierstown 1, Ross 2 (O'Hara 2008b) and Lismullin 1 (O'Connell, chapter 2; 2007a; 2007b).[3] Newman (1997, 183–5) described seven mounds (destroyed since 1829) that flanked the junction of the Castletown Tara–Jordanstown–Blundelstown townland boundaries and which, if archaeological in origin, may have delimited territorial units in that area. Moore (2007) argues for human remains deposited in the Late Iron Age landscape of Britain being part of the formulation and maintenance of territorial relationships, whereby evidence of human remains at landscape boundaries may have had importance in reaffirming earlier boundaries and a community's actual or mythical connection to their landscape. The 'territorial marker' argument should not be overstated in relation to the Gabhra valley, however, if one considers the distribution of recorded funerary monuments in the wider valley and the potential for any number of sites to survive as yet undetected below ground. There are early mythological references to important burial grounds in this area. Skreen, 1.5 km north-east of Collierstown 1, was by repute the burial place of Achall, daughter of Cairpre Nia Fer, a mythical king of Leinster, who was buried on the hill and who gave her name to the area before the 10th century AD, after which it was named after the ecclesiastical site of Scrín Colm Cille (Bhreathneach 1996).

The adult profile of the burials of Groups 1–3 is perhaps indicative of restricted burial practice at the cemetery—that burial there was reserved for adults and adolescents, rather than children, with a focus on female adults evidenced by Burial 48 and the dominance of females in Group 2. Just who these people were is an unanswerable question. It is perhaps premature to consider theories of outside aggrandisement or legitimising intruders' claims to an area through the possession of their burial places. Such instances occurred: the Norse may have sought to do so when placing their dead in ninth-century cemeteries at Islandbridge and Donnybrook, Co. Dublin (O'Brien 2005). O'Brien (2003) has also argued that intruders to an area could choose existing sites for burials, intertwining themselves with the myths and stories associated with such monuments and reinforcing territorial claims through 'possessing' such myths and manipulating myths in the same way that family genealogies were manipulated in the period. Collierstown, as part of the medieval kingdom of Brega, was witness to a succession of intruders during this time. At the beginning of the period, the Laigin were replaced by the Ciannachta and then the Southern Uí Néill dynasties (Price 1950; Byrne 2001). Changes in political supremacy do not necessarily indicate population upheaval; in fact, despite the regular political upheaval caused by early medieval politics, there is strong evidence to suggest that local populations were relatively stable across the period—indeed most of the prominent pre-seventh-century dynasties in Brega survived as landed families into the 12th century AD (Bhreathnach 1999).

Based on the current evidence, it seems likely that Collierstown 1 originated before or during the fourth century AD and subsequently became a focus for inhumation burials into the sixth century AD, at least, and for an unspecified period thereafter. The earliest burials may have been pre-Christian, although the cemetery is likely to have received both pagan and Christian members of the local community. The difficulty in determining religious beliefs based on funerary rites in this period is well documented (O'Brien 1992; 2003). Burial was, until the eighth century AD and for an unknown period thereafter, a secular matter, and both pagans and Christians received largely identical rites, which were essentially unaccompanied inhumation. Beyond this, however, there was enormous variety in the method of burial (see O'Sullivan & Harney 2008). The difficulty of distinguishing between burials is not a recent phenomenon, as seventh- and eighth-century AD texts relate. Muirchú and Tírechán, two biographers of St Patrick, both wrote during the seventh century AD about the confusion in distinguishing pagan and Christian burials, particularly in cemeteries were they occurred together (O'Brien 1992). It is unsurprising, then, to find an apparently pagan practice, such as the placing of an antler tine in a burial, in the same period that post-holes, perhaps indicating wooden crosses, and a possible earthen shrine were erected in the site.

Discarded animal bone, both burnt (currently unidentified) and unburnt, was found in the fills of some graves. Unburnt bone recovered from Burials 31 & 48 (Group 1) has been confirmed as coming from cattle and horse (H Foster, pers. comm.). This bone was not formally placed around these burials and possibly made its way into the grave fill from associated feasting or ritual activity. Stout & Stout (2008) have arrived at similar conclusions for Site M, Knowth, Co. Meath. Burnt animal bone has been identified among the fills of eight graves spread across Groups 1–3, but particularly Group 3. This, of course, could reflect the higher number of graves assigned to this phase and/or the amount of truncation caused by this group.

The recovery of discarded animal bone may suggest the consumption of significant amounts of food at the site during its use as a cemetery (Table 5.1). As conclusive evidence for settlement at or around the cemetery was not forthcoming, this debris can perhaps be interpreted as the remains of mortuary or commemorative feasts at the site. The seventh- or eighth-century AD text *Di Dligiud Raith Somaine La Flaith* declared that clients were duty-bound to attend the commemorative feast of their lord (Kelly 2001; Charles-Edwards 2003). Feasting, being part gift exchange, may have been central to the reciprocated gestures of subjection and submission that defined the lord/client relationship in the early medieval period. The tradition of feasting could owe something to early Judaeo-Christian traditions based on the Last Supper, but the early Church may also have borrowed aspects of pre-Christian celebrations.

Table 5.1—Recorded faunal specimens across all phases at Collierstown 1 (minimum number of individuals [MNI], with %MNI per phase in parentheses).

	Cattle	Sheep/goat	Pig	Horse	Dog	Cat	Red deer	% of total assemblage
Phase 1	3 (50%)	1 (17%)	1 (17%)	1 (17%)	—	—	—	8
Phase 2	15 (42%)	10 (28%)	5 (14%)	2 (6%)	2 (6%)	1 (3%)	1 (3%)	47
Phase 3	8 (36%)	4 (18%)	5 (23%)	4 (18%)	1 (5%)	—	—	29
Phase 4	5 (42%)	3 (25%)	2 (17%)	1 (8%)	1 (8%)	—	—	16

That wine played an important role in feasting at Collierstown 1 was suggested by the recovery of sherds of imported amphorae, although wine could also be transported in wooden casks, evidence for which was also found at Collierstown 1. Wine is referred to in various early medieval texts, and the widespread distribution of E-ware pottery, which probably accompanied shipments of wine, in sixth- and seventh-century AD deposits from ecclesiastical and secular sites indicates its popularity and reflects a strong trade link with western France (for a discussion of this see O'Hara, chapter 4). The wine trade did not arrive with Christianity, of course. The aristocracy of pre-Christian Late Iron Age Ireland were acquiring wine, as evidenced by fragments of goblets and flagons excavated from the Rath of the Synods on the Hill of Tara (Raftery 1994, 212). This trade perhaps came directly from the Mediterranean or France, but Celtic tribes in southern Britain were also huge importers of wine and olive oil before the Roman invasion (Stead & Rigby 1989; O'Sullivan & Breen 2007). O'Brien (2003) has suggested that slab-lined inhumations were an important rite between the fifth and the seventh century AD, because they could represent Christian individuals buried among their pagan brethren or ancestors. The generally low numbers of such grave types at these sites in relation to unlined graves may support this hypothesis (O'Sullivan & Harney 2008, 156–69). The overall number of slab-lined graves at Collierstown 1 throughout its use is of interest in this respect. All of the graves of Group 1 were earth-cut graves, although two had associated stones that possibly held wood lining in place. In Group 2 there were seven earth-cut graves, four stone-lined burials and three wood-lined burials (two had extant wood, while the remains of a third, Burial 60, suggested that the body decomposed in a cavity formed by wood lining, thus allowing some of the bone to become dislodged before the cavity filled in). In Group 3 there were six slab-lined and three partially stone-lined graves, in addition to 13 earth-cut graves. Preserved wood lining was found in four burials. In Group 4 there were five dug graves, six stone-lined graves and one wood-lined burial (although one of the stone-lined graves also had wood lining). Following O'Brien (2003), this corresponds to a larger proportion of stone-lined burials in each successive group (0% in Group 1; 29% in Group 2; 41% in Group 3; and 50% in Group 4). These simply calculated figures may not stand up to stringent statistical scrutiny, but they may signal a population growing progressively stronger in its Christian belief.

The small percentage of wood-lined burials in each phase is also interesting. Elizabeth O'Brien (pers. comm.) suggests that such graves, which are rare in Ireland, are potentially indicative of the influences of Anglo-Saxon burial practices, notably those of Finglesham and Ozengel in Kent, which produced numerous wood-lined graves dating to the sixth and seventh centuries AD. The clearest Irish parallel for the Collierstown 1 graves is a burial at Rathangan, Co. Kildare, excavated by the National Museum in 1987 (E O'Brien, pers. comm.). Such burials cannot be considered coffin burials as the wooden components were not nailed together. The eight Collierstown 1 examples belonging to Groups 2–4 survived as poorly preserved strips of organic material between the cut and the skeleton. A timber covering placed over the bodies was suggested in most examples by a thin strip of wood preserved between the legs of the individuals. This practice was used for both men and women.

The burials at Collierstown 1 belong to the transitional period between pre-Christian and Christian Ireland in the early centuries AD. That such a transformation was a slow and complex process can be seen in the variety of burial rites that characterise this period, and the excavation of Collierstown adds significantly to the corpus of information relating to burial practices at this time. We know of many sites like Collierstown, and there are undoubtedly many more waiting to be discovered. Collierstown provides a platform for future research into the Christianising of traditional burial sites in the early medieval period. In terms of what one would hope to find at such places, this site fulfils a number of criteria, including post-holes perhaps indicating the erection of wooden crosses and the construction of a possible earthen shrine, both of which are mentioned in seventh-century texts, as well as evidence for feasting and its accoutrements (e.g. bowls and amphorae imported from the eastern Mediterranean).

Sometime near the end of prehistory, a ditch was excavated to form a burial mound erected over a woman's final resting place. Many more would be buried at this location in the following centuries, although with time the cemetery fell out of use and was eventually forgotten. Was it serendipitous, a quirk of fate, that centuries later an earthen mound would be placed at precisely the same location and draw attention to what lay beneath?

Notes

1. Collierstown 1: NGR 294743, 258825; height 112 m OD; excavation reg. no. E3068; Ministerial Direction no. A008/015; excavation director Robert O'Hara.
2. Dunboyne 1: NGR 302510, 242487; height 66 m OD; excavation reg. no. E3029; Ministerial Direction no. A017/007; excavation director Linda Clarke.
   Ardsallagh 2: NGR 289171, 262980; height 50.97 m OD; excavation reg. no. E3087; Ministerial Direction no. A008/034; excavation director Linda Clarke.
3. Ross 2: NGR 294455, 259025; height 115 m OD; excavation reg. no. E3381; Ministerial Direction no. A008/082; excavation director Robert O'Hara.
   Lismullin 1: NGR 293437, 261602; height 77 m OD; excavation reg. no. E3074; Ministerial Directions nos A008/021 & A042; excavation director Aidan O'Connell.

6
MILITARY LORDS AND DEFENSIVE BEGINNINGS: A PRELIMINARY ASSESSMENT OF THE SOCIAL ROLE OF AN IMPRESSIVE RATH AT BARONSTOWN

Stephen J Linnane and Jonathan Kinsella

Baronstown 1 was a large and impressive rath that occupied a strategic place in its immediate landscape (the term rath is preferable to ringfort, given that 'rath' was used by the people of early medieval Ireland themselves to describe a range of different enclosures).[1] This paper will discuss its social role within the local community through an assessment of the archaeological, historical and cartographic evidence. It is suggested that Baronstown was initially constructed as a defensive fort, possibly used only intermittently in times of danger, but its function altered over the centuries as it became predominantly a farmstead with an emphasis possibly on crop husbandry. This paper is based on preliminary archaeological findings, and interpretations may be subject to change as radiocarbon dates, environmental samples analysis and further post-excavation results are obtained.

Illus. 6.1—Aerial view of Baronstown pre-excavation, from the south-west (Studio Lab).

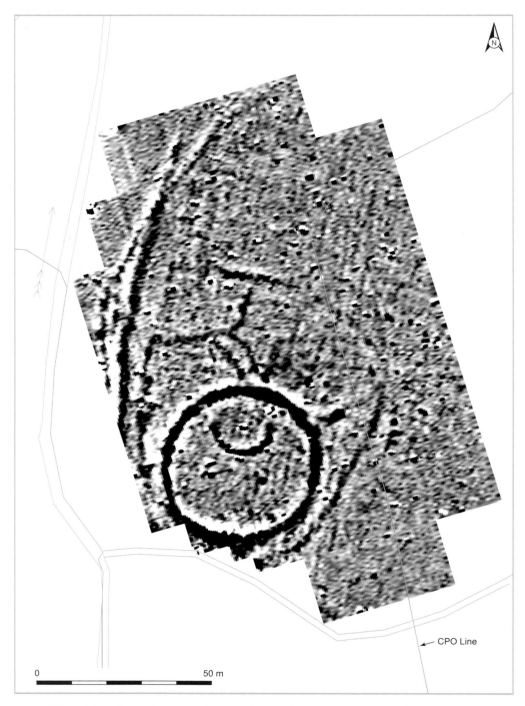

Illus. 6.2—Greyscale image showing the geophysical survey results from Baronstown (Archaeological Consultancy Services Ltd based on an image produced by GSB Prospection Ltd).

The previously unknown site at Baronstown (see site location map on page xiv; Illus. 6.1) was discovered by archaeological investigations before the construction of the proposed M3. The site was first located by geophysical survey (Shiel et al. 2001), undertaken on behalf of Margaret Gowen & Co. Ltd as part of the Environmental Impact Assessment. The survey provided clear evidence of a large circular ditch, with additional internal and external features (Illus. 6.2). The site was provisionally classified as a ringfort with a large outer enclosure. These findings were further enhanced by test-trenching and excavation of a selection of features as part of the archaeological testing before the full excavation of the site (Clarke 2004b).

Landscape setting

The site was on a low hill on the eastern bank of the Gabhra River, some 2.5 km east of the Hill of Tara and 1.4 km south-west of the village of Skreen. The principal part of the site was on level ground with a high point at 112 m OD, but the ground then sloped steeply down to the river to the west and more gently to the north. The lower ground in these areas would have been subject to flooding before canalisation of the river, which could have enhanced the defensive nature of the site (Illus. 6.3).

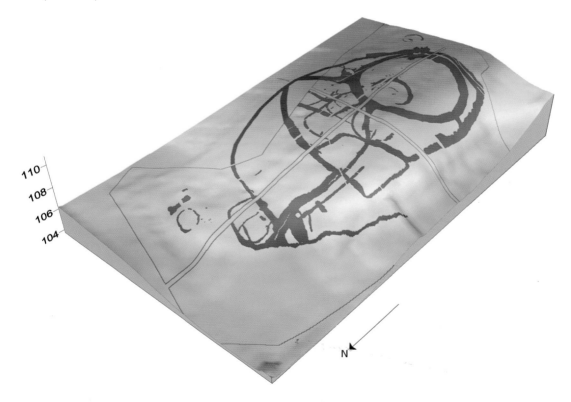

Illus. 6.3—Enhanced topographical survey of site (Archaeological Consultancy Services Ltd).

The site was located in an irregularly shaped field under pasture, with a curving field boundary to the south that formed the division between the townlands of Baronstown and Collierstown (Illus. 6.1). Excavation demonstrated that the field boundary was not contemporary with the rath because it cut through the backfilled outer ditch, and the builders appear at the time of its construction to have had no knowledge of the previous existence of the rath. Its curving nature may be explained by the fact that it followed what was probably a seasonal water-course.

Site description

Inner ditch

The principal feature on the site was the rath, a circular ditch with an internal diameter of 40 m. This inner ditch was, on average, 4 m wide and mostly followed the 112 m contour around the highest point in the immediate landscape (Illus. 6.4 & 6.5). To the west the ditch descended the valley side slightly and became narrower and shallower, with a width of 3.3 m and depth of 2 m; however, the defensive nature of the ditch was enhanced in this area by the slope of the hill and

Illus. 6.4—Aerial view of site post-excavation, from the north-east (Studio Lab).

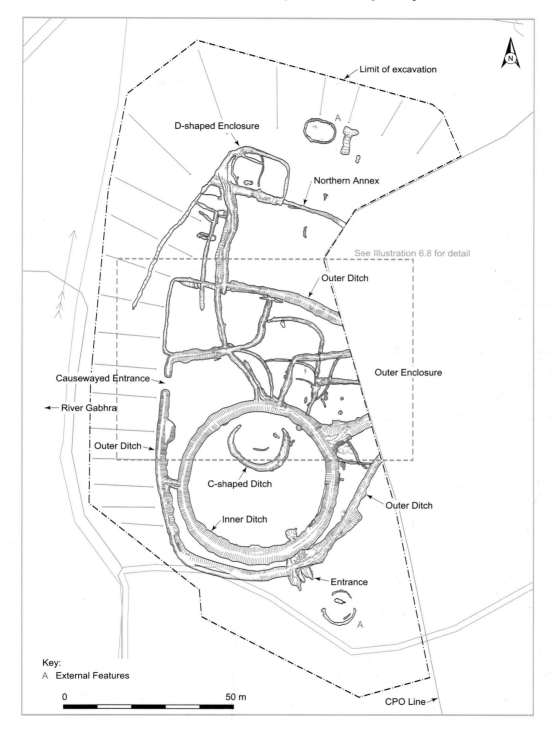

Illus. 6.5—Post-excavation plan of site (Archaeological Consultancy Services Ltd).

the proximity to the River Gabhra. The ditch was at its greatest to the south, where the entrance was located and where the approach to the rath was across level ground; in this area the ditch was 5 m wide and 3 m deep. The ditch also widened to the north, where it was 4 m wide and 2.3 m deep. In profile the ditch formed a truncated V with a flat base varying between 0.6 m and 1 m in width (Illus. 6.6). It had multiple re-cuts, and each re-cut tended to be smaller than its predecessor and also moved towards the inner edge of the ditch, indicating that, as time progressed, less effort was expended on maintaining the defensive function of the rath.

It is assumed that the material created by excavating the ditch was used to build an internal bank, and this has been estimated as being 4 m wide and 2 m high, with a 2 m-wide walkway along the top, possibly equipped with a timber palisade. Even after construction of the bank, the amount of earth left over from excavation of the inner ditch would have been sufficient to raise the ground level of the interior, with a diameter of 32 m, by approximately 0.5 m. This could have been done in order that the raised platform would be better drained. This theory perhaps explains why so few features were found in the area enclosed by the inner ditch after both bank and platform had eroded or otherwise disappeared.

Clearly, the rath builders at Baronstown were concerned with defence. The fort was strategically located on higher ground, when approached from the north and west, and the latter approach was also protected by the river. The entrance, on the southern side, was the most vulnerable area, being located on level ground. However, this was alleviated somewhat by widening and deepening the enclosing ditch in this area. It is also a distinct possibility that the surrounding bank was at its greatest height at either side of the entrance. Considerable effort was spent on fortifying Baronstown, and this fort would have been impressive when approached from any direction.

Features within the rath or inner ditch

The most significant feature enclosed by the inner ditch was a C-shaped enclosure, with the open ends of the C-shaped ditch located to the north, 3 m from the internal edge of the inner ditch (Illus. 6.7). The internal bank of the rath would have been located in this area, and this could explain why the ditch terminated here, abutting the back of the internal bank. The ditch had an internal diameter of 14 m and at its greatest was 2.8 m wide and 0.93 m deep. The ditch was at its widest to the south and decreased in width and depth to the north, ending in rounded terminals with a gap of 12 m between them. The profile of the ditch varied but tended towards a truncated V with a flat base 0.5–1 m wide. Two re-cuts were noted in the ditch fills.

Features within the C-shaped enclosure included a short stretch of curving ditch, a very short and shallow ditch running between the two terminals, and a cluster of post-holes and pits located on the inner and outer edges of the ditch to the south-east (Illus. 6.7 & 6.8). Although there is no supporting evidence, it is possible that this enclosure was the location of the principal house within the rath. Generally, however, roundhouses within raths are found towards the centre, and later rectangular dwellings are usually located closer to the bank (Lynn 1978; 1994). Therefore, it is possible only to hypothesise about the location of the house, but perhaps the ditch was used not only as an aid to drainage but also as further protection for the house. If this was the case, it further

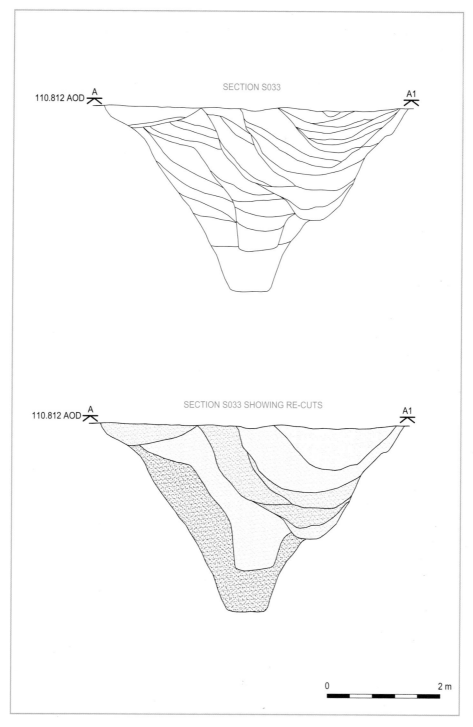

Illus. 6.6—Section through inner ditch showing the complex series of re-cuts
(Archaeological Consultancy Services Ltd).

Illus. 6.7—View of C-shaped enclosure, from the north-east (Hawkeye).

supports the defensive or military aspect of Baronstown because dwellings within early medieval enclosures are not typically surrounded by large internal ditches.

Outer ditch

It is as yet uncertain whether there was an early phase of occupation on the site when the inner ditch existed as a simple univallate rath before the construction of an outer ditch and bank, which created an additional defensive feature and expanded the enclosed area considerably (Illus. 6.3–6.5). The outer ditch was, on average, 2.7 m wide by 1.4 m deep and had a truncated V-shaped profile with a flat base 0.5 m wide. It was concentric with the inner ditch on the southern half, but on the northern side it diverged, eventually creating an outer enclosure to the north of the rath measuring 71 m west–east by 31 m. On the southern half it is assumed that the c. 2.5 m distance between the two ditches contained a bank formed of the spoil excavated from the outer ditch. Along the course of the outer ditch to the north-west of the inner ditch was a gap of 3.5 m, which provided a causewayed access from the outer enclosure to the Gabhra River. Two re-cuts were noted in the ditch fills and, as with the inner ditch, they tended to become smaller with each successive re-cut.

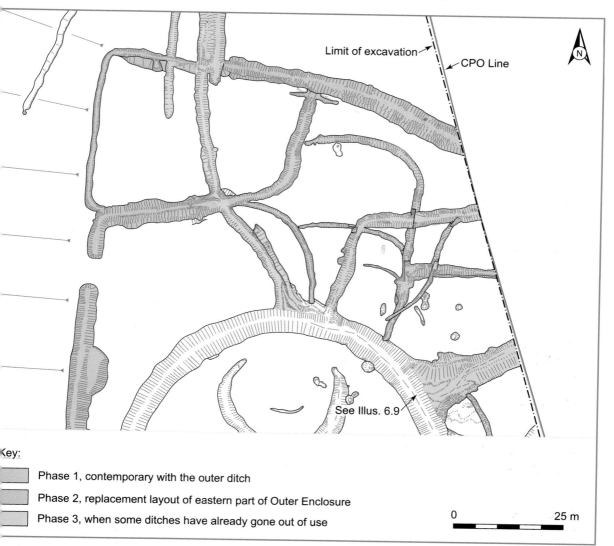

Key:

■ Phase 1, contemporary with the outer ditch

■ Phase 2, replacement layout of eastern part of Outer Enclosure

■ Phase 3, when some ditches have already gone out of use

0   25 m

Illus. 6.8—Outer enclosure showing complex of phased ditches (Archaeological Consultancy Services Ltd).

Entrance

The main entrance to the rath was located to the SSE and consisted of linear cuts into the natural subsoil extending from the internal edge of the inner ditch across the area between it and the outer ditch and further beyond the outer edge of the latter. It would appear that large timbers (possibly split tree trunks) were placed in the cuttings in order to form the base of a bridge that may then have been planked. Successive layers of metalling were found to the south of the outer ditch in this area, reinforcing the idea of a bridge crossing here. A scatter of pits and post-holes in the vicinity of the bridge crossing may indicate the location of a timber gatehouse within the internal bank of the rath. The surviving features were too truncated to allow any form of accurate reconstruction of the putative gatehouse. O'Kelly (1963) suggested that the entranceway to the rath at Garryduff, Co. Cork, was accompanied by a gatehouse. Examples of early medieval gatehouses are very rare and they must only have supported settlements that required extra protection, or perhaps they were constructed as a means of adding to the prestige of the site. Both interpretations could equally be relevant to Baronstown.

A particularly interesting detail was the burial of a horse's skull in a pit central to the internal edge of the bridge crossing, which was possibly a foundation deposit, revealing the continuation of pagan practices, or at least demonstrating a continuation of past traditions or superstitions after the arrival of Christianity.

Internal divisions within the outer enclosure

To the north and west of the rath, and mostly internal to the outer ditch, was a complex sequence of subsidiary ditches designed to create smaller plots within the enclosure. The sequence of interaction between the internal ditches, their various re-cuts and the principal inner and outer ditches has not yet been finalised (Illus. 6.9). The ditches would have functioned both as an aid to drainage and as physical divisions within the outer enclosure. It is possible that these subdivisions were intended to demarcate plots for vegetable and/or cereal crops or, alternatively, for use as enclosures for livestock.

A particularly large ditch ran from west to east, linking the inner and outer ditches on the eastern side of the outer enclosure, and this also had a history of re-cutting and silting, ending with a substantial causeway being built over the backfilled ditch (Illus. 6.5). The causeway surface consisted of an area of large stone slabs worn smooth by use and apparently intended to cross the ditch, which by this time had gone out of use. The feature measured 4 m running north-west to south-east by 2 m. To the west of the causeway were a series of stone alignments that appeared to be the remnants of very poorly constructed walls or, alternatively, low walls that could have supported a timber superstructure (Illus. 6.9). The wall alignments appeared to form a square chamber measuring 2 m by 2 m, with another wall extending to the north-west for a distance of 3 m. The stonework extended over the fills of the inner ditch, which, by this phase, must have been mostly backfilled. A very irregular metalled surface to the south of the stone causeway extended for 3 m west–east by 2 m.

Northern annex

An additional enclosure was appended to the north of the outer enclosure. The geophysical survey (Illus. 6.2) indicated that the new enclosure began at the north-eastern edge of the outer enclosure (beyond the road corridor) and proceeded northwards before curving to the west and entering the area of excavation. The ditch ran westwards for 40 m before turning sharply to the SSW. The ditch then petered out after running for 45 m; at this point there was a splayed gap of 8.5 m between it and the western side of the outer ditch. Although unlikely, it is possible that

Illus. 6.9—Possible stone wall foundations sealing ditch (Archaeological Consultancy Services Ltd).

this gap was intended to function as an entranceway into the northern annex interior. The maximum dimensions of the ditch were 2.8 m wide by 0.46 m deep, and the profile indicated that there had been at least one re-cut, but this was not readily visible within the fills.

Annexed enclosures are common additions to rath complexes (Cagney & O'Hara, chapter 7; Williams 1983), and a D-shaped enclosure was added to the exterior of the northern annex at Baronstown in the final enlargement of the complex. The D-shaped enclosure measured 21 m west–east by 10 m. The enclosing ditch was irregular in profile, at its greatest being 1.15 m wide by 0.34 m deep. It seems probable from its size that this ditch was intended to aid drainage for arable or cereal farming rather than to be an enclosure for livestock. A cereal-drying kiln was located in its interior, but this may have been coincidental and the two features may not have been contemporaneous.

Isolated features

There were numerous pits, depressions and small lengths of ditch that could not be reasonably explained within a coherent site narrative at the time of writing, and these features are not described in this interim paper. Two classes of feature, however, although occurring in isolation, are considered to be of sufficient interest and importance to the site to be included here.

Cereal-drying kilns

There were eight features excavated and identified as cereal-drying kilns on this site (Illus. 6.5), and a further two were excavated in the adjacent southern field as part of the site known as Collierstown 2.[2] It is generally accepted that kilns were used for drying cereal before grinding and milling, although drying as part of the brewing process or before threshing was also practised (Monk 1981; Monk & Kelleher 2005). In form, the cereal-drying kilns at Baronstown can be classified as figure-of-eight types, and their average dimensions were 2.25 m long with a firespot of 1.15 m diameter, a drying chamber of 0.85 m diameter and a flue length of 0.25 m. The difference in depth between the firespot and the drying chamber was 0.1 m, with the former being the deeper. The surviving depths of the kilns varied greatly, which may be due to differential ploughing in recent times. Kilns would normally be orientated to take advantage of the prevailing wind, and, as cereal drying would have taken place after the harvest, generally during August, the prevailing wind should have been fairly constant. Surprisingly, however, the kilns at Baronstown had widely varying orientations and were distributed randomly across the site, and it is likely that some were not contemporary with the rath occupation.

Hearths

In addition to the cereal-drying kilns a total of 22 pits and depressions displayed evidence of burning either through charcoal-rich fills or the oxidisation of clays. Many of the features were slight depressions in the natural ground, while others appeared to be the result of land clearance owing to tree burning and yet more were associated with the various ditches.

The most common type of hearth was a circular bowl-shaped depression, 0.7 m in diameter and 0.15 m deep, with a charcoal-rich basal deposit overlying the oxidised natural subsoil and overlain by pale grey clay/ash. None provided evidence for industrial activity, but it is hoped that analysis of soil samples will provide an indication of the purpose of at least some of the features. As with the cereal-drying kilns, some of the hearths may not have been contemporary with the occupation of the rath.

External features

Two oval enclosures were excavated beyond the limits of the outer ditches (Illus. 6.5). Both may represent the slight remains of circular houses, or structures, not necessarily contemporary with the rath. The enclosure to the north was associated with a nearby spread that produced a Bann flake (a leaf-shaped stone tool characteristic of the Late Mesolithic period). This enclosure had internal dimensions of 8.2 m west–east by 5.93 m. The ditch had maximum dimensions of 0.74 m in width and 0.25 m in depth and had a very variable profile.

To the south of the site were two lengths of curving ditch that formed an enclosure with internal dimensions of 9 m north–south by 8.2 m. The ditch sections had been heavily truncated by ploughing and did not meet at both west and east. In the south-eastern quadrant of the enclosure was a short length of curving ditch 0.7 m within the enclosure ditch. A cereal-drying kiln was located in the interior of this enclosure, and it is possible that the enclosure was built to hold a wind break around the kiln, but equally the kiln's location could be fortuitous.

Finds assemblage

The collection of finds recovered at Baronstown was not large but contained examples of artefact types typically associated with early medieval settlement sites. Detailed analysis of the finds is continuing, and any observations made here are preliminary.

Prehistoric background

The early medieval site at Baronstown overlay a landscape already containing thousands of years of occupation activity. During the testing stage in 2004, Bronze Age pottery was found within a pit inside the inner ditch (Clarke 2004b). During excavation in 2007, however, the feature proved to be the result of tree burning, and it is uncertain how the pottery found its way there. No prehistoric features were identified during this phase of excavation, but an isolated cremation, contained in an inverted urn and dating to the Bronze Age, was located in the adjacent field to the south at Collierstown 2.

Of approximately 250 finds (excluding waterlogged material), c. 20 % were of flint, the majority of which could be described as débitage. However, among the collection were blades, thumb-nail scrapers, hollow scrapers, a barbed-and-tanged arrowhead and a Bann flake. The majority of the flint artefacts came from stratified early medieval contexts, and the only discernible pattern in their distribution so far noted was the marked concentration of flint finds to the north-east of the rath, possibly indicating a focus of prehistoric activity nearby.

The flint finds indicate occupation in the area from the Late Mesolithic period through the Neolithic period and into the Bronze Age. It has been suggested that prehistoric objects, flint or otherwise, were retained during the early medieval period as items with magical or protective properties (O'Sullivan 2006, 21). The distribution and quality of the prehistoric finds from Baronstown suggest, however, that the finds represent residual survival of the rich prehistoric background to early medieval Baronstown.

Early medieval

As stated previously, the finds collection was small for a site that was apparently occupied for several centuries. Nevertheless, the collection contained artefacts typical of the early medieval period.

Iron finds were not common, and the assemblage is dominated by small tanged knife blades; the longest had a combined blade and tang length of 143 mm, with all of the rest being considerably smaller. All were of the typical curve-backed blade form with a straight cutting edge. Other iron finds included a small ring-pin (40 mm long) and stick-pins of various forms dating to between the latter stages of the 10th century and the early 14th century (O'Rahilly 1998; Scully 1997). More iron finds may prove to be of interest after x-ray and conservation. It is notable that no finds have so far been identified as weapons. This, however, is not too surprising as weapons, such as swords and shield bosses, are rare finds on early medieval sites. The crannog at Lagore, Co. Meath (Hencken 1950), produced a number of swords, but this was a royal site, and only the highest aristocracy had access to specialist weapons. The majority of those engaged in early medieval warfare probably used simple weapons such as spears, axes and arrows.

Decorative bronze work was likewise scant, but fine examples of a spiral-ringed loop-headed pin and a penannular brooch, with zoomorphic terminals in the form of birds' heads, were uncovered (Illus. 6.10). The brooch has parallels with similar types from the crannogs at Lagore (Hencken 1950, 64, fig. 10, a) and Moynagh Lough (Bradley 1991, 21, fig. 9; 1993, 79, fig. 8.6), both in County Meath, and more recently from the enclosure and cemetery at Parknahown 5, Co. Laois (O'Neill 2006; 2007). The only production site so far discovered was located at Dunadd, the capital of Dalriada in Scotland, where casts for such brooches were found (Campbell & Lane 1993). These brooches appear to date to the seventh century AD, as might the spiral-ringed loop-headed pin, which generally dates to between the fifth and the eighth century (Fanning 1994). A late medieval ring brooch, with a twisted cable design on one half of the frame, dating to the 13th or 14th century AD was also among the finds (Deevy 1998). This, coupled with the presence of

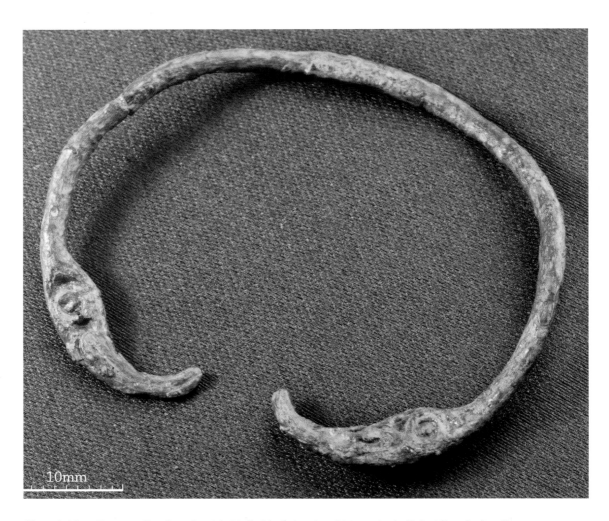

Illus. 6.10—Copper-alloy brooch with bird's head zoomorphic terminals (John Sunderland).

stick-pins, suggests a slight possibility that Baronstown was still in use during the later Middle Ages, but this will not be determined until post-excavation analysis is complete. Other finds of copper alloy included a complete needle, a fragment of curved tubing (6 mm in diameter) from a bracelet and various fragments of uncertain use comprising a total of nine objects.

Bone artefacts included a solitary component of a composite comb, a spindle whorl and nine pins, the largest being 94 mm long. There was also a single glass bead—green with yellow enamel—and a spherical lead weight with broken iron attachment.

The basal deposits of the rath's deep enclosing ditch (the inner ditch) were waterlogged, and an interesting collection of 308 wooden artefacts was recovered. Bucket staves were very common, with over 70 specimens recorded, but of greater rarity were barrel staves, of which three were recovered. All were approximately 580 mm long, and there is a possibility that they came from the same barrel. Barrel staves are rarely recovered from early medieval sites, although one was excavated at the royal crannog at Lagore (Hencken 1950) and another more recently at Roestown 2 (O'Hara, chapter 4). A near-intact, turned wooden bowl was also recovered sitting upright in the ditch fill (Illus. 6.11). The fill of the bowl was very pale in contrast to the surrounding, near-black ditch fills. Before scientific analysis it is suspected that the fill in the bowl was a butter-like substance and that the bowl had been placed in the ditch purposefully, a theory reinforced by a wooden scoop located next to the bowl. The scoop is very similar to two scoops excavated at Lagore.

Illus. 6.11— Wooden bowl and scoop in situ *in the inner ditch* (Archaeological Consultancy Services Ltd).

Numerous fragments of planking were recovered, and it is hoped that their analysis will provide information concerning carpentry techniques of the early medieval period and indeed about the wooden fixtures and fittings to be found in a rath. Many of the finds appeared to have been burnt, and again it will be fascinating to learn whether part of the collection is from a disastrous episode that befell the rath and its occupants.

Agriculture and environment

A massive quantity of animal bone was recovered from the site, the majority coming from the inner ditch. The animal bone has yet to be analysed, but a preliminary survey indicated that the majority was from cattle. The preponderance of cattle in the assemblage is in accord with the findings from similar sites and possibly indicates the importance of dairying to the occupants of the site (McCormick 1995). Other animals from the assemblage include pig, sheep/goat, horse, deer and dog. Such large quantities of bone suggest that animal husbandry, particularly cattle and dairying, was a dominant aspect of the economy of the site, but the presence of cereal-drying kilns and the shallow nature of some of the enclosure ditches provide some balance and indicate the importance of cereal cultivation. The environmental analysis of soil samples from the kilns should reveal the nature of the crops concerned. Pollen samples were taken from all phases of the inner ditch, and hopefully analysis will reveal further information about crop growth on-site, in addition to information about the wider landscape.

It is interesting that the majority of the animal bone came from the rath ditch. McCormick and Murray's (2007) recent research has identified a shift in the early medieval economy from one based on pasture to one where tillage increased in importance from approximately the ninth century. When the faunal assemblage is fully analysed and dates are obtained from the various phases of the rath and outer enclosing ditches (it may transpire, for example, that the excavation of the outer ditch post-dates the rath's construction phase), as well as the cereal-drying kilns, it may be possible to determine whether Baronstown follows this pattern.

Baronstown and its immediate landscape

The rath at Baronstown occupied a prominent place in the landscape, as it was strategically placed to afford commanding views in three directions: to the north, west and east. Its location, more so than the majority of raths, which were located on sloping, well-drained land, was particularly prominent, and views towards the settlements and lands in the immediate landscape appear to have been important for the occupants—at least during the initial use of the fort. There are a small number of recorded monuments in the surrounding landscape that can be classified as ringforts or raths and that are likely to be contemporaneous with the Baronstown settlement. Extant raths exist at Cabragh (Record of Monuments and Places [RMP] no. ME032-054), Castleboy (ME031-033009), Collierstown (ME038-003), Lismullin (ME032-025) and Skreen (ME032-032). The M3 excavations, however, have highlighted the capacity for substantial settlement complexes to exist below ground with no surface indication.

We can argue, however, that the contemporaneous early medieval landscape around Baronstown was more densely settled than the archaeological record currently indicates. The Hill of Tara is situated c. 2.5 km to the west of Baronstown (Illus. 6.12). The written evidence, from approximately the seventh century, unequivocally cites Tara as the mythical capital of Ireland, and its title later became synonymous with the high-kingship of the country (Bhreathnach 1999; 2005a; 2005b). The majority of the monuments on the hill are considered to be prehistoric, and, although there have been suggestions that some are early medieval—for example, the bivallate enclosure known as Tech Cormaic (Newman 1997, 180)—this is impossible to determine without excavation. The historical sources, limited excavations and morphology of the features suggest that Tara was not occupied in a conventional sense during the early medieval period, although it remained of great mythological and political importance. Therefore, based on current archaeological and cartographic evidence, it appears that the Hill of Tara and the lands further to the west feature monuments that pre-date the construction of Baronstown.

When Baronstown's local landscape is examined, a very different picture is evident, as a range of contemporaneous domestic, burial, ecclesiastical and farming features are apparent that demonstrate an area teeming with human activity. The small townland is bounded by Cabragh, Skreen, Collierstown and Ross. The two former townlands feature a souterrain, rath and church, while an earthwork, which was marked 'fort' on the first-edition (1837) Ordnance Survey in Cabragh, may have been a rath (Moore 1987, 50–1, 144–5, 110). Skreen is recorded in early historical documents that declare that it was plundered by both the Irish and the Scandinavians between the 10th and the 12th century, indicating its importance during this period (Bhreathnach 1996; 1999). Although phasing of the site is continuing, it is possible, as indicated by the recovery of a variety of stick-pins, that Baronstown was occupied throughout these centuries, at a time when conflict and war were endemic.

Excavations before construction of the M3 of a circular cropmark recorded in the RMP at Ross 1 to the south revealed a large probable rath that was devoid of contemporaneous features and produced only a moderate amount of animal bone and a handful of artefacts.[3] Its function is unclear at present. It may have been occupied, with all habitation traces having been removed owing to centuries of farming activity, but it is more likely, however, that it served as a livestock enclosure. Another upstanding rath is recorded in Collierstown (Moore 1987, 65), and a forgotten early medieval cemetery was also discovered and excavated before the M3 in this townland (O'Hara, chapter 5).[4]

Finally, evidence of further human activity to the north of Baronstown survives in the form of raths and a souterrain at Castletown Tara, approximately 3 km to the north-east (Moore 1987, 51, 64, 98), and two souterrains are recorded in the townland of Lismullin (ibid., 53, 79). A souterrain and a number of cereal-drying kilns have also been discovered and excavated before construction of the M3 at Lismullin (O'Connell, chapter 2).[5]

Baronstown must be considered in relation to its immediate settlement and burial landscape, as understood from the record of known sites and those recently discovered and excavated, including Ross 1, Collierstown 1 and Lismullin 1. Baronstown, no doubt, occupied the most prominent local position here, and, through an investigation of the archaeological, landscape and historical

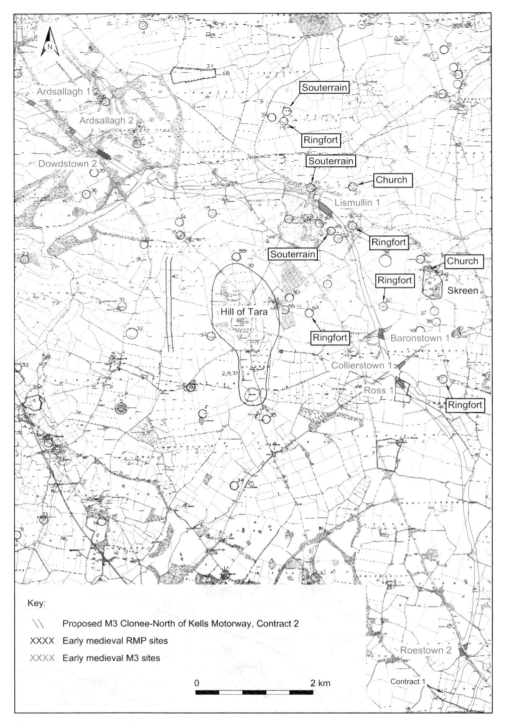

Illus. 6.12—Surrounding RMP sites and sites mentioned in text (Archaeological Consultancy Services Ltd based on 1996 RMP).

evidence, the preliminary discussion below proposes to see how these sites and the people that used them interacted with each other and to assess their role within the local community.

Baronstown: a defensive fort

When the rath at Baronstown was constructed, the builders deliberately chose the highest point in the immediate landscape that gave the fort its prominent position. The size and scale of its enclosing defences were another factor that added to the impressiveness of the site. This would have been a truly dominating piece of architecture when approached from lower ground and represented a strategic and deliberate choice by those who were to fortify the rath during its initial years.

Unusually for a rath of this scale, and given the fact that it was probably used over many centuries, the artefact assemblage from Baronstown is small. If, for example, the finds from other early medieval settlements occupied over a prolonged period in County Meath are compared—such as the crannog at Lagore (Hencken 1950), the settlement and cemetery complex at Raystown (Seaver 2005b; 2006) and the recently excavated enclosures at Roestown 2 (see O'Hara 2007; chapter 4) and Castlefarm 1 (O'Connell, chapter 3)—Baronstown lags far behind in terms of quantity and quality. This may be best understood if it was used or occupied only intermittently, perhaps in times of danger, when the fort was primarily used for its defensive capabilities. The site produced large amounts of animal bone throughout its various phases, and this may indicate that regular feasting events occurred. The specialised nature of the site is suggested by the limited quantity of finds, with the presence of mainly high-status items, such as the bird-headed brooch, and objects possibly representing ritual deposition, including the deliberately placed wooden bowl within the enclosing ditch and the burial of a horse's skull in a pit central to the internal edge of the bridge crossing. Therefore, given the scale of the enclosure defences, the type of finds and the prominent site location, it is possible that Baronstown was a distinctive place used by a social group with access to labour, wealth and economic resources.

There are a small number of excavated early medieval enclosures that provide landscape, morphological and material culture evidence similar to Baronstown. These sites include Ballycasey Beg (Carey 2002) and Beal Boru (O'Kelly 1962), both in County Clare, and Narraghmore, Co. Kildare (Fanning 1972). What all have in common is their strategic defensive location—occupying high vantage points over the lower-lying terrain—impressive defences—taking a variety of forms including wide and deep ditches and tall banks and palisades—and a general lack of occupational evidence in the form of houses and artefacts.

By combining the preliminary archaeological, cartographic and historical evidence it is possible to hypothesise the role that Baronstown played in its local community. In the absence of a detailed chronology for the site, which awaits radiocarbon dates, this interpretation will be based on the role of the fort during the seventh and eighth centuries for a number of reasons. Firstly, the presence of the penannular brooch with bird-headed terminals demonstrates that Baronstown was occupied in the seventh century, and the spiral-ringed loop-headed pin may also belong to this time, although, while it is not yet known for how long Baronstown was used, the numerous re-cuts throughout the site and the presence of stick-pins suggest prolonged activity. Also, law-texts written during the seventh and eighth centuries offer insights into the various social grades and their role in early medieval society. Therefore, we can investigate and compare a time when Baronstown was occupied, during the seventh century, with contemporaneous documents that offer insights into the social fabric of early medieval society in Ireland.

The impressive fort at Baronstown initially functioned as a defensive or military-type site. Archaeologically, this is recognisable by the size of its defences and its landscape setting. The ritual depositions may have been offerings for the protection of the community, crops and animals from neighbouring kingdoms that were based on older pagan beliefs and superstitions, which must still have resonated and held meaning for many people in the early medieval period—Christians or not—for centuries after the arrival of Christianity. The uncovering of the penannular brooch may be significant because generally only the highest-ranking members of early medieval society had access to items of personal adornment. It is likely that the brooch was manufactured in Dunadd, the early medieval Irish-ruled royal site of the Scottish Dalriada, and the Baronstown example can be added to other County Meath examples, including those from the high-status crannogs at Lagore and Moynagh Lough. The distribution of such brooches in Ireland, and notably in the early medieval kingdom of Brega, probably reflects processes such as gift-exchange and tribute between Irish and Anglo-Saxon lords.

The role of the Baronstown fort, in both its immediate and its regional landscape, can be further interpreted alongside information derived from the law-texts. These refer to the *aire forgill* and the *aire ard*, who were high-ranking lords with military functions. One of these functions was the protection of distrained livestock, namely animals that were seized by force from neighbouring kingdoms, so their settlements were usually situated centrally within the *tuath* (Stout 1997, 123). In the distant past the term *tuath* signified a clan or tribal family. In later times it came to mean a unit of territory, namely the ancestral or patrimonial lands of a tribe or tribal grouping. The *tuath* could be described as the smallest unit of land over which a local taoiseach or clan chief exercised control. In terms of size its closest parallel is the parish, and, in fact, a remarkable coincidence will sometimes be seen in the boundaries of these two divisions. A lord in early medieval Irish society could command military service from his clients, so it was imperative that they were located close by. In terms of Baronstown's location and if this was the residence, or a fort used intermittently in times of danger, of a high-ranking lord, the people in the surrounding raths of Cabragh, Skreen, Ross and Collierstown would have been easily accessible and probably visible from this central and prominent vantage point. Critically, they could be quickly called upon to offer military assistance in times of danger. Also, if the interpretation of Ross 1 as a livestock enclosure is accurate, this would have functioned well for the protection of cattle during raids or attacks owing to its large size and proximity to Baronstown. Indeed, this possibility is increased through an analysis of the law-texts, which refer to an enclosure known as a *bódún* (cow-fortress) where cows of the whole neighbourhood were brought for protection against cattle raiders (Kelly 1997, 366).

At a more regional level, Baronstown occupied a secure and roughly central position in the modern barony of Skreen, which corresponds approximately in size to the early medieval demesne of Tara (Bhreathnach 2005a, 4). Therefore, the fort and its neighbouring raths were advantageously central in their own kingdom and sufficiently removed from neighbouring *tuath* borders to limit the chance of attack and to offer the greatest protection to the community and any livestock seized from neighbouring kingdoms.

At a more intimate level, it is interesting that the main entrance to Baronstown faced the cemetery at Collierstown 1, c. 2.5 km to the south-east, and there may have been a direct relationship between its occupants and the deceased at the latter site. Perhaps the cemetery at Collierstown 1 contained the ancestors of this local community. In times when warfare and violence were endemic, and given Baronstown's initial military use, there may have been a much deeper resonance and meaning linking those occupying Baronstown and those buried a short distance away at Collierstown 1.

Conclusions

Two aspects become apparent when examining the development of the site at Baronstown. The first is that the site expanded over time, with the construction of additional enclosures to the north of the site so that, at its greatest, it measured 130 m north–south by 90 m. The small size of the later ditches indicated that they could be for no other purpose than agriculture, probably for crops rather than livestock. It is also apparent that over time all of the major ditches of the site shrank, as they silted up and each successive re-cut became smaller. The defensive nature of the original ditches apparently became increasingly less important to the site's occupants, either because defence was no longer felt essential or because the occupants could no longer command the labour force that would enable the maintenance of such large-scale ditches.

This suggests that the original construction at Baronstown was inspired by the need for strong defences and was carried out by someone with sufficient authority to command a considerable labour force. As time passed, the authority of the occupants seems to have decreased; they were still interested in expanding the holding for agricultural purposes, yet without the desire or authority to maintain a militaristic appearance. How such a sequence might be interpreted in the light of the known historical and social events of the period in the region will be possible only with the establishment of a dated sequence of events (pending radiocarbon dating) enabling each phase of activity to be tied into a chronological framework.

At the time of writing, the post-excavation programme is progressing, with the cleaning and processing of animal bone—a massive job—the processing and conservation of finds and, ultimately, analysis and synthesis. As yet, work is not complete on any of the various post-excavation tasks, and so all identifications and opinions expressed in this paper must be considered to be preliminary observations that will almost certainly be subject to alteration when completed analysis begins to become available to assist in the interpretation of this key site and its contemporaneous landscape.

Notes

1. Baronstown 1: NGR 294401, 259365; height 112 m OD; excavation reg. no. E3070; Ministerial Direction no. A008/017; excavation director Stephen Linnane.

2. Collierstown 2: NGR 294443, 259178; height 112 m OD; excavation reg. no. E3069; Ministerial Direction no. A008/016; excavation director Stephen Linnane.

3. Ross 1: NGR 294753, 258471; height 124 m OD; excavation reg. no. E3092; Ministerial Direction no. A008/077; excavation director Kenneth Wiggins.

4. Collierstown 1: NGR 294743, 258825; height 120 m OD; excavation reg no. E3068; Ministerial Direction no. A008/015; excavation director Robert O'Hara.

5. Lismullin 1; NGR 293437, 261602; height 77 m OD; excavation reg. no. E3074; Ministerial Direction nos A008/021 & A042; excavation director Aidan O'Connell.

7
AN EARLY MEDIEVAL COMPLEX AT DOWDSTOWN 2

Lydia Cagney and Robert O'Hara

A prominent escarpment overlooking the River Boyne was chosen as the site for an early medieval ringfort or rath. Over time the site developed into a large complex of annexed field systems and became a hub of cereal processing activity. This paper presents the preliminary results of the archaeological excavation of this site, designated Dowdstown 2 (see site location map on page xv).[1] The site was first identified by geophysical surveying (Shiel et al. 2001; Illus. 7.1) and was evident as cropmarks during a subsequent aerial survey of the site before excavation (see Deevy 2005, 88, illus. 5). That these features were archaeological in nature was confirmed by archaeological testing in 2004 (04E0419; Linnane 2004c). Excavation of the site occurred between September 2005 and December 2006.

Setting

Dowdstown 2 was situated on the brow of an east–west-running moraine ridge, with the land falling away sharply to the north and merging with the floodplain of the River Boyne, which was approximately 80 m to the north of the site, forming the townland boundary with Ardsallagh and the barony boundary with Lower Navan. The site appears on the 1837 first-edition Ordnance Survey six-inch map as a densely wooded area in demesne parkland surrounding Dowdstown House (Deevy 2005, 89). It would appear that a great deal of the site was reclaimed by this stage; however, flood prevention measures carried out in the mid-20th century saw substantial re-landscaping of the area (T Molten, pers. comm.), which was probably responsible for much of the truncation of the features at the site.

Outline chronological sequence

The initial focus of this site was a ringfort or rath (Enclosure 1). It was circular in plan, approximately 30 m in diameter, and extended partly beyond the road corridor (Illus. 7.1 & 7.2). Abutting this enclosure to the east was a series of large, rectangular, annexed fields (Enclosures 2 & 3). These were replaced by a large D-shaped settlement enclosure (Enclosure 4) that succeeded Enclosure 1. Situated immediately north of these features, within the floodplain, was a large

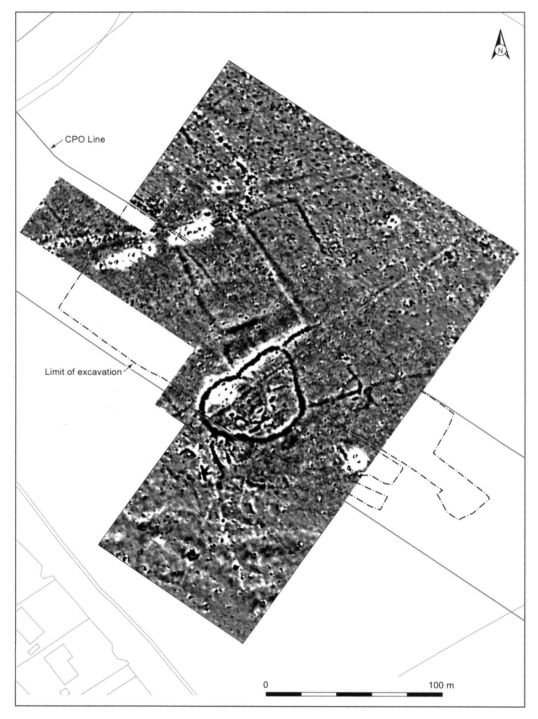

CPO Line

Limit of excavation

0   100 m

Illus. 7.1—Greyscale image of the site at Dowdstown 2 as identified by geophysical survey (Archaeological Consultancy Services Ltd based on a geophysical image produced by GSB Prospection Ltd).

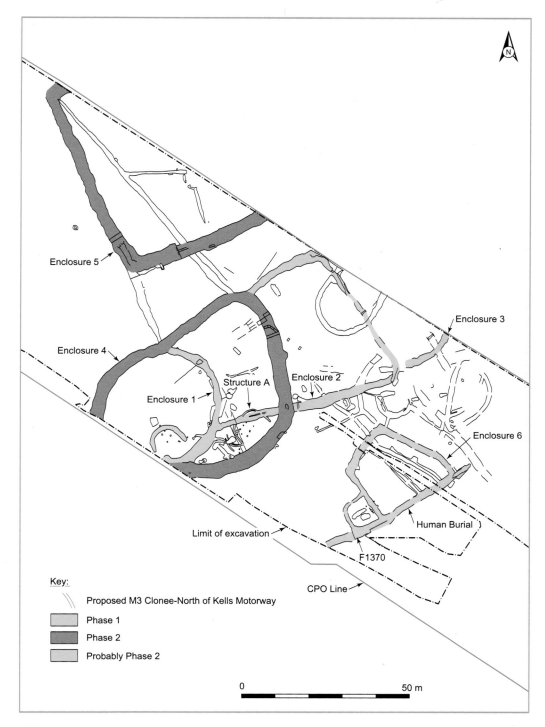

Illus. 7.2—Post-excavation plan of Dowdstown 2 showing the phasing of the site (Archaeological Consultancy Services Ltd).

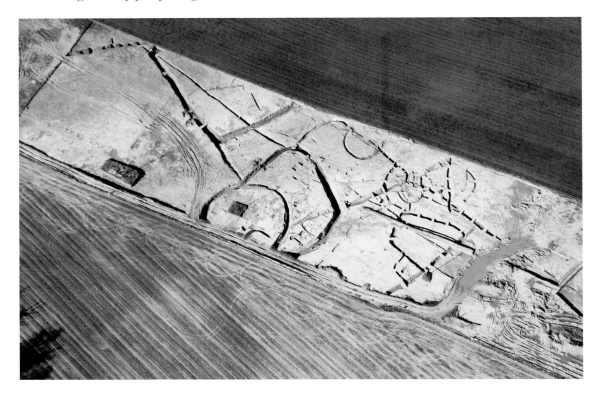

Illus. 7.3—Aerial view of the site, from the south (Studio Lab).

rectangular enclosure (Enclosure 5) that was probably contemporary with Enclosure 2. Additional enclosures or field systems developed to the south of the site, where several cereal-drying kilns were identified. A broad two-phase development of the site is presented in this paper (Illus. 7.2).

Phase 1

The earliest enclosure (Enclosure 1) was a typical early medieval ringfort with a ditch 1.8 m wide by 0.85 m deep (Illus. 7.3). It had been significantly truncated by later activity (Enclosure 4; see below), and significant soil reduction had occurred at the site as a result of reclamation work in the mid-20th century. Available radiocarbon dates from fragments of cattle bone recovered from Enclosure 1 suggest a sixth- or seventh-century AD origin for this enclosure (AD 420–620, Beta-220119; AD 554–651, UB-7039; see Appendix 1 for details of radiocarbon dating results), which was re-cut on at least two subsequent occasions. Animal bone was found throughout the ditch; artefacts found in the fills of the ditch included an iron knife, a bone handle and a rotary quern. No formal entrance to this enclosure was identified, although there was an indication in its later stages of an informal path across the ditch, possibly leading into adjacent fields formed by annex enclosures (Enclosures 2 & 3; see below) to the east.

There was a general absence of internal features in Enclosure 1. Continuous and intensive post-medieval farming may account for the removal of associated remains: frequent plough marks were noted at this location. A semicircular ditch (16.25 m by 1.2 m by 0.95 m) appeared to have originally abutted an inner bank associated with Enclosure 1 and may thus be contemporaneous. Similar-shaped internal ditches were identified at Roestown 2 (see O'Hara, chapter 4) and Baronstown 1 (see Linnane & Kinsella, chapter 6) and may reflect a local design preference. This ditch may have enclosed a cluster of post-holes potentially forming a square or rectangular structure; however, one of these post-holes was truncated by the ditch, suggesting that some, if not all, of these post-holes were earlier than the semicircular ditch. A rectangular structure (Structure A) was located outside the ringfort and pre-dated the construction of Enclosure 2. Structure A was formed by a minimum of eight post-holes arranged in a rectangular pattern. The post-holes were enclosed within a curvilinear gully that probably functioned as a drip gully, the extent of which suggested that Structure A had maximum dimensions of 10 m by 6 m, its long axis orientated north-east–south-west. Given the degree of post-occupation truncation of the site, it is perhaps as a consequence of being sealed beneath the later bank of Enclosure 4 that this structure survived. This explanation may also account for the survival of many of the neighbouring features, which included two cereal-drying kilns. A rectangular structure located externally to an early medieval ringfort, in an area also containing cereal-drying kilns, suggests that Structure A may have been a barn, used for storing kiln-dried grain. Contemporaneous law-texts record that any prosperous farmer was expected to possess a barn (Kelly 1997, 369).

A large sub-rectangular annex (Enclosure 2) abutted the eastern side of the ringfort. It enclosed an area of approximately 40 m by 46 m; however, potentially this large area was originally subdivided into two equal-sized fields, any evidence of which was removed by the expansion of the site in Phase 2 (see below), when a large D-shaped enclosure (Enclosure 4) truncated Enclosures 1 and 2. An additional annex (Enclosure 3) attached to the eastern side of Enclosure 2 was noted in the area of excavation, with further annexes extending eastwards noted on the geophysical survey (see Illus. 7.1). It was not immediately obvious whether these annexes were constructed as a single event over the duration of Phase 1 or they represented protracted development over following phases.

Phase 2

The large D-shaped enclosure (Enclosure 4) constructed at the site replaced the ringfort and a portion of Enclosure 2. The residents of the site may have continued to use the eastern portion of Enclosure 2. Enclosure 4 (60 m by 40 m) was a substantial multi-phase ditch (4.26 m wide by 1.62 m deep), which was re-cut on at least three occasions. The evidence to date suggests an organic expansion of the site that changed in tandem with the shifting requirements of its occupants over time. Available radiocarbon dates for this enclosure suggest activity in the late seventh to the ninth century (AD 680–890, Beta-220117; AD 660–790, Beta-220120).

Early medieval enclosures of non-circular morphology are well attested in the archaeological record, with investigated or excavated sites including Ballynoe, Co. Antrim (Lynn 1980), Balriggan, Co. Louth (Delaney & Roycroft 2003), Clonva, Co. Cork (Doody 1995), Colp West (Clarke &

Murphy 2001) and Johnstown, Co. Meath (Clarke 2004c; Clarke & Carlin 2008), Killickaweeny, Co. Kildare (Walsh 2008), and particularly Newtown, Co. Limerick, (Coyne & Collins 2003; Coyne 2005; 2006) and Roestown 2 (O'Hara, chapter 4), both of which have a number of superficial morphological similarities to Enclosure 4 in Phase 2 at Dowdstown 2. Recent hypotheses forwarded on this subject have proposed that such sites, termed plectrum-shaped enclosures (Coyne & Collins 2003; Coyne 2005; 2006), are a previously unrecognised type of high-status settlement. Ultimately, the shape of any early medieval settlement may have come down to a particular preference on the part of the builders, but factors such as topography and underlying geology could also have been important and would have become obvious only during construction. At Roestown 2 the distinctive shape of the main enclosure from the outset was probably due to the presence in the eastern part of the site of bedrock immediately below the topsoil. Delaney & Walsh (2004), the excavators of the enclosures at Killickaweeny and Balriggan, argue against Coyne & Collins (2003) that their site plans were the result of topographical constraints. Ó Ríordáin (1942; 1949) noted at both Garranes, Co. Cork, and Carraig Aille II, Co. Limerick, that regular deviations in the ground plans occurred, the most likely explanation being inconsistencies in topography (although Ó Ríordáin saw uncoordinated building and poor forward-planning as the reason at Garranes). The expansion to a D-shaped enclosure at Dowdstown appeared to be an amalgamation of an existing annex (Enclosure 2) and the ringfort, a consequence of expansion in an existing site.

Currently, the large rectangular enclosure (Enclosure 5) located 15 m north of Enclosure 2 and within the River Boyne floodplain is also assigned to this phase of activity. This large field (60 m by 47 m) was formed by a large ditch up to 3m deep and was only partially within the limit of excavation. A radiocarbon date (AD 605–762, UB-7009) from a primary deposit in this ditch indicates that it was broadly contemporary with Phase 2. Presumably as a consequence of the sandy nature of the subsoil in this area, there was a tendency for this ditch to become filled rapidly with silt; this was accentuated by its location in the river floodplain. It also appeared that this ditch received run-off from the Enclosure 4 ditch via an interconnecting drain system. Access to this enclosure was through a narrow unexcavated causeway between the ditch terminals on the western side. It was not clear whether there were additional entrance points beyond the road corridor. A shallow drain that cut through this causeway may have acted as an overflow channel, allowing some movement of water between the southern and northern portions of the ditch. The positioning of Enclosure 5 is potentially highly significant for interpretations of land-use patterns in the early medieval period. The construction of the enclosure here may have been intended to exploit nutrient-rich deposits laid down by winter floods, which could then be spread within the enclosed area, resulting in rich grazing during the dry summer months that would allow cattle to be put out to pasture (Kinsella 2008, 105) and reduce the need to drive herds to highland summer pastures (transhumance) (Feehan 2003, 56, 75).

To the south-east of Enclosures 1 and 4 a complex palimpsest of ditch and drain features developed, the stratigraphy of which was complicated by frequent instances of truncation and by post-occupation disturbance. The principal early medieval features here were a ditch (F1370) with a sub-rectangular annex (Enclosure 6). This annex had internal dimensions of 21 m by 19 m. The ditch appeared to delimit the southern expansion of the site. Unfortunately, at the time of writing, radiocarbon dates are pending, and it is difficult to place these features in the overall sequence of the site, although they are considered probably to be contemporary with Phase 2. A stone-lined cereal-drying kiln was constructed at the base of the enclosure ditch and produced a significant quantity of charred cereal remains. This kiln was formed by large boulders placed against the side of the ditch, forming a rectangular chamber (Illus. 7.4). Eight features interpreted as cereal-drying kilns were recorded at the site. The charred seeds from these features are currently being studied as part of the post-excavation analysis for the scheme; when complete, this should provide a comprehensive account of the range of arable agriculture undertaken at the site.

Illus. 7.4—Stone-lined kiln constructed within ditch of Enclosure 6 (Archaeological Consultancy Services Ltd).

Human remains

A single human burial was identified in the site. It was a west–east-aligned inhumation, buried in a flexed position in a simple dug grave. The burial cut into the backfilled ditch F1370 and is therefore unlikely to pre-date the early medieval period.

Artefacts

Approximately 400 flint artefacts were recovered during the excavation, and the identification of scrapers, arrowheads, unfinished tools, cores and flakes (Illus. 7.5) among this material is probably indicative of a prehistoric element to the site. These finds are residual, however, and do not relate to any of the excavated features.

The majority of other artefacts recovered are relatively common from early medieval excavations, including bronze ringed pins, bone combs, spindle whorls and iron knives or shears (see Illus. 7.6 & 7.7). Two bronze pins, one spiral-headed and the other loop-headed, were

Illus. 7.5—Selection of prehistoric flint objects recovered from Dowdstown 2 (John Sunderland).

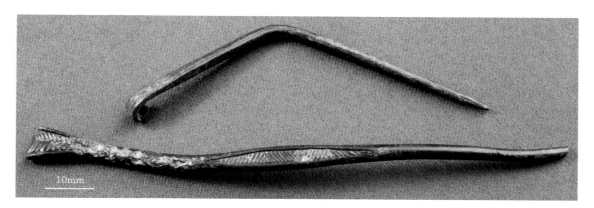

*s. 7.6 (above)—Selection of
~er-alloy pin fragments from
~dstown 2
~n Sunderland).*

*s. 7.7 (right)—Selection of
~e objects from Dowdstown 2
~n Sunderland).*

*s. 7.8 (below)—Billhook
~ Dowdstown 2
~n Sunderland).*

retrieved from deposits associated with Enclosure 2 and Enclosure 5, respectively. These types are known to be among the earlier ones in the chronology of ringed pins (Fanning 1994). A fragment of a decorated bronze penannular brooch was also found in Enclosure 2 deposits. It is likely to date to the seventh century AD and has parallels with a series of brooches and a belt buckle from Lagore, Co. Meath (Hencken 1950). The cultivation of crops and preparation of cereals are further indicated by finds such as a billhook (Illus. 7.8) and a rotary quern-stone. Textile production was evident from the various associated finds, including bone needles and spindle whorls.

A fine example of an early medieval spearhead was retrieved from Enclosure 4. Spears would have been used for hunting (Kelly 1997, 272), and the Dowdstown example was discovered imbedded in a pig's pelvis. Kelly (ibid., 496) relates that a prosperous farmer of *mruigfer* rank would have among his tools a spear for killing livestock. How, or if, this spear differed from the spears used for hunting is not clear. Spearheads are only occasionally encountered in early medieval contexts (Hencken 1950; Edwards 1990), and they were generally absent from the assemblages of the other major early medieval sites excavated along the M3 (Castlefarm 1, Roestown 2 and Baronstown 1).

Function

The River Boyne, an imposing natural boundary, formed the division between the over-kingdoms of Northern and Southern Brega from the seventh century AD onwards. It is plausible that the site on which the current Ballinter Bridge stands, some 100 m west of the site, was an established fording point in this period. The prominent position of the Dowdstown 2 site relative to the fording point is important. A large settlement in proximity to a possible crossing point through a significant territorial boundary indicates that Dowdstown 2 was perhaps more than a wealthy farmer's residence.

The layout of the site is also noteworthy. The settlement sprawled across the brow of the escarpment, which in itself was not unusual. At Roestown 2, for example, the settlement developed on a prominent ridge surrounded by low-lying marshy ground, and its expansion was in part constrained by its location (O'Hara 2007; chapter 4). At Dowdstown 2 there was a deliberate linear bias to the arrangement of annexes. Perhaps this reflects a deliberate manipulation of the landscape to present an imposing façade to anyone approaching from the north, dominating the horizon by obscuring the landscape to the south—a suitable display of wealth and power at an established point of entry. Perhaps the regimented shape and positioning of certain annexes reflect a design catered to the storage of goods and material moving in and out of the region. Dowdstown 2 may have served a number of purposes: part homestead and farmstead, part border barracks, part customs facility.

Conclusions

Dowdstown 2 was a complex and extensive early medieval settlement. The principal economy of the site was agriculture, with cereal processing being particularly important (cereal-drying kilns were the most abundant feature encountered). The associated annexes and field systems indicate that a thriving community prospered at the site for many generations, to which the complete billhook (Illus. 7.8) is a fine testament. There was ample evidence for animal husbandry in all phases also. As mentioned earlier, little evidence of domestic structures survived at the site, likely a consequence of post-occupational activity and soil erosion. Structure A was the only readily identifiable structure in the site. It pre-dated Enclosure 2; however, its relationship to the ringfort (Enclosure 1) was unclear. It is suggested before radiocarbon dating that this structure was contemporary with the ringfort but became redundant with the construction of Enclosure 2. It is plausible that it functioned as a barn associated with cereal drying carried out in the vicinity.

Dowdstown 2 was remarkably similar to the other major early medieval sites excavated along the M3 in terms of its origin, chronology and evidence for prolonged development. The extended occupation of the site and the continuing alterations and modifications to existing features reflect a stable local community modifying their landscape over successive generations. While radiocarbon dates are pending for the later phases of activity at the site, it is probable that Dowdstown continued in use into the 11th or 12th century AD. Its apparent abandonment before the arrival of the Anglo-Normans in the 12th century can be paralleled at the contemporaneous site of Baronstown 1; however, further radiocarbon dates are required to confirm that this was the case.

Note

1. Dowdstown 2: NGR 289684, 262547; height 44–49 m OD; excavation reg. no. E3086; Ministerial Direction no. A008/033; excavation director Lydia Cagney.

8
BOYERSTOWN: A REDISCOVERED MEDIEVAL FARMSTEAD

Kevin Martin

Introduction

In AD 1172 Hugh de Lacy granted to Joceline de Angulo (anglicised as Joceline Nangle) the area of Navan and the lands of Ardbraccan in County Meath (Murphy 2006c). Joceline quickly began to fortify the town and its surroundings and is associated with the building of two large mottes located at Moathill, 0.5 km west of the town, and at Athlumney, directly to the south-east and strategically overlooking the River Boyne. Before the turn of the 13th century a wave of Anglo-Norman settlers had arrived and established themselves in boroughs, fortified farmsteads and manorial villages throughout the surrounding area and across the county (ibid.). Following a previously published overview of the site (Martin 2007), this paper presents preliminary excavation results from the medieval settlement at Boyerstown 1, 3.5 km west of Navan (see site location map on page xv).[1]

The site, in level pastureland and bounded on its north-western side by the present N51 Navan–Athboy road, was first identified as a potential medieval farmstead in 2004 during test-trenching (Fairburn 2004). The testing revealed the remains of drystone walling, metalled surfaces and associated linear ditches. Fifteen sherds of 13th- to 14th-century pottery of Dublin-type Ware were found in association (McCutcheon 2006). A subsequent metal detector survey recovered a number of additional medieval artefacts, including a bodkin-type armour-piercing arrowhead, two knife blades, two copper-alloy belt buckles and an ornately decorated silver ring brooch (Gallagher 2006; Deevy 2006). The finds, coupled with the archaeological testing evidence, indicated that a potentially important medieval site awaited being fully uncovered. Excavation of the site by the author began in May 2006 and continued until April 2007.

Excavations results

The archaeological remains uncovered at Boyerstown 1 extended over an area measuring 300 m by 50 m. The primary features recorded on the site consisted of the partially surviving remains of two drystone-built houses and associated house wall remains, metalled stone surfaces, inter-cutting and connecting drainage ditches, and various-sized pits and wells. These features are interpreted as representing the remains of a medieval farmstead or burgage plot that was settled, potentially by an Anglo-Norman free tenant, sometime during the early 13th century for a period of approximately 400 years. During the excavation the site was divided into two areas (Areas 1 & 2) based on the location of a post-medieval field boundary that ran the full width of the road corridor across the site (Illus. 8.1). This paper focuses on the archaeological remains uncovered in Area 1 as it was the larger area excavated and contained more features. Area 2 contained a series of large drainage ditches and deeply cut wells that were contemporary with the Area 1 features.

Medieval buildings

The structural remains were located towards the centre of Area 1 and abutted the edge of the N51 Navan–Athboy road (Illus. 8.1–8.4). The topsoil was removed by hand and dry sieved because of the high density of metal artefacts recovered in the metal detector survey and the sensitivity of the drystone structural remains underneath. After topsoil removal and clean back, it was evident that the buildings, recorded as House 1 and House 2, had been thoroughly levelled. Both were aligned north-west–south-east, and they abutted each other at their gable ends, with a gap of less than 1 m between them. They were constructed on a plateau of natural, silty sand. Approximately 30–40 % of their lower wall courses survived. A substantial deposit of collapsed stones was recorded overlying a square metalled yard on the north-eastern side of House 1. It was from within this deposit that two squared and dressed wall stones (quoins) were recovered. The paucity of dressed stonework recovered from the site is surprising, given the wealth of the artefact assemblage, and it is perhaps a good indicator that the dressed stone from the structures had been quarried away previously. The two examples recovered exhibited punch dresswork, which dates them approximately to the mid-13th century (D Sweetman, pers. comm.).

House 1, the larger of the two buildings, was rectangular in plan and measured 12 m by 5.5 m. Its walls partially survived on the south-western gable end for a length of 7 m and on the south-eastern side for 7 m. The walls were constructed directly onto the natural, compact, sandy surface, with no evidence for the use of foundation trenches or structural post-holes. No remains of the north-western or the north-eastern wall survived. The straight edge of a metalled surface that abutted the structure on its north-western side was interpreted as the original edge line of its north-western wall. A drainage ditch post-dating the house construction truncated its north-eastern side, although a 2.5 m section of wall uncovered here likely indicates its original extent.

The surviving walls at their widest point were up to 1.2 m thick. There was no evidence for the use of mortar in their construction. The best-preserved section of the House 1 walls was at its south-western gable end, which indicated that the construction method of the lower walls was of drystone courses with a central rubble core. The walls survived to a height of up to three courses (c. 0.50 m high). The specific character of the superstructure of House 1 remains uncertain. The remaining walls did not have any slots evident for positioning upright timbers. It is likely that a wooden frame of perhaps wattle plastered with mud formed the upper levels of the walls. It is also possible, given the large quantity of iron nails (over 1,000) found in the vicinity of the house, that its roof may have been made of nailed wooden shingles.

A possible entrance to House 1 was identified midway along its south-eastern side wall, facing onto a squared metalled yard, where the metalling extended from the yard into the house interior

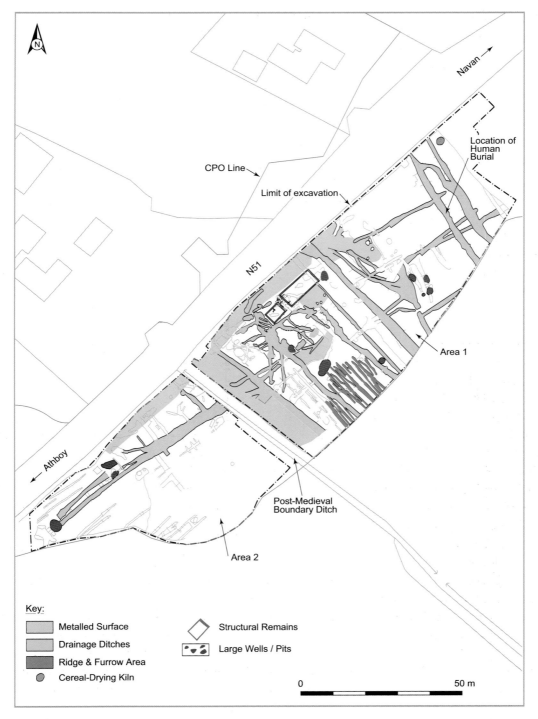

Illus. 8.1—Plan of Boyerstown 1 showing main archaeological features (Archaeological Consultancy Services Ltd).

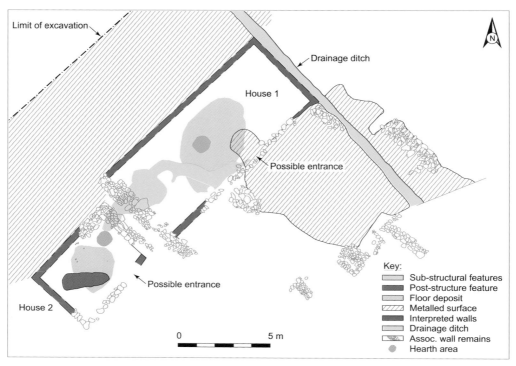

Illus. 8.2—Detailed plan of structures and associated features (Archaeological Consultancy Services Ltd).

Illus. 8.3—Aerial view of the settlement at Boyerstown 1, looking north (Studio Lab).

Illus. 8.4—Elevated view of the Boyerstown 1 structures and associated drainage ditches, looking south (Hawkeye).

(Illus. 8.4). In the interior a compact, clayey, sand floor deposit (8 m by 5 m and up to 0.20 m deep) was identified, sampled and excavated. Fragments of animal bone, pottery and crushed shell were noted during its excavation. A number of stake-holes and two irregular, perpendicular, shallow cuts truncated this surface, potentially indicating the location of a temporary screen or division in the house. Towards the centre of the interior area and within the floor deposit a hearth (1.3 m by 1.2 m) was identified. Numerous sherds of medieval pottery including glazed Dublin-type Ware, Dublin-type Fine Ware and unglazed, soot-blackened domestic Leinster Cooking Ware, along with a number of decorated copper-alloy belt buckles and iron blades, were recovered during the excavation of the House 1 walls and interior. The pottery established a date for occupation of the building sometime during the 12th to the 14th century (N Doyle, pers. comm.).

House 2 was also rectangular, but smaller (6 m by 4.5 m), and was located directly south-west of House 1. Its wall construction was the same as House 1. An entranceway was identified in its south-eastern wall. In the north-eastern corner of the interior a floor surface of flat paving partially survived, along with a small hearth (1.8 m by 0.90 m) (Illus. 8.5). A number of stake-holes were identified in association with the hearth, perhaps indicating the location of a frame. The floor surface was largely made up of a compact, sandy, clay layer that the paving stones overlay. At some

Illus. 8.5—Close-up view of House 2 during excavation, looking south-east (Archaeological Consultancy Services Ltd).

point during the occupation of House 2 a large pit was cut into the already built-up floor layers. The function of this pit is unknown. A number of sherds of green-glazed medieval pottery were recovered from its lower fill.

Sub-structural evidence

After removal of the walls of both houses it was evident they had been built over a number of features. These consisted of a large, elongated pit (5 m by 2 m), a curvilinear gully and clusters of stake-holes (40+), some of which cut into the base of the elongated pit and also around its edges (Illus. 8.6). The function and date of these features remain uncertain. The pit was primarily filled in its upper layers with large stones relating to the collapse of the gable walls of both houses, indicating that it was partially open during this time. The curvilinear gully truncated the northern side of the pit and extended towards the area of the south-eastern wall of House 1. Its function seems to have been to provide drainage for the pit. No scorching or industrial processes were evident in either of these features. Environmental samples retrieved from these features may contain evidence relating to their original function.

Illus. 8.6—Sub-structural features below House 1 and House 2, looking south-east (Archaeological Consultancy Services Ltd).

The floor layer of House 1 partially filled the underlying gully. It is hypothesised that House 1 was built while this gully and the elongated pit were still open and therefore may have been using these features as a dumping pit and internal drain for the house. This suggests that the house may have been a byre dwelling where a number of animals were kept at one side of the structure during the winter months to provide extra heat for the occupants. The gully would have allowed the animal waste to be removed from the house more efficiently. Given the amount of metalled gullies around the houses, it is surprising that the occupants of Boyerstown 1 chose not to line the gully with stone. The function or use of this area of the house changed over time, and the gully was subsequently filled in.

Drainage ditches and metalled yards

Surrounding the perimeter of the houses was an elongated, metalled, stone surface recorded up to 90 m in length and 5 m in width, which ran across the northern area of the site, extending into Area 2 parallel to the N51 Navan–Athboy road (Illus. 8.1–8.2). It was evident during the uncovering of this surface that it had previously extended beyond the northern limits of the excavation and ultimately under the current N51 roadway. It is conceivable that the surface extended or was part of the original medieval routeway from Navan to Athboy. Within the site boundaries numerous drains and gullies were incorporated into this surface so as effectively to channel and pool water away from the vicinity of the houses. Indeed it was frequently noted during the wettest days of excavation that the structures and the areas around them were always the driest parts of the site, indicating that the metalled surface and drains performed their intended functions very efficiently (Illus. 8.5).

A smaller rectangular metalled surface (8 m by 6 m) was uncovered at the south-eastern side of House 1 (Illus. 8.7). The metalling here was noticeably very finely set compared with the other metalled areas on site. Currently there are two interpretations of the function of this metalled surface. The first is that it previously functioned as an outside yard of House 1 and was probably enclosed on its sides by low walling or fencing, as indicated by a number of wall sections that were uncovered around its perimeter. The second interpretation is that this was an internal floor surface of a larger structure, which either preceded the construction of House 1 or was contemporary and connected with it. There also remains the possibility that it functioned initially as an internal surface and subsequently as an outdoor yard for House 1. The surviving wall remains do not allow

Illus. 8.7—Close-up view of metalled yard abutting House 1, looking north (Archaeological Consultancy Services Ltd).

for a more definitive conclusion to be drawn. It was noted that the construction method of the walls around the metalled surface was the same as the two houses. Also, it was evident that the metalled surface was laid first, as the walls directly overlay the edge of it. Two pits had been incorporated into the surface during its construction and may have been used for water/food storage. The largest density of artefacts found on site was in this area. Interestingly, the well-preserved remains of a human skull accompanied by a white seashell were found in an elongated pit nearby. In addition to the skull, an adult skeleton was recovered from a large north-west–south-east-aligned ditch located over 60 m north-east of the houses (Illus. 8.1). The body was placed carefully on its back into the partially filled ditch, and two earmuff stones were positioned next to the head. No grave goods or datable artefacts accompanied the burial. A number of medieval pottery sherds were recovered from the lower fills of the ditch, and it is interpreted as medieval in date. The skeleton awaits radiocarbon analysis.

Directly south of the houses and metalled surfaces the archaeology on the site took the form of re-cut and inter-cutting gullies and drainage ditches, which extended from the elongated metalled surface south-east across the site (Illus. 8.3–8.4). The phasing between these features was very short, as most had not filled by one-third before being truncated and re-cut. Most of the gullies contained occasional sherds of medieval green-glazed pottery. The gullies were up to 20 m long, 0.3–1.8 m wide and 0.3–1.2 m deep. The edges and bases of some of the larger ditches were stone lined, making them easier to clean out. A number of the gullies had been deliberately backfilled and metalled over during the site's occupation. It became clear during the excavation of this area that water control and water management were of primary concern to the site's occupants. The natural subsoil on the site was a mixture of boulder clay and compact gravels. The highest concentration of drainage gullies was evident in the boulder clay areas, owing to the poor drainage characteristics of the clay.

Two large, north-west–south-east-aligned drainage ditches ran either side of the settlement area across the full 50 m width of the road corridor (Illus. 8.1, 8.3 & 8.4). Initially, it was thought that they may be defensive ditches around the settlement area, potentially defining the site as a moated site. However, after excavation their function as large drainage ditches was evident as each was found to contain a stone-lined drain along the centre of its cut. Both ditches were also less than 1 m deep and 2–2.5 m wide, which does not point towards a defensive interpretation. Although not defensive in nature, the ditches delimit the core farmstead from the outlying farmed and worked areas. A large number of finds were recovered from both ditches—mostly medieval and post-medieval pottery but also a number of iron nails and a fine, gilded, copper-alloy, flower-motif brooch, most likely dating to the medieval period. It was clear during excavation of the ditches that they extended beyond either side of the road corridor. It is proposed that a geophysical survey will be undertaken in the area next to the site on the south-eastern side in an attempt to identify the south-eastern edge of the settlement and termini of the large drainage ditches.

Pits and wells

A number of large pits (over 2 m diameter and up to 2 m deep) were excavated in the main settlement area. The largest pit (4.8 m by 2.8 m by 1.8 m deep) was stone lined and is interpreted

Illus. 8.8—Large stone-lined well mid-excavation, looking east (Archaeological Consultancy Services Ltd).

as a well (Illus. 8.8). It was located 23 m south of the houses. A linear gully extended from its northern edge and skirted the edge of a metalled surface; this would have channelled water from the surface into the well. A clay fill at its base was waterlogged and preserved small amounts of organic remains, including charred seeds and worked timber fragments. Animal bone and medieval pottery were also recovered from the lower fills of this feature. No leather fragments or wooden bowls or staves were retrieved, as have been found in medieval wells at Castlefarm (O'Connell, chapter 3). Such finds are ubiquitous in waterlogged deposits on contemporaneous urban sites, and, in light of the wealth of other finds on site, their absence is perhaps surprising at Boyerstown.

A large assemblage of animal bone, mostly cattle, was recovered from the topsoil and stratified within the fills of a number of ditches and pit features. The distribution of the animal bone did not suggest that specific areas of the site were being used for butchery or processing purposes. The animal bone did not exhibit clear signs of butchery but is currently being assessed by a bone specialist. Preliminary indications reveal that cattle, sheep, pig, horse, dog and cat are present.

Ridge and furrow cultivation

The remains of medieval ridges and furrows were located along the south-eastern edge of Area 1, enclosed within the area of the two large drainage ditches (Illus. 8.1 & 8.3). Ridges and furrows are more commonly associated with potato cultivation during the 18th–20th centuries. This type of activity is based around aiding drainage and ensuring that the seeds and crops are not exposed to excessive moisture, particularly in soils subject to poor drainage or high levels of rainfall (O'Sullivan & Downey 2007). It seems that both factors were prevalent at Boyerstown 1.

The excavated area with ridge and furrow activity measured 24 m by 18 m. A total of 22 furrows were identified, and it was clear that they extended beyond the road corridor. On average they were between 0.3 m and 0.5 m wide (although the widest furrow was 1.1 m) and up to 0.2 m deep. Their cut profiles were consistent with the use of both a plough and a spade in their creation, as they varied from straight sided and flat bottomed to more concave profiles along their lengths. The narrow spacing and evident truncation of a number of furrows by each other are indicative of prolonged use of this area for cultivation. The ridges created from the upcast material from the furrows did not survive at Boyerstown. Typically, ridges in medieval Ireland were smaller, on average 1.5–2 m wide, than those recorded in medieval England, which were up to 8 m wide (ibid.). If a 2 m-wide ridge is taken as the standard for Boyerstown, two groups of contemporaneous furrows can be identified.

In the Middle Ages, ridge and furrow cultivation was typically used to grow cereals such as oats and barley. Given the amount of furrows recorded, it seems likely that the settlers at Boyerstown were growing cereal for their own use. The finding of six hand disc quern fragments suggests that they were processing the grain on site and near the houses and that cereal cultivation was not being carried out on a large scale. In the most north-western area of the site, approximately 80 m from the houses, an oval cereal-drying kiln (2.1 m by 1.8 m by 0.2 m deep) was excavated. The kiln was stratigraphically isolated from the other archaeological features but is currently interpreted as being contemporary with the medieval activity on the site. Samples retrieved from its fill contained large quantities of charred grains and indicate that the last attempt to use it went badly wrong. The size and simplicity of the kiln construction further indicate the small-scale nature of the production and processing of cereals that occurred at Boyerstown.

Artefact assemblage

The artefact assemblage from the site was quite extensive and varied for a rural settlement site. A total of 10,206 artefacts were recovered during the excavation phase alone. The largest amount of artefacts was recovered from the topsoil, at nearly 7,600 finds, and mostly consisted of medieval pottery sherds. A total of 2,606 finds were retrieved from stratified contexts. Overall, medieval pottery was the most common find type on the site, with over 7,000 sherds recovered. These comprised various-sized fragments of base, body, handle and rim sherds of large glazed jugs and pots, smaller glazed drinking vessels and coarsely finished domestic cooking pots (Illus. 8.9). The majority were regionally produced; however, imports of Bristol and Ham Green Ware from Britain

Illus. 8.9—Selection of decorated medieval pottery recovered from Boyerstown (John Sunderland).

Illus. 8.10—Decorated silver ring brooch with Latin inscription (John Sunderland).

and Saintonge from France also featured. A preliminary assessment of the pottery by Niamh Doyle has suggested occupation of the site from sometime during the 12th to 14th century. The pottery is being analysed in detail, and, given that a large amount of the features contained pot fragments in their fills, this may allow a more detailed phasing to be established for some of the main features on the site.

In addition to the pottery assemblage, a large number of medieval metal finds were recovered. These were mostly concentrated in and around the areas of the houses and metalled surfaces. In fact the density of metal finds dramatically decreased outside of the main settlement area. The metal artefacts included high-quality silver and copper-alloy pieces, and a number of items of jewellery stand out in particular. These include a finely worked 13th-century silver ring brooch, with traces of red enamel decoration (Illus. 8.10). This was found during the original metal detection survey of the site. A Latin inscription on the front of the brooch, 'IESVS NAZARENUS REX IVDAMEORVM', which translates as 'Jesus of Nazareth, King of the Jews', is clearly discernible and reflected both the religious devotion of the period and also perhaps a perceived amuletic power for its owner (Deevy 2006, 26; 1998). Interestingly, a ring brooch with the same inscription was found in Trim, 12 km south-west of Boyerstown (Deevy 2006, 26). A second brooch, from one of the large linear drainage ditches, made of gilded copper alloy, was modelled in the shape of a flower (Illus. 8.11). A perforation in the middle of the flower may have held a precious or semi-precious stone. A collection of 30 coins included four silver and copper medieval examples. Other notable finds were a silver crucifix pendant, iron and copper-alloy belt buckles, 47 various-sized iron blades, six iron keys, five iron barrel padlocks, over 1,087 iron nails, 25 copper-alloy buttons and 22 lead objects (including two lead weights and four musket balls).

Two of the medieval coins uncovered have been preliminarily dated to the 14th and 15th centuries. One has been identified as a four-penny piece of Henry VI struck in Calais between 1424 and 1427 (Illus. 8.12). The other is a penny of Edward III minted at Canterbury in 1327–35 (J Stafford-Langan, pers. comm.). This coin was heavily worn, indicating that it had seen considerable circulation.

In addition to the pottery and metal finds, six disc quern-stone fragments, two whetstones and a partially broken stone mortar were recovered.

The scale of the artefact numbers is similar to that of an urban medieval excavation and attests to the importance and status of the site's occupants. The artefacts represent the functional, as well as personal adornment tastes of the period. Geographically, Boyerstown 1 was well situated in the medieval landscape. It lay adjacent to a probable medieval route and would have offered its residents access to the market centres of Navan, Athboy, Kells and Trim, each of which was within 20 km of the site. Given the sheer quantity of the medieval pottery from the site, which includes examples of imports, the occupants would almost certainly have been engaging with the larger market centres of Dublin and Drogheda. This may also explain the origin of the finely decorated metal artefacts recovered.

Illus. 8.11—Decorated copper-alloy gilded flower brooch (John Sunderland).

10mm

Illus. 8.12—Silver four-penny piece of Henry VI minted between 1424 and 1427 (John Sunderland).

10mm

Comparative medieval sites

O'Conor (1998) has highlighted the scarcity of excavations of rural medieval houses in Ireland. Since then, apart from a number of recently excavated examples such as Mountdaniel, Co. Cork (Quinn 2005), and Tullykane, Co. Meath (Baker 2002), the situation has largely remained unchanged. The majority of the medieval houses previously excavated in Ireland were rectangular and over 10–15 m long. A central hearth is a recurring feature, and they occasionally contained internal partitions. The recorded wall construction includes the use of drystone, mud, timber posts, and wattle and daub. In general it is likely that a combination of two or more of these materials was used during the house construction.

Excavations at Caherguillamore in County Limerick (Ó Ríordáin & Hunt 1942) uncovered two medieval structures of similar size and construction to Boyerstown, which were found to be part of an Anglo-Norman manor. The larger and earlier of the two houses measured 12 m by 4.8 m, and the second, later structure measured 8.4 m by 3.8 m (ibid.). Both contained internal hearths and evidence of a partial floor paving, as seen at Boyerstown. The sites differ enormously in their artefact assemblages. Apart from a silver penny of Edward I (1272–1307), an iron belt buckle and a possible bronze mount for a dagger, Caherguillamore produced what are best described as functional artefacts, including 18 whetstones, 32 quern-stone fragments and 70 sherds of medieval pottery (ibid., 49–63).

The results of the excavations of a medieval two-roomed building at Lough Gur, Co. Limerick (Cleary 1982), illustrate some further similarities with and differences from the remains at Boyerstown. The rooms of the house at Lough Gur were of mixed construction, with the use of foundation trenches, mud walls and drystone walls incorporating a rubble core. The house was larger (22 m by 12 m) than the Boyerstown House 1, although, as previously noted, the original house at Boyerstown may have been much larger and more complex. Artefacts recovered from the Lough Gur excavations included medieval pottery, iron knife blades and nails, a barrel padlock key and bronze stick-pins. The excavator recorded 16 sherds of late 13th- to early 14th-century pottery found in association with the structure (ibid., 61). The artefact numbers were low and potentially indicate the limited wealth of the settlers at Lough Gur compared to Boyerstown.

More recently, the excavation in 2000 of an unenclosed medieval settlement site, only 15 km south of Boyerstown, at Tullykane, near Kilmessan, Co. Meath, offers a close comparison (Baker 2002). At Tullykane two rectangular slot-trench structures (9.5 m by 5 m and 8 m by 4.2 m) were identified, along with associated linear gullies, pits, hearths and shallow drainage ditches. Although it was interpreted as having a short occupation lifespan, 4,028 pottery sherds were recovered, of which over 99 % were identified as medieval (ibid.). This appears to have been a settlement of people of equal social standing and wealth to those at Boyerstown. A more detailed comparative analysis of the two sites as part of post-excavation work may uncover more informative and direct parallels.

Two other, previously unknown, medieval sites at Trevet 1 and Phoenixtown 2, which were also excavated as part of the M3, have uncovered substantial quantities of medieval artefacts and may represent contemporaneous undefended medieval settlements like that at Boyerstown 1.[2] The site at Trevet, located 20 km south-east of Navan, near Dunshaughlin, comprised a large cobbled road surface and associated drainage ditches that led to a crudely built, rubble-walled structure with a cobbled rear yard. Over 3,000 sherds of 13th- to 14th-century pottery were recovered from the site, along with a small quantity of metal objects, including a cruciform strap end, and a number of iron slag pieces (Rathbone 2008). As at Boyerstown, the structure at Trevet had no evident foundation trenches or structural post-holes and was built using drystone rubble walls. It is possible that the structure at Trevet, located 2 km from the historical manorial centre of Trevet, represented an outlying settlement of a free tenant attached to that manor (Kinsella 2006b).

The site uncovered at Phoenixtown, 20 km north of Boyerstown, comprised a rural medieval trackway (not unlike the elongated metalled surface at Boyerstown) and an L-shaped drystone-built structure with associated pits, wells, cereal-drying kilns, drainage ditches and an animal-powered circular mill feature. The site produced approximately 700 medieval pottery sherds, which included local Meath ware, Leinster Cooking Ware and Ham Green and Bristol Redcliffe Ware (Lyne forthcoming; 2008). It was located 1 km south of the church of Martry and likely formed part of the Martry manorial centre (Murphy 2006e).

Apart from the excavations at Boyerstown 1, Trevet and Tullykane, undefended medieval sites generally have not produced substantial quantities of artefacts. The artefacts they do produce tend to be functional, such as pottery, iron nails and knife blades. While these types of finds featured largely in the Boyertown assemblage, the jewellery, coinage and overall scale of the excavated site (15,000 m^2) indicate that its occupants had a relatively important position in the society of the time and more wealth at their disposal than some of their contemporaries. Excavations of medieval rural settlements have shown that the undefended farmstead is becoming more common in the archaeological record in Ireland. These settlements were the homes of free tenants and manorial officers who chose to live outside of the main density of settlement. While this offered a degree of independence, it also left the farmstead more exposed.

Conclusions

The medieval settlement uncovered at Boyerstown offers a very interesting insight into life in rural medieval Meath. The site represents an unfortified rural medieval farmstead that on preliminary indications was occupied for no more than two or three hundred years. The people that lived on the site obviously had wealth and enjoyed a comfortable lifestyle, as evidenced by the extensive archaeological and artefactual record that they left behind. One of the more important, and as yet unanswered, questions is: are we able to identify more precisely who lived at Boyerstown?

Consultant historian Margaret Murphy has investigated evidence for the site and its environs in the historical sources (Murphy 2006d). Although a specific reference to the settlement or its owners has not been identified, a tentative link between Boyerstown and the manorial village of Ardbraccan, only 2 km to the north-west, has been suggested. Its relationship with Ardbraccan may mirror a similar relationship between the settlement excavated at Trevet 1 and the manorial centre of Trevet mentioned previously, or that between Phoenixtown and the Martry manor. The present-day Ardbraccan House is thought to have been built over the former residence of the Bishop of Meath. As Boyerstown was situated in the medieval parish of Ardbraccan, it may have been the residence and farm of a free tenant of the bishop, or that of a manorial officer (ibid.). A manorial officer of the bishop would certainly have enjoyed a privileged and comfortable life during this time. Records of the Irish exchequer indicate that Ardbraccan remained a demesne manor of the bishop throughout the 14th and 15th centuries. They also record that in 1321–2 significant annual profits were being generated for the manor, amounting to £23 10s 1d (ibid.). The ecclesiastical link seems more credible based on the religious associations of some of the artefacts (i.e. the silver crucifix pendant and the inscription on the ring brooch). However, it is prudent to remember that this was at a time when laypeople were particularly religious and 'god fearing'. The ecclesiastical motifs visible on some of the jewellery may simply reflect the fashions of the day.

Without a specific historical reference, it is impossible to know how much land a free tenant at Boyerstown could have leased. Leased land holdings among free tenants in County Meath during the 14th century varied from 15 acres to over 600 acres (Murphy 2006c). The farmstead area excavated at Boyerstown amounted to nearly 4 acres. It was evident that the archaeological features continued to the north and south beyond the excavation area. The southern extent of the farmstead may be determinable through a forthcoming geophysical survey of this area. Based on the results of this survey it may be possible to estimate accurately the overall landholding at Boyerstown.

What prompted the abandonment of the site is unknown. In 1470 King Edward IV authorised the collection of tolls on all goods coming for sale into Navan town, and for three miles around it, in order to build up the walls and maintain the pavements (ibid.). It seems that the raiding by native Gaelic chiefs was intensifying during this period and was prompting the Anglo-Normans to refortify their positions. This is reflected in the building of a stone castle next to the motte at Athlumney, 1 km south-east of Navan, during this time. Boyerstown, located in quite a prominent position fronting onto the probable route from Navan to Athboy and undefended as it was, is likely to have been quite vulnerable to these types of raids. A fortified motte at Moathill, over 3 km east of the site, would have offered little protection in the climate of opportunistic raiding that prevailed. The *Annals of Loch Cé* record that in 1539 Conn O'Neill and Magnus O'Domhnaill attacked Meath and that the town of Navan was completely pillaged (ibid.).

In 1654 Boyerstown was recorded as containing 90 acres of arable land, 6 acres of meadow and 40 acres of pasture. No buildings or upstanding features were noted, but at Ardbraccan there were two castles, a church, a hall and a quarry (Murphy 2006d). The site had likely been abandoned by this stage, and it would be another 350 years before it was rediscovered.

Notes

1. Boyerstown 1: NGR 283589, 265799; height 67.74m OD; excavation reg. no. E3105; Ministerial Direction no. A023/013; excavation director Kevin Martin.
2. Trevet 1: NGR 295858, 256608; height 132.73m OD; excavation reg. no. E3067; Ministerial Direction no. A008/014; excavation director Stuart Rathbone.
   Phoenixtown 2: NGR 279305, 271332; height 61.65 m OD; excavation reg. no. E3129; Ministerial Direction no. A029/011; excavation director Ed Lyne.

9
RURAL SETTLEMENT IN MEATH, 1170–1660: THE DOCUMENTARY EVIDENCE

Margaret Murphy

Introduction

The aim of this paper is to present a summary of current scholarship on rural settlement in Meath based largely on documentary source material. The period covered extends from the arrival of the Anglo-Normans in the area in 1170 to c. 1660, when major changes in landholding and settlement patterns occurred as a result of the Cromwellian conquest and confiscations. The area under investigation is that occupied by the present county of Meath rather than that which formed the much larger medieval lordship or liberty of Meath. The paper endeavours to provide background and context for the late medieval sites and material excavated recently along the route of the M3 Clonee to North of Kells motorway scheme. While the paper presents an overview of the entire county of Meath, it attempts, where possible, to draw examples from areas of particular relevance to the excavations.

Anglo-Norman settlement in Meath was intensive and enduring. The fertile farmland of the county acted as a magnet to enterprising colonisers with the skill to exploit agrarian resources and generate profit. The political situation was secure by the standards of medieval Ireland, and, for at least the first 120 years of Anglo-Norman rule, resources could be concentrated on developing the manors that were the key settlement form through which the Anglo-Norman agrarian economy operated.

The study of rural settlement in medieval Ireland is currently the focus of a great deal of interest among archaeologists, historians and historical geographers. Much remains to be investigated and understood about, for example, the layout and organisation of the medieval manor. The later medieval sites that are currently being researched along the route of the planned M3 have the potential to reveal to us something of the way in which that manorial system operated. In particular, they may add to our understanding of continuity of site-use from early to later medieval periods and expand our knowledge concerning the features associated with dispersed tenant settlement and agricultural practices. The documentary sources can provide a great deal of evidence about rural settlement, but this evidence needs to be evaluated and combined with the archaeological record. The aim of collaborative study of the type that has characterised the M3 investigations is to maximise the contribution that the excavations can make to future archaeological and historical research.

The documentary sources

Meath is relatively well served by surviving documentary sources, although they vary considerably in the type and quality of information they contain. The initial phases of Anglo-Norman conquest and colonisation are described in chronicle sources such as the *Song of Dermot and the Earl*, a French poem composed shortly after the invasion, and the *Expugnatio Hibernica*, a chronicle of events in Ireland from the 1160s to the 1180s, completed in 1189 by Giraldus Cambrensis.[1] Such chronicle sources are valuable but suffer from the shortcomings of documents of this type—chiefly omissions, vagueness and bias. Official deeds such as charters, leases and grants give more specific chronological and spatial information. One of the most important collections of deeds for Meath is contained in the Gormanston Register, which was compiled for the Preston family in 1397–8 and includes documents going back to 1172.[2] Cartularies and registers of religious houses contain similar material, and several survive for houses that had interests in Meath. These include the Dublin abbeys St Thomas's and St Mary's (Illus. 9.1) and the Hospital of St John the Baptist, as well as the monasteries of Llanthony Prima in Wales and Llanthony Secunda near Gloucester.[3]

There are several other types of ecclesiastical records that shed light on settlement, land-use and land-ownership. For example, the early 14th-century assessments for the ecclesiastical taxation of the diocese of Meath provide information on relative levels of ecclesiastical wealth and settlement density at a parochial level, and the extents of former monastic possessions made in 1540–1 show the property owned by each religious house at the time of its dissolution.[4]

The system of central and local government established in Ireland by the Anglo-Normans produced voluminous records, of which only a small fraction survive.[5] Of particular importance for Meath are the records of the Irish exchequer such as the Pipe Rolls, which contain, *inter alia*,

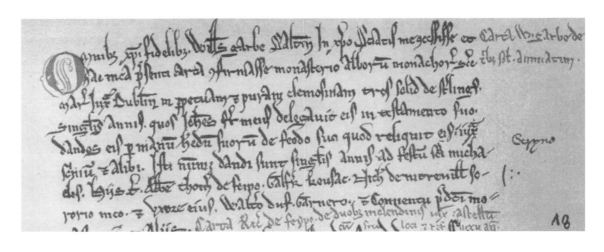

Illus. 9.1—Charter of 1185 from William Garbe to St Mary's Abbey, Dublin, granting rent from lands near Skreen, Co. Meath (Chart. St Mary's, frontispiece).

the audited accounts of seneschals of liberties and custodians of lands in the king's hands. All surviving rolls in this series were destroyed in 1922, but the Pipe Roll for 1211–12 had been copied and provides the earliest information on the organisation of the manorial economy in Meath.[6] There is also a summary in English of Pipe Rolls from 1229 to 1348, as well as a calendar of the rolls produced by the medieval Irish chancery, both of which contain much of relevance to Meath.[7] These can be used in conjunction with a number of important compilations of documents that are still extant in the National Archives of the UK.[8]

One type of document that has particular importance for the study of medieval rural settlement, especially the morphology and function of manors, is the extent. The essential function of an extent was to provide information on the value of manorial resources.[9] A typical extent itemised the major types of land-use on the manorial demesne (arable, meadow, pasture and wood) and any other resources (mills, dovecots, warrens, fishponds etc.), attaching a monetary valuation to each. In addition, some extents provide details on the holdings of the manorial tenants and their dues, both as money rents and as labour services. This information is extremely valuable for research into settlement, shedding light on the internal organisation of manors and on the ethnic and social diversity that existed in the communities that made their living on the manors. A number of extents relating to manors and granges in Meath survive, and, although they vary in the quantity and quality of information they contain, taken together they provide much-needed statistical information relating to land-use, as well as valuable data on buildings and the make-up of manorial tenantry (Table 9.1 & Illus. 9.2).

The next systematic body of data relating to land-use in Meath dates from the 17th century and comprises the records of the Civil and Down Surveys, drawn up between 1649 and 1659 after the Cromwellian conquest of Ireland.[10] Both sources were compiled before the extensive landscape alterations of the 18th century, from which the present landscape of County Meath

Table 9.1—Extents relating to manors and granges in Meath in the late medieval period.

Manor (barony)	Date	Source
Colp (Lower Duleek)	1408	St John Brooks 1953, 178–82
Donacarney (Lower Duleek)	?	Mills &McEnery 1916, 8–9
Dowth (Upper Slane)	1253	Sweetman 1877, 27
Duleek (Lower Duleek)	1381	St John Brooks 1953, 289–95
Dunmoe (Lower Navan)	1415	Dryburgh & Smith 2005, 62
Dunshaughlin (Ratoath)	1344	Dryburgh & Smith 2005, 59
Gormanston (Upper Duleek)	1310	TNA: PRO C134/21/6
Martry (Lower Navan)	1323	TNA: PRO C143/168
Moyglare (Upper Deece)	1344	Dryburgh & Smith 2005, 59
Rathfeigh (Skreen)	1322	TNA: PRO C47/10/18/13
Ratoath (Ratoath)	1333	TNA: PRO C135/36
Slane (Slane)	1370	TNA: PRO C135/218

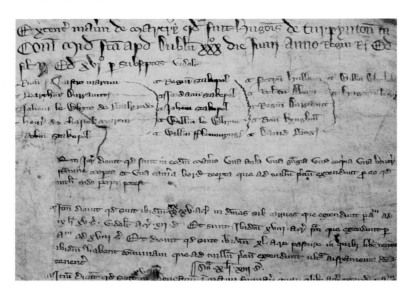

Illus. 9.2—Part of the 1323 extent for the manor of Martry (Barony of Lower Navan) (The National Archives (UK): PRO C143/168).

emerged. Although patterns of settlement were by no means static throughout the period, it is generally accepted that the mid-17th-century evidence substantially reflects the settlement pattern established by the Anglo-Normans in the late medieval period.[11]

From conquest to colonisation

In April 1172 King Henry II granted to Hugh de Lacy, a major baron with holdings concentrated in the border counties between England and Wales, 'the land of Meath with all its appurtenances as Murchada Ua Mael Sechlainn held it' to hold for the service of fifty knights.[12] The process that de Lacy then initiated involved the carving up of this huge territory, which extended to almost 325,000 hectares, between himself and his barons and chief followers. These men, many of them from families who held land from him in Herefordshire, had accompanied de Lacy to Ireland in 1172. This process, known as subinfeudation because the land was granted in expressly feudal terms, was described in the *Song* by use of the verb *herberger*, 'to plant'.

E Huge de Laci, qui tant iert fer,	And Hugh de Lacy, who was so fierce,
Pur sa terre herberger	Set out for Meath
Vers Mithe s'en est turné	With many renowned vassals
Od meint vassal alos	To plant his territory[13]

The territory granted to de Lacy did not exactly correspond to any single existing political unit; however, it contained an established pattern of territorial divisions related to focal points of settlement.[14] These divisions and settlements formed the basis for de Lacy's grants. Retaining Clonard, Duleek, Ratoath and Trim as his own demesne manors, he established seven followers in areas equivalent to entire baronies.[15] These were William le Petit (Dunboyne), Jocelin de Nangle (Navan), Gilbert de Nangle (Morgallion), Richard le Fleming (Slane), Adam de Feypo (Skreen), Hugh de Hose (Deece) and William de Muset (Lune). In addition, de Lacy granted several smaller parcels of land to various knights. Some of the original charters granted by Hugh to his followers have survived, and their language underlines the extent to which pre-existing territorial divisions were used in the subinfeudation. For example, de Hose was granted 'all the land of Deece which MacGillaSeachlainn held,' while Gilbert de Nugent was granted Delvin in Westmeath, 'which the O'Phelans held in the time of the Irish'.[16]

The next stage of the colonisation process saw the establishment of strongholds in the form of mottes and ringwork castles suitable for the garrisoning of forces. These strongholds played a vital role in initiating colonisation as they offered security to the settlers who were necessary for the establishment of manors. All over eastern and southern Ireland (and Wales and Scotland also) the castles built by the Anglo-Normans quickly developed from centres of domination to foci of non-military settlement and springboards for economic exploitation.[17] The Irish were well aware that the building of fortifications by the newcomers signalled their intention to put down roots, and their resistance in Meath in 1173–5 was focused on the destruction of the new castles. This caused a temporary setback to the process of colonisation, but it was quickly overcome. From 1175 on, the complete occupation of Meath was accomplished, and, in the words of the *Song*, 'the noble and renowned vassals were able to put down firm roots'.[18]

The entry in the *Annals of Loch Cé* that recorded the death of Hugh de Lacy in July 1186 stated that the lordship of Meath 'from the Shannon to the sea was full of castles and of foreigners'.[19] It is believed that by this date ringwork or motte castles had been constructed by de Lacy at Trim, Ratoath, Kells, Clonard, Dunshaughlin, Drogheda and Duleek, while his barons—the recipients of principal land grants—had erected fortifications of this type at Navan, Nobber, Slane, Skreen, Dunboyne, Athboy, Dollardstown and Rathkenny.[20] The comparative ease with which this level of penetration and colonisation was achieved in 14 years suggests that the Anglo-Normans were moving into an area that had already seen a high degree of settlement and organisation and that had infrastructural elements in place such as roads, trading links, mills and so on.

The extent to which pre-Norman ecclesiastical sites and the royal residence or status sites of pre-Norman kings were adapted and re-used in Meath must be stressed.[21] Continuity in the use of sites on a lower level of the settlement hierarchy was perhaps also common, although it is much harder to document. In this context the excavated evidence from sites such as Castlefarm (O'Connell, chapter 3) and Roestown (O'Hara, chapter 4) is particularly interesting. Both of these sites display evidence for continuity and/or re-use from the early medieval to the late medieval period. Not all early medieval enclosure sites continued in use or were re-used in the later medieval period, of course. In contrast to Castlefarm and Roestown, the enclosure site at Dowdstown (Cagney & O'Hara, chapter 7) was abandoned long before the arrival of the Anglo-Normans, who established their manorial centre and parish church to the south-east of the earlier site. Similarly at Cookstown, 9 km east of Roestown, where a late medieval settlement comprising a house, garden and forge was excavated by CRDS Ltd as part of the N2 Finglas–Ashbourne road scheme, a pre-existing ringfort there did not appear to have been occupied by the Anglo-Normans, although it may have been incorporated into the settlement's boundaries and enclosures.[22]

The hiatus following Hugh de Lacy's death, during which the lordship of Meath was taken into the king's hand, did not significantly slow down the pace of colonisation. Once he had taken control of his father's lands in c. 1194, Walter de Lacy continued the process of settlement, and it was during the 50 or so years of his lordship that Meath was comprehensively manorialised.[23]

An early and well-documented stage in territorial organisation was the establishment of a parish church and the granting of the tithes—the ecclesiastical dues of the parishioners—to a religious house. This process can be seen in operation in various parts of Meath in the last decades of the 12th century, and the recipients of the tithes were frequently the large religious houses of Dublin and the houses of Llanthony Prima in Monmouthshire and Llanthony Secunda near Gloucester, which had close associations with the de Lacys. Parochial organisation in Skreen, for instance, began when Adam de Feypo assigned tithes to the chapel of St Nicholas, which he had founded at his castle there, and then granted the church to St Mary's Abbey, Dublin.[24] In Dunboyne, William le Petit, shortly after constructing his castle, granted the church and the tithes of the parishioners to Llanthony Prima.[25] In both of these cases the first incumbents of the parish churches were the brothers of the manorial lords—Thomas de Feypo, who went on to become a Cistercian monk at St Mary's, and Ralph le Petit, who held the bishopric of Meath from 1227 to 1230. This close association between secular and religious authority strengthened the colonial grip on the countryside. Moreover, some of the earliest-recorded grants of manorial lands were to religious houses, and this also forged close links between ecclesiastical and lay estates.

The Anglo-Normans founded or developed 18 boroughs in Meath—the majority of them in the last quarter of the 12th and early in the 13th century.[26] Boroughs served a twofold purpose: they were centres of trade, places where markets and fairs could be held to facilitate exchange and exploit further the economic potential of the countryside; and they attracted settlers seeking the privileges of burgage tenure. These privileges included the possession of a burgage plot at a fixed rent with freedom to pass it to one's heirs or sell it without lordly interference. In addition, the community of a borough also had freedom to regulate its affairs in its own court. Some of these boroughs, through a combination of the advantages of their sites and the power of their lords, grew into walled urban centres—Athboy, Drogheda-in-Meath, Kells, Navan and Trim. Others, such as Duleek, Dunboyne, Dunshaughlin, Nobber, Ratoath, Skreen and Slane, functioned as the centres of the major land-grants of the subinfeudation and as ecclesiastical and market centres. A handful, such as Colp, Drumcondra, Greenoge, Mornington and Siddan, despite their borough status, appear to have been little more than agricultural settlements. They, along with others that may have had borough status of which no evidence survives, have been classified as 'rural boroughs'.[27]

In 1212, 40 years after the first arrival of the newcomers, the Pipe Roll of 14 John presents a detailed picture of the economy and agriculture of Meath. The royal officials who were administering the sequestered de Lacy lands were obliged to set down in great detail all sources of profit and expense in these areas. This document presents Meath as a deeply settled, highly organised rural economy. It is illuminating to compare the language used to describe settlements in Meath with that used in reference to Tipperary, much of which was also in the king's hands during the period covered by the Pipe Roll. While a dozen settlements in Meath are called 'manors', the term is notably absent from the Tipperary entries, which record income from a number of castle territories. Hennessy has concluded that the Tipperary landscape 'was still very much under construction in 1212' and that there is little evidence for a substantial colonist presence.[28] It is clear that in the early 13th century there was still a considerable degree of regional variation in the depth and density of Anglo-Norman settlement.

It would appear that settlement in Meath had developed substantially beyond the 'castle territory' phase by 1212. The quantity of grain that was being harvested from the various granges in the county implies agrarian exploitation on a large scale. This type of agriculture required substantial labour inputs, as did the widespread repair work on castles also recorded in the Pipe Roll. Much of the labour force would have been made up of colonists recruited by the de Lacys and their tenants-in-chief from their homelands in England. Numerous servants and farm workers such as ploughmen are mentioned (but not named) in the Pipe Roll, but references to classes of manorial tenant—apart from betaghs—are absent.

The presence of betaghs, servile Irish tenants, is a reminder that a significant number of the native population were incorporated into the evolving manorial structure. The payments that the Pipe Roll record to a latimer or interpreter also indicate positive interaction between native and coloniser.[29] There is evidence that the Anglo-Normans made use of the native labour force from the early days of the colonisation and that the Irish in turn pragmatically accepted the change of overlord. According to Giraldus, Hugh de Lacy went to great trouble to conciliate those who had been conquered and forcibly ejected from their lands: 'He restored the countryside to its rightful cultivators and brought back cattle to pastures which had formerly been deserted'.[30] A charter survives in which de Lacy granted lands in Ballinakill in Moyfenrath barony to members of the Uí Caindelbáin family, and charters of land by the new overlords to persons of Gaelic stock were probably much commoner than has been realised. A partial explanation for the apparent speed with which military conquest turned to colonisation and economic exploitation in Meath may therefore be the presence of a largely unchanged workforce in some areas. The fact that the native Irish were incorporated into the colonisation does not mean that they were necessarily integrated with the colonists or that they were economically on a par with them. For most Irish the conquest resulted in a definite loss of status, and the excavated evidence at sites like Castlefarm (O'Connell, chapter 3) may underline this decline.

Manors and tenants

Keegan has recently written that manorial settlement did not consist of 'a single [archaeological] site but a composite system of different settlement components interacting within a defined area'.[31] The residence of the manorial lord was only one of the settlement components, but the nature of documentary evidence results in its being the one most often described. The records show that the manorial caput comprised some type of fortified building with such associated agricultural structures as stables, bake houses and granaries, augmented by mills, warrens, dovecots and fishponds, resources that are sometimes labelled 'seigneurial monopolies'.[32] The manorial centre was generally situated close to the parish church and attracted a degree of nucleation, ranging from a collection of cottiers' cottages to the fully fledged borough with its burgesses. Graham has postulated 98 manorial villages in Meath, places that always contained a church and generally, but not always, a castle and mill.[33]

The collection of extents for manors and granges that survives for Meath gives some idea of the range of buildings that were associated with manorial centres (Table 9.2). The evidence varies considerably, both chronologically and in the level of detail given, but indicates that these centres differed considerably in the complexity of their structural make-up.

The above evidence suggests that there was no such thing as a typical manorial centre, but in general the *location* of the manorial caput, with associated buildings, at the centre of the lord's demesne farm is fairly unproblematic. Similarly, although it is never possible to be completely confident of territorial boundaries, it is usually accepted that in Meath the principal manors of de Lacy's subinfeudation often equated to baronies (e.g. Dunboyne, Ratoath, Skreen), while the sub-manors that were granted by the barons were usually coterminous with parishes. Within the geographical boundaries of the manors, however, the location of tenants' lands and habitations is by no means clear. The question of how manors were organised and developed socially and spatially is seen as one of the core issues for investigation in the field of medieval rural settlement studies.[34] Much of the debate in recent years has centred on the relative importance of dispersed versus nucleated settlement types and, by extension, the size and location of tenant holdings.

Table 9.2—Buildings and resources on Meath manors (source: manorial extents).

Manor/grange	Date	Buildings/resources
Dowth	1253	Garden, dovecot, fishery.
Duleek	1381	Chapel, hall, kitchen, dairy, stable, long room with closet, room called the knight's room, cellar, larder, bakery and brew-houses with kiln and oven, granary, pigsty, byre/ox-house, sheepcot, gatehouse, kilnhouse, garden, 2 dovecots, watermill.
Dunmoe	1415	Castle with houses called 'the gatehouse' and 'the cartstable', close, fishpond, watermill, weir, fishery.
Dunshaughlin	1344	Messuage, hall, stable, ox-house and kiln.
Gormanston	1310	Mill, warren.
Martry	1323	Hall, grange, kitchen, ox-house, cottage, orchard, dovecot, watermill.
Moyglare	1344	Stone tower, hall, chamber, bakehouse, grange and dovecot.
Rathfeigh	1322	House, capital messuage, garden, dovecot.

The tenants of a manor were usually organised into different groups. Meath extents indicate that some or all of the following groups were present on the manors of the county in the medieval period—free tenants, tenants 'at will', farmers (tenants who leased land for a term of years), cottagers, betaghs and burgesses. It is clear, however, that conditions of tenure, size of landholding and ethnic origin of members of these groups varied considerably. For example, there were nine free tenants on the manor of Dowth in 1260 who held land 'infra villam et extra', both inside and outside the vill. Three of the free tenants had distinctly Irish names, and some owed labour services, in addition to rent, for their holdings, which varied between 15 and 240 acres.[35] There were, in addition, an unspecified number of cottagers who held gardens and 85 acres of land between them. This is the only surviving 13th-century extent, and its evidence appears to point to a manor consisting of a nucleated core where the cottars and some of the smaller free tenants lived, surrounded by the 132 acres of demesne farm in which were located a dovecot and two mills. The holdings of the larger free tenants were probably those situated outside the vill, and they may have lived on these holdings at a distance from the manorial centre. It would appear that the tenantry was of mixed English and Irish origin.

In her studies of Duleek and Colp, Simms set out to investigate the spatial implications of a manorial extent in order to gain insight into the morphology and functions of Anglo-Norman rural settlement and 'rural boroughs'.[36] More recently, Seaver has explored how space, structures and routeways were used in three manors in the barony of Slane.[37] With reference to Duleek and Colp, Simms concluded that the manorial core consisted of a parish church, buildings of the demesne farm, houseplots of the burgesses, and cottages of the cottars and tenants at will.[38] The more substantial free tenants held land in separate townlands surrounding the manorial centre. Because of the small size of villages and their identification with one manor only, they functioned primarily as centres of estate administration and did not form true village communities similar to those in England and on the Continent. Seaver's conclusions with regard to the barony of Slane are broadly in agreement, and in particular he states, with reference to Siddan, that beyond the townland of that name—which contained the borough and demesne lands—'the territory of the manor was probably held by free tenants who held townlands of their own'.[39]

It has been pointed out, however, that the proposition that free tenants held land independent and distant from the manorial centre is largely based on late 14th- and even 15th-century sources, and it is possible that different arrangements of manorial settlement pertained in an earlier period.[40] Dispersed settlement may have been a feature of a secondary movement of tenants out of nucleated villages in the period after the Black Death, possibly as a response to greater land availability.

The medieval farmstead excavated at Boyerstown (Martin, chapter 8) would appear from its size and the complexity of the artefactual assemblage to represent the dwelling of a fairly substantial free tenant household. Provisional dating indicates that the farmstead was first settled in the early 13th century, suggesting that in this area dispersed settlement was a feature of the primary phase of manorialisation. The site offered a number of locational and environmental advantages, being placed in fertile farmland with access to several transport arteries. It was some distance from the episcopal manor residence at Ardbraccan and may therefore have been the residence of a free tenant of this manor or even a member of the bishop's *familia*, or household. Defence does not appear to have been a major consideration in its construction or early occupation, but its vulnerable position may have been the reason for its eventual desertion.

The dwellings of important free tenants would have been associated with other features linked with occupation and agricultural processing and may have appeared as mini-manorial caputs. The site at Phoenixtown 2 excavated by Ed Lyne of Irish Archaeological Consultancy Ltd can perhaps be interpreted as one such holding.[41] Located midway between Navan and Kells, this site comprised a series of field systems, pits and the remains of a horse mill. A section of a metalled medieval roadway was also uncovered, and, although only one possible house site was identified, more may have been located outside the excavated area. Documentary research revealed that in the 14th century Phoenixtown was occupied by free tenants of the manor of Martry in return for an annual cash rent of 15 shillings.[42]

Cottars or cottagers are mentioned in virtually all of the Meath extents. They had holdings of an acre or less, which generally consisted of a small plot or croft around their cottage. Their customary services had probably been commuted to money payments by the late 13th century, and they would have provided waged labour for the manorial demesne. They would have lived in a nucleated group around the manor centre. Similarly, where there was a borough, the burgesses no doubt lived on their burgage plots. The location of the dwellings of the last grouping of tenants mentioned in extents—the betaghs—is, however, open to debate.

The records tend to refer to the betaghs and their holdings communally, leading to the proposition that, on many Anglo-Norman manors in Ireland, these servile Irish tenants occupied a quite separate area to other manorial tenants, perhaps a definite townland.[43] It has been argued, for example, that betagh settlements were pre-existing bond settlements that the Anglo-Normans incorporated into their manorial structures.[44] Graham has identified at least a hundred medieval settlements in Meath that he has classified as 'house clusters' and that he considers may in fact have been betagh settlements.[45] Virtually all of these settlements were located within 4 km of manorial villages.

It would be erroneous to believe that Irish manorial tenants were always to be found in dispersed settlements. It is evident from the documents that Irish tenants also occurred in the classes of free tenants, farmers and cottars, although burgess names appear to be exclusively of English origin. A study of the manorial village of Killeen (barony of Skreen) based on a 15th-century manuscript partly compiled in the area concluded that the local population had remained largely Irish in its descent.[46] Of 88 individuals named in the document, at least 47 had surnames of Irish origin. Given the location of Killeen, securely within the Pale, it was not deemed plausible that the Irish names represented a re-Gaelicisation of an English settlement. Rather, it was concluded that the individuals were descended from the Irish population that had been assimilated into the manorial village when it was founded.

Land-use and agriculture

The upper limit for Anglo-Norman settlement in Ireland as a whole is considered to have been around 150 m, or 500 ft, above sea level.[47] This was fundamentally linked to the arable farming regime, which was an intrinsic part of manorial organisation. Graham found that in Meath the zone below 60 m (principally composed of the lowland valleys of the Boyne and Blackwater) exerted the most powerful positive influence on the distribution of Anglo-Norman settlement, while land over 120 m had a corresponding negative effect.[48] The 120 m contour therefore effectively marked the upper limit of Anglo-Norman settlement in the area. Virtually all of lowland Meath has fertile soils suitable for arable. While bogland was certainly present in the medieval period, it was not a major land-use.

It is generally accepted that the Anglo-Normans substantially changed the practice of agriculture in Ireland. However, the belief, expounded first in the works of Giraldus Cambrensis, that arable cultivation was largely absent from pre-Norman Ireland has been considerably revised.[49] There are several indications that cereal growing was of economic significance in the pre-Norman period. These include the abundant references in monastic literature to mills and milling, which led Lucas to the conclusion that 'the mill must have been one of the commonest features of the countryside'.[50] The increasing archaeological evidence for cereal-drying kilns and for early mill sites such as Raystown, Co. Meath, and Killoteran, Co. Waterford, adds further weight to the argument.[51] Moreover, the Annals frequently refer to the loss of a cereal crop due to wet or windy weather and record the burning of corn as a technique of warfare in the 11th and 12th centuries.[52] A recent commentator has written that in Ireland 'traditions of arable cultivation were already well established by 1170. The cultivated area had increased between the 6th and the 12th centuries to feed a growing population, and some trade in grain is implied by the urban developments of the east coast.'[53] There are some indications that commercial grain production may have been carried on in Meath before the arrival of the Anglo-Normans. In the early 13th century Walter de Lacy confirmed the right of the men of Chester to buy all kinds of corn, malt and flour from his Irish lands, as they had been accustomed to doing in the past.[54]

Arable cultivation was, however, greatly intensified under the Anglo-Normans, as the 1211–12 Pipe Roll testifies.[55] The introduction of the eight-ox heavy plough facilitated the cultivation of much greater areas. Very large numbers of oxen were present to provide traction for the eight-ox plough, and cows were also plentiful—both for dairying and to breed replacement oxen. For example, 86 cows were delivered to the stock of Kilmore (manorial village/parish in Upper Deece) and 26 to the stock of Galtrim (parish in Lower Deece), and 173 were put in the forest of Trim. In addition, 180 sheep and 68 pigs were also delivered to the stock of Galtrim.

It is possible to use the information on demesne land resources provided by medieval extents to calculate the proportion of arable versus other land-uses on a number of manors across Meath. These figures (Table 9.3) emphasise the preponderance of arable over other land-uses, with only one manor (Donacarney in Lower Duleek) showing arable at less than 77% of the land classified. It is highly likely that pasture was underestimated in documents of this type. Demesnes frequently had access to the communal pasture of their tenants, and, furthermore, fallow arable land was used for pasturing animals, which is often not stated in the extents. Even with these caveats, the evidence appears to point to arable being by far the most important land-use in late medieval Meath.

The extents also indicate that arable land was highly valued and often given the same value as mowable meadowland. The extent of the manor of Martry (Illus. 9.2), some 8 km to the north-west

Table 9.3—Demesne acres under different land-uses, 1322–1408 (source: manorial extents).

Manor	Date	Arable	Meadow	Pasture	% arable
Colp	1408	115	5	26	79
Donacarney (Lower Duleek)	?	221	21	97	65
Duleek	1381	233	33	—	88
Dunshaughlin	1344	280	20	—	93
Gormanston (Upper Duleek)	1310	920	17	—	98
Martry	1323	195	18	40	77
Moyglare	1344	240	30	—	89
Rathfeigh	1322	330	18	—	95

of Navan beside the River Blackwater, records that in 1323 there were 195 acres of demesne land under the plough, worth 12d per acre, 18 acres of meadow, also valued at 12d per acre, a 2-acre orchard, worth 24d per year, and 40 acres of pasture, worth nothing beyond 'easements' because the free tenants of the manor had common grazing there.[56]

The proportion of arable land can also be calculated for various manors and other holdings in Meath and Louth listed in the dissolution extents of Irish monastic possessions that were drawn up in the late 1530s. In the extensive estate of Mellifont Abbey, straddling the Meath–Louth border west of Drogheda, permanent grassland seems to have been scarce, and some 90% of land is classified as arable. At Oldbridge, on the south bank of the Boyne, 168 acres of arable but only 15 acres of pasture and 5 acres of meadow were recorded, an arable proportion of 89%.[57] Smaller holdings, such as the 34 acres held by the Dublin Hospital of St John the Baptist at Dardistown, 5 km south of Drogheda, display a similarly pronounced bias towards arable.[58] Further up the Boyne, the former demesnes of the abbeys of Bective and Navan are recorded as 89% and 83% arable, respectively. These proportions are maxima and would, of course, include those parts of the arable fields that were fallow in any given year. By the time of the Civil Survey in 1654, Meath was still primarily an area of mixed farming in which arable cultivation played the dominant role. In well over half of the townlands surveyed, arable accounted for over 70% of the land area.

There is some, though not much, evidence regarding the practice of agriculture and the organisation of arable lands on the manors of the medieval county. It is clear from the evidence of the 1211–12 Pipe Roll that the ox was the pre-eminent beast of traction on the demesnes of Meath at this date. In all, 906 oxen are found on the de Lacy manors, with up to eight plough teams in some places. By contrast, only 18 affers or draught-horses are mentioned. These affers were probably the heavy breed of horses introduced by the Anglo-Normans. It is difficult to assess the degree to which oxen were used outside of the demesnes, as the sources for peasant agriculture and smallholdings are so sparse.

The extents for some manors indicate that the arable land on many demesnes was organised into large blocks, or *sesona*, which may be translated as 'sowing areas'. For example, in 1322 the jurors at Rathfeigh reported that there were '300 acres of arable, that is in each seysona 100 acres'.[59] This might be interpreted as meaning that each *sesona* comprised a large open field and that a three-field system, with perhaps wheat in one, oats in another and a third fallow, was in use.

There is also a certain amount of evidence to demonstrate that in Meath, as elsewhere in Ireland, some individual holdings were made up of a collection of small strips located in a number of different fields.[60] This suggests a system of cultivation that would have been familiar in the homelands of the colonisers. There is mention of unenclosed land alongside multiple small parcels of arable in the 1381 extent for Duleek, and Simms interpreted this as pointing towards an open field system with intermixed parcels.[61] A grant in 1344 of land in Slane appears to offer clear evidence of strip holdings on this manor.[62] The land being granted to a burgess of Drogheda consists of 17 separate parcels, some of them of less than an acre. They are carefully described:

> two and a half acres between the land of Roger White on the west and the land of William Carrigg on the east; two acres between the land of the lord of Slane on the west and the land of John Passauaunt on the east…half an acre between the land of John Flemyng on the east and the land of John Facy on the west.

The grain produced on the arable lands of Meath and in particular on the demesne lands was overwhelmingly of just two types—wheat and oats. The 1211–12 Pipe Roll indicates that Meath had an early prominence in the production of oats, with 7,740 crannocks of oats being harvested from the granges of Meath, as opposed to 5,462 crannocks of wheat.[63] (A crannock is an old Irish measure of wheat, containing 8 bushels, although a crannock of oats contained 16 bushels.) Similarly, in a purveyance (compulsory purchase) of 1244, Drogheda was commanded to supply to the king 300 crannocks of dry oatmeal, as well as 300 crannocks of wheat, while Dublin, Cork and Waterford were asked only for wheat.[64] Later purveyances under Edward I and II similarly required the Drogheda purveyors and the sheriffs of Meath and Louth to supply large quantities of both wheat and oats, augmented on occasion by very small quantities of beans and maslin, a mixture of wheat and rye.[65]

Conclusions

Godard Orpen and, more recently, Brian Graham have stated that Meath was more fully occupied by the Anglo-Normans than any other rural area in Ireland—with the exception of the area around Dublin. If Anglo-Norman settlement in Meath was deep-rooted, it was also long-lasting. By the standards of late medieval Ireland, the area experienced a high degree of political and military stability. Family names encountered during the primary settlement are still to be found centuries later. Consequently, the Anglo-Norman influence on the landscape was maximised, and many of their settlements survived until the 17th century and beyond.

The first generations of the lords of Meath achieved this level of settlement over a vast area by a process that has become known as subinfeudation. While retaining large demesnes to supply their own needs, they divided substantial parcels of their territory between their followers and relations. These people, in turn, subdivided their holdings and introduced the free tenants, cottars and burgesses who were to populate their manors. A study of the administrative boundaries of the county indicates, however, that pre-existing territorial divisions were utilised at all levels of settlement and that these played an important role in determining the structure and layout of Anglo-Norman manors.

There was a considerable movement of settlers into the county, but there is also evidence for the continuation of Gaelic settlement in many, if not most, areas. An examination of the range and variety of townland names in different parts of Meath sheds light on the interaction of Gaelic and Anglo-Norman cultures in the Middle Ages.[66] In Meath the process whereby military conquest changed into colonisation and economic exploitation was very rapid. One possible explanation for this is that the area was already densely settled and substantially involved in arable agriculture when the Anglo-Normans arrived. The presence of Irish tenants on the manors not just as betaghs but also as free tenants from the early days of colonisation may indicate a rapid assimilation into the new order, which facilitated agrarian exploitation. The intensive cultivation of land in order to produce surplus grain for sale and export is generally believed to have been introduced by the Anglo-Normans. It is likely, however, that in this area, as in so many others, they merely accelerated a process that was already under way.

By introducing a network of manorial centres, parishes and rural boroughs, in addition to the towns, the Anglo-Normans *did* fundamentally change the character of rural settlement. These settlements are revealed, in a sporadic but invaluable way, by manorial documents, especially the extents made by the lords themselves or by royal government. The picture they present, particularly in reference to the layout of the manorial centres and the organisation of demesne and tenant holdings, is one of great variability. In these areas it must be concluded that there was no 'typical manor'. The information regarding land-use and agricultural practice is more consistent, however. Arable emerges as by far the most important land-use across the county and during the entire late medieval period.

Despite the relative richness of the documentary sources for rural settlement in medieval Meath, there remain many gaps in our knowledge and unanswered questions that only the archaeological record can attempt to answer. The data from sites recently excavated along the M3 such as Castlefarm and Roestown can make a direct contribution to the debates on continuity between the pre- and post-invasion periods and the incorporation of the indigenous rural population into the Anglo-Norman manorial system. The excavation of undefended rural farmsteads, of which Boyerstown is a prime example, is adding immeasurably to the growing corpus of information concerning dispersed rural settlement types and the phasing of colonisation. As post-excavation analysis continues in tandem with historical research, the potential of these sites to increase our knowledge of medieval rural settlement in Meath and in Ireland will be fully realised.

Notes

1. Mullally 2002; Scott & Martin 1978.
2. Mills & McEnery 1916.

3. Gilbert 1889; Gilbert 1884; St John Brooks 1936; St John Brooks 1953.

4. The National Archives of the United Kingdom (hereafter TNA) TNA: PRO E101/233/21; Sweetman 1886, 252–70; White 1943.

5. Connolly 2002, 14–37.

6. Davies & Quinn 1941.

7. Tresham 1828.

8. Sweetman 1875; 1877; 1886; Sayles 1979; Dryburgh & Smith 2005.

9. Lennard 1929.

10. Simington 1940. The Down Survey maps are in the Library Map Room, Trinity College Dublin.

11. Graham 1975, 225.

12. Mills & McEnery 1916, 177.

13. Mullally 2002, 128.

14. Bhreathnach 1999, 16–17.

15. Graham 1976, 39.

16. Orpen 2005, 184.

17. Davies 1990, 42.

18. Mullally 2002, 135.

19. Hennessy 1871, s.a. 1186.

20. Graham 1980, 45–7.

21. Bhreathnach 1999, 15; Graham 1976, 42.

22. Clutterbuck (forthcoming).

23. For a detailed examination of Walter's career see Hillaby 1992–3.

24. See, for example, Otway-Ruthven 1964.

25. St John Brooks 1953, 74–5, 216–17.

26. Bradley 1988–9.

27. Otway-Ruthven 1965, 79; Glasscock 1970.

28. Hennessy 1996, 121.

29. Davies & Quinn 1941, 45.

30. Scott & Martin 1978, 191.

31. Keegan 2005, 18.

32. See Hennessy 2004.

33. Graham 1975, 225. Nineteen were identified from earthwork remains, and 80 from descriptions in the Civil and Down Surveys.

34. O'Keeffe 2005; O'Conor 1998, 41–71.

35. Sweetman 1877, 179.

36. Simms 1979; 1988.

37. Seaver 2005a, 70–104.

38. Simms 1988, 313.

39. Seaver 2005a, 101.

40. Graham 1993, 74.

41. Lyne 2008.

42. Murphy 2008.

43. Otway-Ruthven 1951, 3.

44. McCourt 1971, 143.

45. Graham 1975, 244.

46. Benskin 1991, 73–4.

47. Otway-Ruthven 1958–9, 184.

48. Graham 1975, 237.

49. O'Meara 1982, 34–5.

50. Lucas 1960.

51. For a recent synthesis of the documentary and archaeological evidence for milling see Brady 2006.

52. Ó Corráin 1972, 51.

53. Britnell 2004, 195.

54. Thacker 2003, 29.

55. Davies & Quinn 1941.

56. TNA: PRO C143/168.

57. White 1943, 216.

58. White 1943, 60.

59. TNA: PRO C47/10/18/13.

60. Otway-Ruthven 1951.

61. Simms 1979, 167.

62. Mills & McEnery 1916, 55.

63. Davies & Quinn 1941, 33.

64. Sweetman 1875, 400.

65. For example, TNA: PRO E101/16/21.

66. Duffy 2000, 203–4.

APPENDIX 1—
RADIOCARBON DATING RESULTS

Notes

1. Radiocarbon ages are quoted in conventional years BP (before AD 1950), and the errors for these dates are expressed at the one-sigma (68% probability) level of confidence.

2. Calibrated date ranges are equivalent to the probable calendrical age of the sample material and are expressed at one-sigma (68% probability) and two-sigma (95% probability) levels of confidence.

3. Dates obtained from Beta Analytic in Florida (Beta lab code) were calibrated using the IntCal04 calibration dataset (Reimer et al. 2004) and the Talma & Vogel (1993) calibration programme. Dates obtained from Queen's University Belfast (UB lab code) were calibrated using datasets from Stuiver & Reimer (1993) and Reimer et al. (2004) and the CALIB 5.0.2 calibration programme (Stuiver et al. 2005).

Lab code	Site	Sample/context	Yrs BP	Calibrated date ranges
Chapter 1. Ardsallagh 1 & 2				
Beta-220128	Ardsallagh 1	Cattle (*Bos taurus*) bone (metapodial) from main fill of ring-ditch	1620 ± 40	AD 400–450 one sigma AD 370–540 two sigma
Beta-220129	Ardsallagh 1	Cattle (*Bos taurus*) bone (right metacarpal) from main fill of ring-ditch	1510 ± 40	AD 530–610 one sigma AD 440–640 two sigma
Beta-222061	Ardsallagh 1	Sheep/goat (*Ovis/Capra*) bone (metacarpal) from primary fill of ring-ditch	1600 ± 40	AD 410–530 one sigma AD 390–550 two sigma
Beta-221186	Ardsallagh 1	Human bone from a single individual from inurned cremation burial	2820 ± 40	1010–920 BC one sigma 1060–880 BC two sigma
Beta-222014	Ardsallagh 1	Human femoral shaft fragment (Burial 2) inside ring-ditch	1470 ± 40	AD 560–640 one sigma AD 530–650 two sigma
Beta-222015	Ardsallagh 1	Human rib shaft fragment (Burial 4) north of ring-ditch	1620 ± 40	AD 400–450 one sigma AD 370–540 two sigma

Lab code	Site	Sample/context	Yrs BP	Calibrated date ranges
Chapter 1. Ardsallagh 1 & 2				
Beta-222016	Ardsallagh 1	Human femoral shaft fragment (Burial 16) entranceway of ring-ditch	1560 ± 40	AD 430–550 one sigma AD 410–600 two sigma
Beta-227862	Ardsallagh 1	Human rib shaft fragment (Burial 13) north-west of ring-ditch	1460 ± 40	AD 570–640 one sigma AD 540–650 two sigma
Beta-229294	Ardsallagh 1	Elm (*Ulmus*), hazel (*Corylus*) & ash (*Fraxinus excelsior*) charcoal from fill of pit immediately south of ring-ditch containing cremated bone	2140 ± 40	360–190 BC one sigma 380–160 BC two sigma
Beta-236026	Ardsallagh 1	Cremated long-bone shaft from fill of pit west of ring-ditch	2120 ± 40	200–90 BC one sigma 350–40 BC two sigma
Beta-237058	Ardsallagh 1	Human femur (left) fragment (Burial 9)	1440 ± 40	AD 590–650 one sigma AD 450–650 two sigma
Beta-237059	Ardsallagh 1	Human femur (right) fragment (Burial 11)	1490 ± 40	AD 550–610 one sigma AD 450–640 two sigma
Beta-237060	Ardsallagh 1	Human tibia (right) fragment (Burial 29)	1460 ± 40	AD 570–640 one sigma AD 540–650 two sigma
Beta-233923	Ardsallagh 1	Cremated bone from deposit in ditch	1890 ± 40	AD 70–140 one sigma AD 30–230 two sigma
Beta-229295	Ardsallagh 1	Ash (*Fraxinus excelsior*), hazel (*Corylus*), pomoideae, blackthorn (*Prunus spinosa*), elm (*Ulmus*) and alder (*Alnus*) charcoal from pit	2220 ± 40	370–200 BC one sigma 390–180 BC two sigma
Beta-220121	Ardsallagh 2	Pomoideae, alder (*Alnus*) and willow (*Salix*) charcoal from pit at terminus of Ring-ditch 1	3590 ± 40	1970–1890 BC one sigma 2030–1870 BC two sigma
Beta-220122	Ardsallagh 2	Hazel (*Corylus*) charcoal from pit inside entrance of Ring-ditch 1	3560 ± 50	1950–1870 BC one sigma 2030–1750 BC two sigma
Beta-220123	Ardsallagh 2	Alder (*Alnus*) charcoal from pit at north end of site	3480 ± 40	1880–1740 BC one sigma 1900–1690 BC two sigma
Beta-220124	Ardsallagh 2	Blackthorn (*Prunus spinosa*) and ash (*Fraxinus excelsior*) charcoal from re-cut of Ring-ditch 3	1330 ± 40	AD 660–700 one sigma AD 650–770 two sigma
Beta-220125	Ardsallagh 2	Hazel (*Corylus*) charcoal from burial inside Ring-ditch 1	3520 ± 40	1900–1760 BC one sigma 1940–1740 BC two sigma
Beta-220126	Ardsallagh 2	Alder (*Alnus*) charcoal from cremation pit	3520 ± 40	1900–1760 BC one sigma 1940–1740 BC two sigma
Beta-220127	Ardsallagh 2	Oak (*Quercus*) charcoal from pit	3740 ± 50	2210–2040 BC one sigma 2290–2010 BC two sigma
Beta-222060	Ardsallagh 2	Cattle (*Bos taurus*) teeth from fill in Ring-ditch 3	1500 ± 40	AD 540–620 one sigma AD 450–640 two sigma
Beta-221184	Ardsallagh 2	Unidentifiable bone from Cordoned Urn cremation	3420 ± 40	1750–1680 BC one sigma 1870–1620 BC two sigma
Beta-221185	Ardsallagh 2	Human bone from Vase Urn cremation	3510 ± 50	1900–1750 BC one sigma 1950–1700 BC two sigma
Beta-237584	Ardsallagh 2	Ash (*Fraxinus excelsior*) charcoal from timber in base of Ring-ditch 1	2040 ± 40	90 BC–AD 10 one sigma 170 BC–AD 50 two sigma

Lab code	Site	Sample/context	Yrs BP	Calibrated date ranges
Chapter 2. Lismullin 1				
Beta-230460	Lismullin 1	Ash (*Fraxinus excelsior*) and hazel (*Corylus*) charcoal from post-hole of outer enclosure	2360 ± 40	410–390 BC one sigma 520–380 BC two sigma
Beta-230461	Lismullin 1	Ash (*Fraxinus excelsior*) and hazel (*Corylus*) charcoal from post-hole of outer enclosure	2360 ± 40	410–390 BC one sigma 490–370 BC two sigma
Beta-233922	Lismullin 1	Cattle (*Bos taurus*) bone from fill of refuse pit north of the post enclosure	980 ± 40	AD 1030–1160 one sigma AD 990–1160 two sigma
Beta-233921	Lismullin 1	Bone from dog (*Canis familiaris*) burial	930 ± 40	AD 1020–1120 one sigma AD 1020–1210 two sigma
Beta-237057	Lismullin 1	Cattle (*Bos taurus*) bone from backfill of souterrain construction trench	1000 ± 40	AD 1010–1040 one sigma AD 980–1150 two sigma
Chapter 3. Castlefarm 1				
Beta-220131	Castlefarm 1	Cattle (*Bos taurus*) bone (left distal tibia) from fill of inner enclosure ditch	1500 ± 40	AD 540–620 one sigma AD 450–640 two sigma
Beta-220132	Castlefarm 1	Cattle (*Bos taurus*) bone (left distal humerus) from fill of outer enclosure ditch	1170 ± 40	AD 790–900 one sigma AD 770–980 two sigma
Beta-220133	Castlefarm 1	Sheep (*Ovis aries*) horn core from primary fill of outer enclosure ditch	1160 ± 40	AD 810–960 one sigma AD 780–980 two sigma
Beta-229298	Castlefarm 1	Human bone fragment (right femur shaft) from Burial 1	1570 ± 40	AD 420–550 one sigma AD 410–580 two sigma
Beta-229299	Castlefarm 1	Human bone fragment (left fibula shaft) from Burial 7	1530 ± 40	AD 450–580 one sigma AD 420–610 two sigma
Chapter 4. Roestown 2				
Beta-219002	Roestown 2	Chicken (*Gallus gallus*) bone from Enclosure 3	1320 ± 40	AD 660–710 one sigma AD 650–780 two sigma
Beta-219003	Roestown 2	Dog (*Canis familiaris*) bone from Enclosure 6	1360 ± 40	AD 650–680 one sigma AD 630–710 two sigma
Beta-219005	Roestown 2	Pig (*Sus* sp.) bone from re-cut of Enclosure 3	1380 ± 40	AD 640–670 one sigma AD 620–690 two sigma
Beta-220114	Roestown 2	Dog (*Canis familiaris*) bone from Enclosure 1 (F404)	1200 ± 40	AD 780–890 one sigma AD 710–960 two sigma
Beta-220115	Roestown 2	Cattle (*Bos taurus*) bone from Enclosure 1 (F405)	1480 ± 40	AD 550–630 one sigma AD 530–650 two sigma
Beta-220116	Roestown 2	Dog (*Canis familiaris*) bone from Enclosure 1 (F450)	1170 ± 40	AD 790–900 one sigma AD 770–980 two sigma
Chapter 5. Collierstown 1				
Radiocarbon dates pending.				
Chapter 6. Baronstown 1				
Radiocarbon dates pending.				
Chapter 7. Dowdstown 2				
UB-7039	Dowdstown 2	Cattle (*Bos taurus*) bone (tibia shaft) from fill of Enclosure 1	1454 ± 33	AD 585–641 one sigma AD 554–651 two sigma

Lab code	Site	Sample/context	Yrs BP	Calibrated date ranges
Chapter 7. Dowdstown 2				
UB-7009	Dowdstown 2	Cattle (*Bos taurus*) bone (proximal end left tibia) from fill of Enclosure 5	1369 ± 33	AD 642–673 one sigma AD 605–762 two sigma
Beta-220119	Dowdstown 2	Cattle (*Bos taurus*) bone (left metatarsal) from fill of Enclosure 1	1540 ± 40	AD 450–570 one sigma AD 420–620 one sigma
Beta-220117	Dowdstown 2	Cattle (*Bos taurus*) bone (left humerus) from fill of Enclosure 4	1240 ± 40	AD 710–860 one sigma AD 680–890 two sigma
Beta-220120	Dowdstown 2	Cattle (*Bos taurus*) bone (left radius) from fill of re-cut to Enclosure 4	1300 ± 40	AD 670–770 one sigma AD 660–790 two sigma
Chapter 8. Boyerstown 1				
Radiocarbon dates pending.				

BIBLIOGRAPHY

Primary sources

The National Archives of the United Kingdom
   TNA: PRO C47/10/18/13—Extent for the manor of Rathfeigh, Co. Meath, 1322.
   TNA: PRO C134/21/6—Extent for the manor of Gormanston, Co. Meath, 1310.
   TNA: PRO C135/218—Extent for the manor of Slane, Co. Meath, 1370.
   TNA: PRO C143/168—Extent for the manor of Martry, Co. Meath, 1323.
   TNA: PRO C135/36—Extent for the manor of Ratoath, Co. Meath, 1333.
   TNA: PRO E101/16/21—Account of royal purveyors at Drogheda, 1323–4.
   TNA: PRO E101/233/21—Ecclesiastical taxation of the diocese of Meath c. 1302–06.

Secondary sources

Ambrosiani, B 1998 'Ireland and Scandinavia in the early Viking Age: an archaeological response', *in* H B Clarke, M Ní Mhaonaigh & R Ó Floinn (eds), *Ireland and Scandinavia in the Early Viking Age*, 405–11. Four Courts Press, Dublin.

Baker, C 2002 'Tullykane, Co. Meath', *in* I Bennett (ed.), *Excavations 2000: summary accounts of archaeological excavations in Ireland*, 266–7. Wordwell, Bray.

Benskin, M 1991 'An English township in fifteenth-century Ireland', *Collegium Medievale*, Vol. 4, 57–84.

Bhreathnach, E 1996 'The documentary evidence for pre-Norman Skreen, County Meath', *Ríocht na Midhe*, Vol. 9, No. 2, 37–45.

Bhreathnach, E 1999 'Authority and supremacy in Tara and its hinterland, c. 950–1200', *Discovery Programme Reports*, No. 5, 1–23. Royal Irish Academy/Discovery Programme, Dublin.

Bhreathnach, E 2005a 'Defining the historical landscape of Tara', *Ríocht na Midhe*, Vol. 16, 1-7.

Bhreathnach, E 2005b 'The medieval kingdom of Brega', *in* E Bhreathnach (ed.), *The Kingship and Landscape of Tara*, 410-22. Four Courts Press, Dublin.

Bieler, L (ed.) 1979 *The Patrician Texts in the Book of Armagh*. Dublin Institute for Advanced Studies, Dublin.

Bonsall, J & Gimson, H 2007 *A magnetic gradiometer survey over the National Monument at Lismullin (R0091)*. Unpublished report to the Department of the Environment, Heritage and Local Government.

Bourke, C 1987 'Irish croziers of the eighth and ninth centuries', *in* M Ryan (ed.), *Ireland and Insular Art, AD 500–1200*, 166–73. Royal Irish Academy, Dublin.

Boyle, M 1937–8 'Suggestions for the dates of four Scottish monuments', *Proceedings of the Society of Antiquaries of Scotland*, Vol. 72, 115–21.

Bradley, J 1988–9 'The medieval towns of County Meath', *Ríocht na Midhe*, Vol. 8, No. 2, 30–49.

Bradley, J 1991 'Excavations at Moynagh Lough, Co. Meath', *Journal of the Royal Society of Antiquaries of Ireland*, Vol. 121, 5–26.

Bradley, J 1993 'Moynagh Lough: an insular workshop of the second quarter of the 8th century', *in* R M Spearman & J Higgit (eds), *The Age of Migrating Ideas: early medieval art in northern Britain and Ireland*, 74–80. National Museum of Scotland, Edinburgh.

Bradley, J 1995 'Moynagh Lough, Brittas', *in* I Bennett (ed.), *Excavations 1994: summary accounts of archaeological excavations in Ireland*, 72–3. Wordwell, Bray.

Bradley, J 1996 'Moynagh Lough, Brittas', *in* I Bennett (ed.), *Excavations 1995: summary accounts of archaeological excavations in Ireland*, 69–70. Wordwell, Bray.

Brady, N 2006 'Mills in medieval Ireland: looking beyond design', *in* S Walton (ed.), *Wind and Water in the Middle Ages: fluid technologies from antiquity to the Renaissance*, 39–68. Arizona Center for Medieval and Renaissance Studies, Tempe.

Britnell, R 2004 *Britain and Ireland, 1050–1530: economy and society*. Oxford University Press, Oxford.

Burbidge, C J & Sanderson D C W 2008 *Luminescence dating of ditch and pit fills from the ACS Ltd excavation of Lismullin National Monument, Republic of Ireland*. Unpublished report to Meath County Council on behalf of Archaeological Consultancy Services Ltd.

Byrne, F J 2001 *Irish Kings and High-Kings*. Four Courts Press, Dublin.

Campbell, E & Lane, A 1993 'Celtic and Germanic interaction in Dalriada: the 7th-century metalworking site at Dunadd', *in* R M Spearman & J Higgit (eds), *The Age of Migrating Ideas: early medieval art in northern Britain and Ireland*, 52–63. National Museum of Scotland, Edinburgh.

Carey, A 2002 'Ballycasey Beg', *in* I Bennett (ed.), *Excavations 2000: summary accounts of archaeological excavations in Ireland*, 14–15. Wordwell, Bray.

Carroll, J 2007 'Darcytown', *in* I Bennett (ed.), *Excavations 2004: summary accounts of archaeological excavations in Ireland*, 108. Wordwell, Bray.

Charles-Edwards, T 2003 'Dliged: its native and latinate usages', *Celtica*, Vol. 24, 65–78.

Clarke, L 2004a *Report on archaeological assessment at testing area 9: Lismullin, County Meath (04E0426)*. Unpublished report to the Department of the Environment, Heritage and Local Government on behalf of Archaeological Consultancy Services Ltd.

Clarke, L 2004b *Report on archaeological assessment at testing area 6: Baronstown, Collierstown and Skreen. M3 Clonee–North of Kells, Co. Meath (04E423)*. Unpublished report to the Department of the Environment, Heritage and Local Government on behalf of Archaeological Consultancy

Services Ltd.

Clarke, L. 2004c *Johnstown 1: archaeological excavation of a multi-period burial, settlement and industrial site (02E0462).* Unpublished report to the Department of the Environment, Heritage and Local Government on behalf of Archaeological Consultancy Services Ltd.

Clarke, L & Carlin, N 2006a 'Life and death in Ardsallagh', *Seanda*, No. 1, 16–18.

Clarke, L & Carlin, N 2006b 'Life and death in County Meath', *Archaeology Ireland*, Vol. 20. No. 4, 22–5.

Clarke, L & Carlin, N 2008 'Living with the dead at Johnstown 1: an enclosed burial, settlement and industrial site', *in* N Carlin, L Clarke & F Walsh, *The Archaeology of Life and Death in the Boyne Floodplain: the linear landscape of the M4*, 55–85. NRA Scheme Monographs 2. National Roads Authority, Dublin.

Clarke, L & Murphy, D 2001 *Report on the archaeological resolution of a multi-period settlement site at Colp West, Co. Meath (99E0472).* Unpublished report to the Department of the Environment, Heritage and Local Government on behalf of Archaeological Consultancy Services Ltd.

Cleary, R M 1982 'Excavations at Lough Gur, Co. Limerick: Part II', *Journal of the Cork Archaeological and Historical Society*, Vol. 87, 7–106.

Cleary, R M 2006 'Excavations of an early-medieval period enclosure at Ballynagallagh, Lough Gur, Co. Limerick', *Proceedings of the Royal Irish Academy,* Vol. 106C, 3–66.

Clinton, M 2001 *The Souterrains of Ireland.* Wordwell, Bray.

Clutterbuck, R forthcoming 'Cookstown, Co. Meath: a medieval rural settlement', *in* C Corlett & M Potterton (eds), *Rural Settlement in Medieval Ireland in Light of Recent Excavations.*

Cogan, A 1874 *The Ecclesiastical History of the Diocese of Meath*, Vol. 1. Dublin.

Collins, T & Coyne, F 2003 'Fire and water… early Mesolithic cremations at Castleconnell, Co. Limerick', *Archaeology Ireland*, Vol. 17, No. 2, 24–7.

Collis, J 1977 'Iron Age henges?', *Archaeologia Atlantica*, Vol. 2, 55–63.

Comber, M 1997 'Lagore crannóg and non-ferrous metalworking in early historic Ireland', *Journal of Irish Archaeology*, Vol. 8, 101–14.

Comber, M 2002 'M.V. Duignan's excavations at the ringfort of Rathgureen, Co. Galway, 1948–9', *Proceedings of the Royal Irish Academy,* Vol. 102C, 137–97.

Connolly, P 2002 *Medieval Record Sources.* Four Courts Press, Dublin.

Cooney, G & Grogan, E 1999 *Irish Prehistory: a social perspective.* Wordwell, Bray.

Coughlan, J 2006 *Report on the human remains from Roestown 2.* Unpublished report to Meath County Council on behalf of Archaeological Consultancy Services Ltd.

Coughlan, J 2007a *Osteological analysis of the human skeletal remains from Lismullin 1, Co. Meath.* Unpublished report to Meath County Council on behalf of Archaeological Consultancy Services Ltd.

Coughlan, J 2007b *The human skeletal remains from Castlefarm 1.* Unpublished report to Meath County Council on behalf of Archaeological Consultancy Services Ltd.

Coughlan, J 2008 *The human skeletal remains from Collierstown 1.* Unpublished report to Meath County Council on behalf of Archaeological Consultancy Services Ltd.

Coyne, F 2005 'Excavation of an early medieval "plectrum-shaped" enclosure at Newtown, Co.

Limerick', *North Munster Archaeological Journal*, Vol. 45, 51–63.

Coyne, F 2006 'Excavation of an early medieval "plectrum-shaped" enclosure at Newtown, County Limerick', *in* J O'Sullivan & M Stanley (eds), *Settlement, Industry and Ritual*, 63–72. Archaeology and the National Roads Authority Monograph Series No. 3. National Roads Authority, Dublin.

Coyne, F & Collins, T 2003 'Plectrum-shaped enclosures—a new site type at Newtown, Co. Limerick', *Archaeology Ireland*, Vol. 17, No. 4, 17–19.

Daly, A & Grogan, E 1993 'Excavation of four barrows at Mitchelstowndown West, Knocklong, Co. Limerick', *Discovery Programme Reports*, No. 1, 44–60. Royal Irish Academy/Discovery Programme, Dublin.

Danaher, E 2007 *Monumental Beginnings: the archaeology of the N4 Sligo Inner Relief Road*. NRA Scheme Monographs 1. National Roads Authority, Dublin.

Danaher, E 2008 *Interim report on archaeological excavation at Blundelstown 1 (A008/022)*. Unpublished report to the Department of the Environment, Heritage and Local Government on behalf of Archaeological Consultancy Services Ltd.

Davies, O & Quinn, D B (eds) 1941 'The Irish Pipe Roll of 14 John, 1211–12', *Ulster Journal of Archaeology*, 3rd ser., Vol. 4, supplement, 1–76.

Davies, R R 1990 *Domination and Conquest: the experience of Ireland, Scotland and Wales, 1100–1300*. Cambridge University Press, Cambridge.

Deevy, M B 1998 *Medieval Ring Brooches in Ireland: a study of jewellery, dress and society*. Wordwell, Bray.

Deevy, M 2005 'The M3 Clonee to North of Kells Road Scheme, Co. Meath', *in* J O'Sullivan & M Stanley (eds), *Recent Archaeological Discoveries on National Road Schemes 2004*, 83–93. Archaeology and the National Roads Authority Monograph Series No. 2. National Roads Authority, Dublin.

Deevy, M 2006 'Strange creatures and mixed messages', *Seanda*, No. 1, 26–7.

Delaney, S & Roycroft, N 2003 'Early medieval enclosure at Balriggan, Co. Louth', *Archaeology Ireland*, Vol. 17, No. 2, 16–19.

Delaney, S & Walsh, F 2004 'Plectrum-shaped enclosures', *Archaeology Ireland*, Vol. 17, No. 4, 6.

Dineen, P S 1927 *Foclóir Gaeilge–Béarla, Irish–English Dictionary*. Irish Texts Society, Dublin.

Doherty, C 1980 Exchange and trade in early medieval Ireland, *Journal of the Royal Society of Antiquaries of Ireland*, Vol. 110, 67–89.

Donaghy, C & Grogan, E 1997 'Navel-gazing at Uisneach, Co. Westmeath', *Archaeology Ireland*, Vol. 11, No. 4, 24–6.

Doody, M G 1995 'Ballyhoura Hills Project, Chancellorsland, Co. Tipperary: interim report', *Discovery Programme Reports*, No. 2, 13–18. Royal Irish Academy/Discovery Programme, Dublin.

Dowling, G 2007 'The liminal boundary: an analysis of the sacral potency of the ditch at Ráith na Ríg, Tara, Co. Meath', *Journal of Irish Archaeology*, Vol. 15, 15–38.

Duffy, P J 2000 'Heritage and history: exploring landscape and place in County Meath', *Ríocht na Midhe*, Vol. 11, 187–218.

Dryburgh, P & Smith, B (eds) 2005 *Handbook and Select Calendar of Sources for Medieval Ireland in the National Archives of the United Kingdom*. Four Courts Press, Dublin.

Edwards, N 1990 *The Archaeology of Early Medieval Ireland*. Batsford, London.

Eogan, G 1968 'Excavations at Knowth, Co. Meath, 1962–65', *Proceedings of the Royal Irish Academy*, Vol. 66C, 299–400.

Eogan, J & Finn, D 2000 'New light on late prehistoric ritual and burial in County Limerick', *Archaeology Ireland*, Vol. 14, No. 1, 8–10.

Eogan, J & Reid, M 2002 'Ninch', *in* I Bennett (ed.), *Excavations 2000: summary accounts of archaeological excavations in Ireland*, 259–60. Wordwell, Bray.

Fairburn, N 2004 *Report on archaeological assessment at testing area 7, Boyerstown, Co. Meath, licence: 0E0580*. Unpublished report to the Department of the Environment, Heritage and Local Government on behalf of Archaeological Consultancy Services Ltd.

Fanning, T 1972 'Excavations of a ringfort at Narraghmore, Co. Kildare', *Journal of the Kildare Archaeological and Historical Society*, Vol. 15, No. 2, 170–7.

Fanning, T 1994 *Viking Age Ringed Pins from Dublin*. Medieval Dublin Excavations 1962–81, Ser. B, Vol. 4. Royal Irish Academy, Dublin.

Feehan, J 2003 *Farming in Ireland: history, heritage and environment*. University College Dublin, Dublin.

Fenwick, J & Newman, C 2002 'Geomagnetic survey on the Hill of Tara, Co. Meath, 1998–9', *Discovery Programme Reports*, No. 6, 1–17. Royal Irish Academy/Discovery Programme, Dublin.

Fredengren, C 2002 *Crannogs: a study of people's interaction with lakes, with particular reference to Lough Gara in the north-west of Ireland*. Wordwell, Bray.

Gahan, A 1998 'Castle Upton, Templepatrick', *in* I Bennett (ed.), *Excavations 1997: summary accounts of archaeological excavations in Ireland*, 3. Wordwell, Bray.

Gallagher, D 2006 *Report on topsoil assessment and metal detection of topsoil at Boyerstown 1*. Unpublished report to Meath County Council on behalf of Archaeological Consultancy Services Ltd.

Geary, B & Hill, T 2007 *Palaeoenvironmental assessment of sites along the proposed M3 Clonee to North of Kells Motorway: interim statement*. Unpublished report to Meath County Council on behalf of Archaeological Consultancy Services Ltd.

Gibson, A 2000 'Circles and henges: reincarnations of past traditions', *Archaeology Ireland*, Vol. 14, No. 1, 11–14.

Gibson, A 2005 *Stonehenge and Timber Circles*. Tempus, Stroud.

Gibson, A, Becker, H, Grogan, E, Jones, N & Masterson, B 1999 'The Walton Basin, Wales: survey, exploration and preservation of the archaeological heritage (SEPAH)', *Archaeology Ireland*, Vol. 13, No. 1, 21–3.

Gilbert, J T (ed.) 1884 *Cartularies of St Mary's Abbey, Dublin, 2 vols*. Rolls Series, London.

Gilbert, J T (ed.) 1889 *Register of the Abbey of St Thomas, Dublin*. Rolls Series, London.

Glasscock, R E 1970 'Moated sites and deserted boroughs and villages; two neglected aspects of Anglo-Norman settlement in Ireland', *in* N Stephens & R E Glasscock (eds), *Irish Geographical Studies in Honour of E. Estyn Evans*, 162–77. Queen's University of Belfast, Belfast.

Gowen, M 1989a 'Westreave', *in* I Bennett (ed.), *Excavations 1988: summary accounts of archaeological excavations in Ireland*, 18. Wordwell, Bray.

Gowen, M 1989b 'Colp', *in* I Bennett (ed.), *Excavations 1988: summary accounts of archaeological excavations in Ireland*, 31–2. Wordwell, Bray.

Gowen, M 1989c 'Smithstown', *in* I Bennett (ed.), *Excavations 1988: summary accounts of archaeological excavations in Ireland*, 34–5. Wordwell, Bray.

Graham, B J 1975 'Anglo-Norman settlement in County Meath', *Proceedings of the Royal Irish Academy*, Vol. 75C, 223–49.

Graham, B 1976 'The evolution of the settlement pattern of Anglo-Norman Eastmeath', *in* R H Buchanan, R A Butlin & D McCourt (eds), *Fields, Farms and Settlement in Europe*, 38–46. Ulster Folk & Transport Museum, Hollywood.

Graham, B J 1980 'The mottes of the Norman liberty of Meath', *in* H Murtagh (ed.), *Irish Midland Studies*, 39–56. The Old Athlone Society, Athlone.

Graham, B J 1993 'The high Middle Ages: c. 1100 to c. 1350', *in* B J Graham & L J Proudfoot (eds), *A Historical Geography of Ireland*, 58–98. Academic Press, London.

Grogan, E 1984 'Excavation of an Iron Age burial mound at Furness', *Journal of the Kildare Archaeological Society*, Vol. 16, 298–316.

Grogan, E 2004 'Middle Bronze Age burial traditions in Ireland', *in* H Roche, E Grogan, J Bradley, J Coles & B Raftery (eds), *From Megaliths to Metals: essays in honour of George Eogan*, 61–71. Oxbow, Oxford.

Grogan, E 2005 'Appendix C. The pottery from Mooghaun South', *in* E Grogan, *The North Munster Project, Vol. 1: the later prehistoric landscape of south-east Clare*, 317–29. Discovery Programme Monograph No. 6. Wordwell, Bray.

Grogan, E 2008 *The Rath of the Synods, Tara, Co. Meath: excavations by S.P. Ó Ríordáin*. Wordwell (in association with the UCD School of Archaeology), Bray.

Grogan, E & Roche, H 2007a *The prehistoric pottery assemblages from the M3 Clonee–North of Kells, Co. Meath: Ardsallagh 1, Ardsallagh 2, Ardsallagh 4, Johnstown 3, Pace 1 and Dunboyne 2–4*. Unpublished report to Meath County Council on behalf of Archaeological Consultancy Services Ltd.

Grogan E & Roche H 2007b *The prehistoric pottery assemblages from the M3 Clonee–North of Kells, Co. Meath: Lismullin preliminary report*. Unpublished report to Meath County Council on behalf of Archaeological Consultancy Services Ltd.

Hall, M undated 'A double-sided hnefatafl board from Cathedral Hill, Downpatrick: time consumed in an early medieval monastic enclosure', at www.downcountymuseum.com/uploads/HnefatafiBoard.doc [last accessed February 2009].

Hencken, H O'N 1936 'Ballinderry crannóg no. 1', *Proceedings of the Royal Irish Academy*, Vol. 43C, 103–240.

Hencken, H O'N 1942 'Ballinderry crannóg no. 2', *Proceedings of the Royal Irish Academy*, Vol. 47C, 1–76.

Hencken, H O'N 1950 'Lagore crannóg: an Irish royal residence of the 7th to 10th centuries AD', *Proceedings of the Royal Irish Academy*, Vol. 53C, 1–247.

Hennessy, M 1996 'Manorial organisation in early thirteenth-century Tipperary', *Irish Geography*, Vol. 29, No. 2, 116–25.

Hennessy, M 2004 'Manorial agriculture and settlement in early fourteenth-century Co. Tipperary', *in* H B Clarke, J Prunty & M Hennessy (eds), *Surveying Ireland's Past: multidisciplinary essays in honour of Anngret Simms*, 99–118. Irish Geographical Publications, Dublin.

Hennessy, W M (ed.) 1871 *The Annals of Loch Cé: a chronicle of Irish affairs from AD 1014 to AD 1590*, 2 vols. Rolls Series, London.

Henry, F 1967 *Irish Art During the Viking Invasions (800–1020 AD)*. Methuen, London.

Henry, M 2001 'Cloongownagh', *in* I Bennett (ed.), *Excavations 1999: summary accounts of archaeological excavations in Ireland*, 268. Wordwell, Bray.

Hillaby, J 1992–3 'Colonisation, crisis-management and debt: Walter de Lacy and the lordship of Meath, 1189–1241', *Ríocht na Midhe*, Vol. 8, No. 4, 1–48.

Hughes, K 1966 *The Church in Early Irish Society*. Methuen, London.

Johnson, R 2005 'A descriptive account of the decoration on the early medieval shrine known as the Corp Naomh', *in* T Condit & C Corlett (eds), *Above and Beyond: essays in memory of Leo Swan*, 303–18. Wordwell, Bray.

Johnston, S A & Wailes, B 2007 *Dun Ailinne: excavations at an Irish royal site, 1968–1975*. Pennsylvania University Museum Publications, Pennsylvania.

Keegan, M 2005 'The archaeology of manorial settlement in west County Limerick', *in* J Lyttleton & T O'Keeffe (eds), *The Manor in Medieval and Early Modern Ireland*, 17–39. Four Courts Press, Dublin.

Keeley, V J 1991 'Archaeological excavation of a burial ground, Greenhills Townland', *Journal of the County Kildare Archaeological Society*, Vol. 27, 180–201.

Keeley, V J 1999 'Iron Age discoveries at Ballydavis', *in* P G Lane & W Nolan (eds), *Laois: history & society. Interdisciplinary essays on the history of an Irish county*, 25–34. Geography Publications, Dublin.

Kelly, A 2008a *Collierstown 1 pottery report: Phocaean Red Slip Ware (PRSW) and Bii Ware*. Unpublished report to Meath County Council on behalf of Archaeological Consultancy Services Ltd.

Kelly, A 2008b 'A Turkish import in County Meath: Mediterranean pottery on the M3', *Seanda*, No. 3, 16–18.

Kelly, F 1997 *Early Irish Farming*. Dublin Institute for Advanced Studies, Dublin.

Kelly, F 2001 *A Guide to Early Irish Law*. Dublin Institute for Advanced Studies, Dublin.

Kiely, J 2004 'Ballydowny', *in* I Bennett (ed.), *Excavations 2002: summary accounts of archaeological excavations in Ireland*, 218–19. Wordwell, Bray.

Kinsella, J 2006a *Research paper on artefacts from Castlefarm, Roestown and Dowdstown Co. Meath*. Unpublished report for Archaeological Consultancy Services Ltd and Meath County Council.

Kinsella, J 2006b *Research for the townland of Trevet*. Unpublished report for Archaeological Consultancy Services Ltd and Meath County Council.

Kinsella, J 2008 'New discoveries and fresh insights: researching the early medieval archaeology of the M3 in County Meath', *in* J O'Sullivan & M Stanley (eds), *Roads, Rediscovery and Research*,

95–115. Archaeology and the National Roads Authority Monograph Series No. 5. National Roads Authority, Dublin.

Laing, L & Laing, J 1995 *Celtic Britain and Ireland: art and society*. Herbert Press, London.

Lennard, R V 1929 'What is an extent?', *English Historical Review*, Vol. 44, 256–62.

Linnane, S J 2004a *Report on archaeological assessment at testing area 17, Ardsallagh, Co. Meath*. Unpublished report to the Department of the Environment, Heritage and Local Government on behalf of Archaeological Consultancy Services Ltd.

Linnane, S J 2004b *Report on archaeological assessment at testing area 16, Ardsallagh, Co. Meath*. Unpublished report to the Department of the Environment, Heritage and Local Government on behalf of Archaeological Consultancy Services Ltd.

Linnane, S J 2004c *Report on archaeological assessment at testing area 15, Dowdstown, Castletown Tara and Ballinter, Co. Meath*. Unpublished report to the Department of the Environment, Heritage and Local Government on behalf of Archaeological Consultancy Services Ltd.

Linnane, S & Kinsella, J 2007 'Fort Baronstown: exploring the social role of an impressive ringfort on the M3', *Seanda*, No. 2, 57–9.

Lucas, A T 1960 'Irish food before the potato', *Gwerin*, Vol. 3, 1–36.

Lynch, P 2004 'Bellinstown', in I Bennett (ed.), *Excavations 2002: summary accounts of archaeological excavations in Ireland*, 127. Wordwell, Bray.

Lyne, E 2008 'Lives through time', *Archaeology Ireland*, Vol. 22, No. 2, 17–21.

Lyne, E forthcoming 'Phoenixtown 2', in I Bennett (ed.), *Excavations 2006: summary accounts of archaeological excavations in Ireland*. Wordwell, Bray.

Lynn, C J 1978 'Early Christian period domestic structures: a change from round to rectangular plans?', *Irish Archaeological Research Forum*, Vol. 5, 29–45.

Lynn, C J 1980 'The excavation of an earthwork enclosure at Ballynoe, County Antrim', *Ulster Journal of Archaeology*, Vol. 43, 29–38.

Lynn, C 1988 'Slices through time', in A Hamlin and C Lynn (eds), *Pieces of the Past: archaeological excavations by the Department of the Environment for Northern Ireland, 1970–1986*. HMSO, Belfast.

Lynn, C J 1994 'Houses in rural Ireland, AD 500–1100', *Ulster Journal of Archaeology*, Vol. 57, 81–94.

MacWhite, E 1945 'Early Irish board games', *Éigse*, Vol. 5, 22–35.

McConway, C 2003 'Ninch', in I Bennett (ed.), *Excavations 2001: summary accounts of archaeological excavations in Ireland*, 311–13. Wordwell, Bray.

McConway, C 2004 'Ninch', in I Bennett (ed.), *Excavations 2002: summary accounts of archaeological excavations in Ireland*, 421–4. Wordwell, Bray.

McCormick, F 1995 'Cows, ringforts and the origins of Early Christian Ireland', *Emania*, Vol. 13, 33–7.

McCormick, F & Murray, E 2007 *Knowth and the Zooarchaeology of Early Christian Ireland*. Excavations at Knowth, Vol. 3, Royal Irish Academy, Dublin.

McCormick, F, Cribben, G, Robinson, M, Shimwell, D & Murphy, E 1995 'A pagan–Christian transitional burial at Kiltullagh', *Emania*, Vol. 13, 89–98.

McCourt, D 1971 'The dynamic quality of Irish rural settlement', in R H Buchanan, E Jones &

D McCourt (eds), *Man and his Habitat: essays presented to Emyr Estyn Evans*, 126–64. Routledge and Kegan Paul, London.

McCutcheon, C 2006 *Medieval Pottery from Wood Quay, Dublin*. Medieval Dublin Excavations 1962–81, Ser. B, Vol. 7. Royal Irish Academy, Dublin.

McGarry, T 2007 'Irish late prehistoric burial practices: continuity, developments and influences', *Trowel*, Vol. 11, 7–21.

McGarry, T in press 'Some exotic evidence amidst Irish late prehistoric burials', *in* O P Davis, N M Sharples & K E Waddington (eds), *Changing Perspectives on the First Millennium BC*. Oxbow, Oxford.

McRoberts, D 1960–1 'The ecclesiastical significance of the St Ninian's Isle treasure', *Proceedings of the Society of Antiquaries of Scotland*, Vol. 94, 301–14.

Martin, K 2007 'Opening the door on a medieval settlement at Boyerstown 1', *Seanda*, No. 2, 60–1.

Mills, J & McEnery, M J (eds) 1916 *Calendar of the Gormanston Register*. University Press, Dublin.

Monk, M 1981 'Post-Roman drying kilns and the problem of function: a preliminary statement', *in* D Ó Corráin (ed.), *Irish antiquity: essays and studies presented to Professor M.J. O'Kelly*, 216–30. Four Courts Press, Dublin.

Monk, M & Kelleher, E 2005 'An assessment of the archaeological evidence for Irish corn-drying kilns in the light of results of archaeological experiments and archaeobotanical studies', *Journal of Irish Archaeology*, Vol. 14, 77–144.

Moore, M 1987 *Archaeological Inventory of County Meath*. Stationery Office, Dublin.

Moore, T 2007 'Perceiving communities: exchange, landscapes and social networks in the later Iron Age of western Britain', *Oxford Journal of Archaeology*, Vol. 26, 79–102.

Mount, C 1999 'Excavation and environmental analysis of a Neolithic mound and Iron Age barrow cemetery at Rathdooney Beg, Co. Sligo', *Proceedings of the Prehistoric Society*, Vol. 65, 337–71.

Mullally, E (ed.) 2002 *The Deeds of the Normans in Ireland: a new edition of the chronicle formerly known as The Song of Dermot and the Earl*. Four Courts Press, Dublin.

Murphy, M 2006a *Late medieval settlement in the barony of Dunboyne*. Unpublished report to Archaeological Consultancy Services and Meath County Council.

Murphy, M 2006b *Roestown—late medieval historical references*. Unpublished report to Archaeological Consultancy Services Ltd and Meath County Council.

Murphy, M 2006c *Late medieval settlement in the barony of Lower Navan*. Unpublished report to Archaeological Consultancy Services Ltd and Meath County Council.

Murphy, M 2006d *Boyerstown—late medieval historical references*. Unpublished report to Archaeological Consultancy Services Ltd and Meath County Council.

Murphy, M 2006e *Phoenixtown—late medieval historical references*. Unpublished report to Irish Archaeological Consultancy Ltd and Meath County Council.

Murphy, M 2008 'Digging with documents: late medieval historical research on the M3 in County Meath', *in* J O'Sullivan & M Stanley (eds), *Roads, Rediscovery and Research*, 95–115. Archaeology and the National Roads Authority Monograph Series No. 5. National Roads

Authority, Dublin.

Myhre, B 1998 'The archaeology of the early Viking Age in Norway', *in* H B Clarke, M Ní Mhaonaigh & R Ó Floinn (eds), *Ireland and Scandinavia in the Early Viking Age*, 3–36. Four Courts Press, Dublin.

Mytum, H 1992 *The Origins of Early Christian Ireland*. Routledge, London.

Newman, C 1993a 'Sleeping in Elysium', *Archaeology Ireland*, Vol. 7, No. 3, 20–3.

Newman, C 1993b 'The show's not over until the fat lady sings', *Archaeology Ireland*, Vol. 7, No. 4, 8–9.

Newman, C 1997 *Tara: an archaeological survey*. Discovery Programme Monographs No. 2. Royal Irish Academy/Discovery Programme, Dublin.

Newman, C 1998 'Reflections on the making of a "royal site" in early Ireland', *World Archaeology*, Vol. 30, No. 1, 127–41.

Nicholls, J & Shiel, D 2006 'Shades of grey', *Seanda*, No. 1, 12–15.

Nicolaysen, N 1882 *Langskibet fra Gokstad ved Sandefjord*. A Cammermeyerm, Kristiania.

O'Brien, C, Ranner, H, Allen, M & Caffell, A 2007 *Ardsallagh 2, M3 Motorway Project, Ireland: environmental analysis (1638)*. Unpublished report to Meath County Council on behalf of Archaeological Consultancy Services Ltd.

O'Brien, E 1992 'Pagan and Christian burial in Ireland during the first millennium AD: continuity and change', *in* N Edwards & A Lane (eds), *The Early Church in Wales and the West: recent work in Early Christian archaeology, history and placenames*, 130–7. Oxbow Monograph 16. Oxbow, Oxford.

O'Brien, E 1999 'Excavation of a multi-period burial site at Ballymacaward, Ballyshannon, Co. Donegal', *Donegal Annual*, Vol. 51, 56–61.

O'Brien, E 2003 'Burial practices in Ireland: first to seventh centuries AD', *in* J Downes & A Ritchie (eds), *Sea Change: Orkney and Northern Europe in the later Iron Age, AD 300–800*, 63–72. Pinkfoot Press, Orkney.

O'Brien, E 2005 *The location and context of Viking burials at Kilmainham and Islandbridge*. Lecture notes for a paper delivered to the Save Viking Waterford Action Group, at http://www.vikingwaterford.com/images_documents/woodstown_lecture_elizabeth_obrien.pdf [last accessed October 2008].

O'Brien, E in press 'Pagan or Christian? Burial in Ireland during the 5th to 8th centuries AD', *in* N Edwards (ed.), *The Archaeology of the Early Medieval Celtic Churches*, 189–214. Society for Medieval Archaeology and the Society for Church Archaeology Monograph.

O'Connell, A 2007a 'Iron Age enclosure at Lismullin, Co. Meath', *Archaeology Ireland*, Vol. 21, No. 2, 10–13.

O'Connell, A 2007b 'The elusive Iron Age: a rare and exciting site type is uncovered at Lismullin, Co. Meath', *Seanda*, No. 2, 52–4.

O'Connor, E 2007 *A projecting ring-headed pin from Lismullin, Co. Meath*. Unpublished report to Meath County Council on behalf of Archaeological Consultancy Services Ltd.

O'Connor, E 2008 'Fragments from the past: the prehistory of the M3 in County Meath', *in* J O'Sullivan & M Stanley (eds), *Roads, Rediscovery and Research*, 83–94. Archaeology and the

National Roads Authority Monograph Series No. 5. National Roads Authority, Dublin.

O'Conor, K D 1998 *The Archaeology of Medieval Rural Settlement in Ireland*. Discovery Programme Monograph No. 3. Royal Irish Academy/Discovery Programme, Dublin.

Ó Corráin, D 1972 *Ireland Before the Normans*. Gill & Macmillan, Dublin.

Ó Corráin, D 2001 'The Vikings in Ireland', *in* A C Larsen (ed.), *The Vikings in Ireland*, 17–28. The Viking Ship Museum, Roskilde.

Ó Donnchadha, B 2002 *M1 Dundalk Western Bypass. Donaghmore excavations: sites 108, 109, 110 and 131*. Unpublished report to the Department of the Environment, Heritage and Local Government on behalf of Irish Archaeological Consultancy Ltd.

O'Donnell, L 2007 *Analysis of the charcoal, Ardsallagh 2, Co. Meath, A008/034*. Unpublished report to Meath County Council on behalf of Archaeological Consultancy Services Ltd.

O'Donovan, J 1836 *The Ordnance Survey Field Name Books for County Meath*. National Archives of Ireland ref. OS 88.

Ó Drisceoil, C 2002 'Recycled ringforts: the evidence from archaeological excavation for the conversion of pre-existing monuments to motte castles in medieval Ireland', *Journal of the County Louth Archaeological and Historical Society*, Vol. 25, No. 2, 189–201.

O'Flaherty, R 1999 'Of gods and drinking men', *Archaeology Ireland*, Vol. 13, No. 1, 33–5.

Ó Floinn, R 1987–8 'Lehinch, Co. Offaly', *in* 'Excavations Bulletin 1977–9: summary accounts of archaeological excavations in Ireland', *Journal of Irish Archaeology*, Vol. 4, 65–79.

Ó Floinn, R 1999 'The date of some metalwork from Cahercommaun reassessed', *in* C Cotter, 'Cahercommaun Fort, Co. Clare: a reassessment of its cultural context', *Discovery Programme Reports*, No. 5, 73–9. Royal Irish Academy/Discovery Programme, Dublin.

O'Hara, R 2007 'Roestown 2, Co. Meath: an excavation on the M3 Clonee to North of Kells motorway scheme', *in* J O'Sullivan & M Stanley (eds), *New Routes to the Past*, 141–51. Archaeology and the National Roads Authority Monograph Series No. 4. National Roads Authority, Dublin.

O'Hara, R 2008a *Report on archaeological excavation at Colp Cross, Painestown, Co. Meath, 07E891*. Unpublished report for Archaeological Consultancy Services Ltd.

O'Hara, R 2008b *Interim report on archaeological excavation at Ross 2 (A008/082)*. Unpublished report to the Department of the Environment, Heritage and Local Government on behalf of Archaeological Consultancy Services Ltd.

O'Keeffe, T 2001 *Medieval Ireland: an archaeology*. Tempus, Stroud.

O'Keeffe, T 2005 'Afterword', *in* J Lyttleton & T O'Keeffe (eds), *The Manor in Medieval and Early Modern Ireland*, 188–97. Four Courts Press, Dublin.

O'Kelly, M J 1962 'Beal Boru, Co. Clare', *Journal of the Cork Historical and Archaeological Society*, Vol. 67, 1–27.

O'Kelly, M J 1963 'The excavations of two earthen ringforts at Garryduff, Co. Cork', *Proceedings of the Royal Irish Academy*, Vol. 63C, 17–150.

O'Meadhra, U 1987 'Irish, Insular, Saxon and Scandinavian elements in the motif pieces from Ireland', *in* M Ryan (ed.), *Ireland and Insular Art, AD 500–1200*, 159–65. Royal Irish Academy, Dublin.

O'Meara, J J (ed.) 1982 *Gerald of Wales: the history and topography of Ireland*. Penguin Books, London.

O'Neill, T 2006 'Parknahown 5: an extensive cemetery at the River Goul', *Seanda*, No. 1, 32.

O'Neill, T 2007 'The hidden past of Parknahown, Co. Laois', *in* J O'Sullivan & M Stanley (eds), *New Routes to the Past*, 133–9. Archaeology and the National Roads Authority Monograph Series No. 4. National Roads Authority, Dublin.

O'Rahilly, C 1998 'A classification of bronze stick-pins from the Dublin excavations 1962–72', *in* C Manning (ed.), *Dublin and Beyond the Pale: studies in honour of Patrick Healy*, 23–33. Wordwell, Bray.

Ó Ríordáin, S P 1942 'The excavation of a large earthen ringfort at Garranes, Co. Cork', *Proceedings of the Royal Irish Academy*, Vol. 47C, 77–150.

Ó Ríordáin, S P 1949 'Lough Gur excavations: Carraig Aille and the Spectacles', *Proceedings of the Royal Irish Academy*, Vol. 52C, 6–111.

Ó Ríordáin, S P & Hartnett, P J 1943 'The excavation at Ballycatteen fort, Co. Cork', *Proceedings of the Royal Irish Academy*, Vol. 49C, 1–43.

Ó Ríordáin, S P & Hunt, J 1942 'Medieval dwellings at Caherguillamore, Co. Limerick', *Journal of the Royal Society of Antiquaries of Ireland*, Vol. 72, 37–63.

Orpen, G H 2005 *Ireland under the Normans, 1169–1333* [reprint]. Four Courts Press, Dublin.

O'Sullivan, A 2006 'Early medieval houses in Ireland: social identity and dwelling spaces', *Peritia*, Vol. 20, 19–30.

O'Sullivan, A & Breen, C 2007 *Maritime Ireland: an archaeology of coastal communities*. Stroud, Tempus.

O'Sullivan, A & Harney, L 2008 *The Early Medieval Archaeology Project: investigating the character of early medieval archaeological excavations, 1970–2002*. Unpublished report for the Heritage Council. UCD School of Archaeology, Dublin.

O'Sullivan, M 2005 *Duma na nGiall: the Mound of the Hostages, Tara*. Wordwell, Bray.

O'Sullivan, M & Downey L 2007 'Ridges and furrows', *Archaeology Ireland*, Vol. 21, No. 4, 34–7.

Otway-Ruthven, A J 1951 'The organisation of Anglo-Irish agriculture in the Middle Ages', *Journal of the Royal Society of Antiquaries of Ireland*, Vol. 81, 1–13.

Otway-Ruthven, A J 1958–9 'The medieval county of Kildare', *Irish Historical Studies*, Vol. 11, 181–99.

Otway-Ruthven, A J 1964 'Parochial development in the rural deanery of Skreen', *Journal of the Royal Society of Antiquaries of Ireland*, Vol. 94, 111–22.

Otway-Ruthven, A J 1965 'The character of Norman settlement in Ireland', *in* J L McCracken (ed.), *Historical Studies, Vol. 5*, 75–84. Bowes and Bowes, London.

Petersen, J 1951 *Vikingetidens Redskaber*. Norske Videnskapsakademi, Oslo.

Price, L 1950 'The history of Lagore, from the annals and other sources', *in* H O'N Hencken, 'Lagore crannóg: an Irish royal residence of the 7th to 10th centuries AD', *Proceedings of the Royal Irish Academy*, Vol. 53C, 18–34.

Pryor, F 2001 *Seahenge: a quest for life and death in Bronze Age Britain*. Harper Collins, London.

Quinn, A 2005 *Mondaniel 3, Co. Cork: excavations on the N8 from Rathcormac to Femoy*. Unpublished excavation report prepared for Archaeological Consultancy Services Ltd and Cork County

Council.

Quinney, P 2006a *Osteological analysis of cremated skeletal remains from Ardsallagh site 2 (A008/034), M3 Clonee to North of Kells Motorway*. Unpublished report to Meath County Council on behalf of Archaeological Consultancy Services Ltd.

Quinney, P 2006b *Osteological analysis of human skeletal remains from Ardsallagh site 1 (A008/035), M3 Clonee to North of Kells Motorway*. Unpublished report to Meath County Council on behalf of Archaeological Consultancy Services Ltd.

Quinney, P 2006c *Osteological analysis of cremated skeletal remains from Ardsallagh site 1 (A008/035), M3 Clonee to North of Kells Motorway*. Unpublished report to Meath County Council on behalf of Archaeological Consultancy Services Ltd.

Quinney, P 2007 'An unusual burial at Ballygarraun West', *Seanda*, No. 2, 30–1.

Raftery, B 1994 *Pagan Celtic Ireland*. Thames & Hudson, London.

Rathbone, S 2007 'Seeing the light at Garretstown, Co. Meath', *Seanda*, No. 2, 55–6.

Rathbone, S 2008 *Interim report on archaeological excavation at Trevet, Co. Meath (A008/014)*. Unpublished report to the Department of the Environment, Heritage and Local Government on behalf of Archaeological Consultancy Services Ltd.

Reimer, P J, Ballie, M G L, Bard, E, et al. 2004 'IntCal04 terrestrial radiocarbon age calibration, 0–26 cal kyr BP', *Radiocarbon*, Vol. 46, No. 3, 1029–58.

Riley, F T 1936–7 'Excavation in the townland of Pollacorragune, Tuam, Co. Galway', *Journal of the Galway Archaeological and Historical Society*, Vol. 17, 44–54.

Roseveare, M J & Roseveare, A C K 2007 *National Monument, Lismullin Co. Meath—geophysical survey report*. Unpublished report to the Department of the Environment, Heritage and Local Government.

Robinson, M E, Coombs, D, Maude, K & Shimwell, D W 2000 'Early Christian inhumations on Kiltullagh Hill, Co. Roscommon', *Emania*, Vol. 18, 65–73.

Russell, I, Mossop, M & Corcoran, E 2002 'Claristown 2: a cemetery and later cairn: excavations for the Drogheda Bypass—M1 Motorway', *Ríocht na Midhe*, Vol. 13, 23–31.

Ryan, F 2001 'Ferns Lower, Ferns', *in* I Bennett (ed.), *Excavations 1999: summary accounts of archaeological excavations in Ireland*, 302. Wordwell, Bray.

Ryan, F 2007 'Darcytown', *in* I Bennett (ed.), *Excavations 2004: summary accounts of archaeological excavations in Ireland*, 106–7. Wordwell, Bray.

Ryan, M 1973 'Native pottery in Early Historic Ireland', *Proceedings of the Royal Irish Academy*, Vol. 73C, 619–45.

St John Brooks, E (ed.) 1936 *Register of the Hospital of St John the Baptist Without the New Gate of Dublin*. Stationery Office, Dublin.

St John Brooks, E (ed.) 1953 *The Irish Cartularies of Llanthony Prima and Secunda*. Stationery Office, Dublin.

Scott, A B & Martin, F X (eds) 1978 *Expugnatio Hibernica: the conquest of Ireland by Giraldus Cambrensis*. Royal Irish Academy, Dublin.

Sayles, G O (ed.) 1979 *Documents on the Affairs of Ireland Before the King's Council*. Irish Manuscripts Commission, Dublin.

Seaver, M 2005a 'Practice, spaces and places: an archaeology of boroughs as manorial centres in the barony of Slane', *in* J Lyttleton & T O'Keeffe (eds), *The Manor in Medieval and Early Modern Ireland*, 70–104. Four Courts Press, Dublin.

Seaver, M 2005b 'Run of the mill? Excavation of an early medieval site at Raystown, Co. Meath', *Archaeology Ireland*, Vol. 19, No. 4. 9–12.

Seaver, M 2006 'Through the mill—excavation of an early medieval settlement at Raystown, County Meath', *in* J O'Sullivan & M Stanley (eds), *Settlement, Industry and Ritual*, 73–87. Archaeology and the National Roads Authority Monograph Series No. 3. National Roads Authority, Dublin.

Scully, O M B 1997 'Metal artefacts', *in* M F Hurley, O M B Scully & S W J McCutcheon (eds), *Late Viking Age and Medieval Waterford: excavations 1986–1992*, 438–90. Waterford Corporation, Waterford.

Shiel, D, Harvey, L & Martinez, C 2001 *Survey results: N3 Navan to Dunshaughlin Road, Co. Meath, 00R064*. Unpublished report prepared for Meath County Council.

Simington, R C (ed.) 1940 *The Civil Survey, 1654–56. Vol. V. County Meath*. Stationery Office, Dublin.

Simms, A 1979 'Settlement patterns and medieval colonization in Ireland: the example of Duleek in County Meath', *in* P Flatrès (ed.), *Paysages Ruraux Européens*, 159–76. Université de Haute-Bretagne, Rennes.

Simms, A 1988 'The geography of Irish manors: the example of the Llanthony cells of Duleek and Colp in County Meath', *in* J Bradley (ed.), *Settlement and Society in Medieval Ireland*, 291–326. Boethius Press, Kilkenny.

Sloane, R 2007a *Lismullin 1 (A008/021): results of bone analysis for dog skeleton F1257*. Unpublished report to Meath County Council on behalf of Archaeological Consultancy Services Ltd.

Sloane, R 2007b *Lismullin 1 (A008/021): results of bone analysis for cattle specimen F901*. Unpublished report to Meath County Council on behalf of Archaeological Consultancy Services Ltd.

Stead, I M & Rigby, V 1989 *Verulamium: the King Harry Lane site*. English Heritage Archaeological Report 12. English Heritage, London.

Stout, G & Stout, M 2008 *Excavation of an Early Medieval Secular Cemetery at Knowth Site M, County Meath, and Related Sites in North-east Leinster*. Wordwell, Dublin.

Stout, M 1997 *The Irish Ringfort*. Four Courts Press, Dublin.

Stout, M 2005 'Early medieval boundaries', *in* T Condit & C Corlett (eds), *Above and Beyond: essays in memory of Leo Swan*, 139–48. Wordwell, Bray.

Stuiver, M & Reimer, P J 1993 'Extended ^{14}C data base and revised CALIB 3.0 ^{14}C age calibration program', *Radiocarbon*, Vol. 35, No. 1, 215–30.

Stuiver, M, Reimer, P J & Reimer, R W 2005 *CALIB 5.0*, http://www.calib.qub.ac.uk/calib/

Sweetman, D 1983 'Reconstruction and partial excavation of an Iron Age burial mound at Ninch, Co. Meath', *Ríocht na Midhe*, Vol. 7, 59–68.

Sweetman, H S (ed.) 1875 *Calendar of Documents Relating to Ireland, 1171–1251*. HMSO, London.

Sweetman, H S (ed.) 1877 *Calendar of Documents Relating to Ireland, 1252–1284*. HMSO, London.

Sweetman, H S (ed.) 1886 *Calendar of Documents Relating to Ireland, 1302–1307*. HMSO, London.

Talma, A S & Vogel, J C 1993 'A simplified approach to calibrating ^{14}C dates', *Radiocarbon*, Vol. 35, No. 2, 317–32.

Thacker, A T 2003 'Early medieval Chester, 400–1230', *in* C P Lewis & A T Thacker (eds), *A History of the County of Cheshire: vol. 5, part 1. The city of Chester: general history and topography*, 16–33. Boydell and Brewer, London.

Thomas, C 1976 'Imported late-Roman Mediterranean pottery in Ireland and western Britain: chronologies and implications', *Proceedings of the Royal Irish Academy*, Vol. 76C, 245–55.

Thomas, C 1981 *A Provisional List of Imported Pottery in Post-Roman Western Britain and Ireland*. Institute of Cornish Studies, Cornwall.

Thomas, C 1990 '"Gallici Nnautae de Galliarum provinciis"—a sixth/seventh century trade with Gaul reconsidered', *Medieval Archaeology*, Vol. 34, 1–26.

Toner, G 2004 '*Baile*: settlement and landholding in medieval Ireland', *Éigse*, Vol. 34, 25–43.

Tresham, E (ed.) 1828 *Rotulorum Patentium et Clausorum Cancellariae Hiberniae Calendarium*. Record Commission of Ireland, Dublin.

Wailes, B 1982 'The Irish "royal sites" in history and archaeology', *Cambridge Medieval Celtic Studies*, Vol. 3, 1–29.

Waddell, J 1988 'Rathcroghan in Connacht', *Emania*, Vol. 5, 5–18.

Waddell, J 1998 *The Prehistoric Archaeology of Ireland*. Galway University Press, Galway.

Walsh, G 1995 'Iron Age settlement in Co. Mayo', *Archaeology Ireland*, Vol. 9, No. 2, 7–8.

Walsh, F 2008 'Killickaweeny 1: high-class early medieval living', *in* N Carlin, L Clarke & F Walsh, *The Archaeology of Life and Death in the Boyne Floodplain: the linear landscape of the M4*, 27–53. NRA Scheme Monographs 2. National Roads Authority, Dublin.

Warner, R B 1994 'The Navan complex: a new schedule of sites and finds', *Emania*, Vol. 12, 39–44.

Warner, R B 2000 'Keeping out the otherworld: the internal ditch at Navan and other Irish hengiform enclosures', *Emania*, Vol. 18, 39–44.

Waterman, D M 1997 *Excavations at Navan Fort 1961–71*. HMSO, Belfast.

White, N B (ed.) 1943 *Extents of Irish Monastic Possessions, 1540–1541*. Stationery Office, Dublin.

Wilde, W R 1861 *A Descriptive Catalogue of the Antiquities of Animal Material and Bronze in the Museum of the Royal Irish Academy*. Hodges & Smith, Dublin.

Williams, B B 1983 'Early Christian landscapes in Co. Antrim', *in* T Reeves-Smyth & F Hamond (eds), *Landscape Archaeology in Ireland*, 233–46. British Archaeological Reports, British Series 116. Oxford.

Williams, H 1997 'Ancient landscapes and the dead: the re-use of prehistoric and Roman monuments as Early Anglo-Saxon burial places', *Medieval Archaeology*, Vol. 41, 1–32.

Williams, H 1998 'Monuments and the past in early Anglo-Saxon England', *World Archaeology*, Vol. 30, No. 1, 90–108.

Wooding, J M 1996 *Communication and Commerce Along the Western Sea Lanes, AD 400–800*. British Archaeological Reports, International Series 654. Oxford.

INDEX

Note: Bold type indicates tables, and italics indicate illustrations.